AFRICAN-AMERICAN FIRSTS

~

Famous, little-known and unsung
triumphs of blacks in America

AFRICAN-AMERICAN FIRSTS

Famous, little-known and unsung triumphs of blacks in America

by

JOAN POTTER

with

CONSTANCE CLAYTOR

Illustrated by
Alison Muñoz

Pinto Press
Elizabethtown, NY

Publisher's Cataloging in Publication
(Prepared by Quality Books Inc.)

Potter, Joan.
   African-American firsts : famous, little-known & unsung triumphs
of Blacks in America / by Joan Potter with Constance Claytor.
   p. cm.
   Preassigned LCCN: 93-84716.
   ISBN 0-9632476-1-1

   1. Afro-Americans--Biography. 2. Afro-Americans--History.   I.
Claytor, Constance. II. Title.

E185.96.P68 1993   973'.0496073
                                        QBI93-21792

Book design by Dale Schroeder and Alison Muñoz
Book illustration by Alison Muñoz

10 9 8 7 6 5 4 3 2 1

Published by

Pinto Press
Elizabethtown, NY

To Julia, Jackson, Rachel, and Christian,
their parents, and their Uncle Steve

Joan Potter

To Louis, Bruce, and Evan

Constance Claytor

CONTENTS

INTRODUCTION

The people you will read about in this book are unusual, not just because their achievements are outstanding, but because, directly or indirectly, they all were forced to contend with racism in their struggle toward goals that required the utmost in dedication and effort. That they were also able to bear the frequent indignity, frustration, and despair caused by the innocent circumstance of race adds greater lustre to all their triumphs.

The people in this book are part of American history—from Crispus Attucks who died at the Boston Massacre defending the birth of America, to the frontiersman James Beckwourth who discovered a new pass through the Rockies, to Mae Jemison, astronaut and NASA mission specialist—and all give continuity to the enduring importance of the African-American presence in the United States.

Over the years there have been many attempts to deny African-Americans their own history: schoolbooks without mention of blacks, historical records rewritten to exclude blacks; even in the 1951 movie, *Tomahawk*, the black mountainman Beckwourth was played by the white actor Jack Oakie.

All this is changing. Significantly, more and more books detailing African-Americans' place in American history are being published. Old documents, records, letters, family histories are being mined to provide ore that not only "sets the record straight" but creates a record where there was none.

African-American Firsts is part of this discovery and rediscovery phenomenon. We wanted to publish it for these reasons: to give a measure of history back to those who made it, and to show that African-Americans have been and are now successfully engaged in all areas of human endeavor.

In a better world this book would be unnecessary. With race not an issue, who would care who the first black police commissioner of New York City was? But in this world the appointment of Commissioner Benjamin Ward was a milestone; to African-Americans it represented one more step toward achieving deserved representation. Until we have what approaches racial amity, achievements or "firsts" like those in this book will be applauded, and deserve to be, as signs of progress, cause for hope and pride.

As you might imagine, in researching the firsts for our book we found many conflicting "facts" and dates, and accounts that lay mostly in the realm of folklore. If there was a question concerning competing claims for a first, we either indicated this in the text, or made a judgment based on the weight of the evidence. We freely confess our inability to arrive at the exact truth in every instance, especially in the distant past where the written record is rare or the oral one has suffered changes. We also regret that there were significant firsts we could not include because of the limited size of our book.

We do, however, assure readers that we have made every effort to give them as factual an account as possible. The impulse to pick this book up and read, whether it arises from hope or pride, deserves to be rewarded with the truth. We have tried to give it to you.

ACKNOWLEDGMENTS

Much of the research for this book was done in various libraries in New York and California and at a desk surrounded by material sent by many generous people. A number of reference librarians provided help, but Mary Lou Grinwis, director of the Elizabethtown (N.Y.) Circulating Library, deserves special thanks for helping amass such a great quantity of valuable books. Thanks also go to Bythema Bagley, for her encouragement at the outset; Richard Hunnicutt and the rest of the staff at the Mansion Inn in Marina del Rey, California, for arranging a perfect working environment; Faye Jonason at the California Afro-American Museum in Los Angeles for providing access to pictures; Paula Woods and Felix Liddell of Los Angeles for their generous advice; Stephen Potter of Venice, California, for his help with photographs; Jean Propp of Pacific Palisades, California, for sending important clippings; Judge James L. Watson of New York for supplying information about his family; Phil Schaap of radio station WKCR in New York City for jazz facts; Joanne McCubrey of Placerville, California, for information about Delilah Beasley; Ruby Ryles of New York Mayor David Dinkins's office for patiently answering questions; and Julie Weaver of the Clinton-Essex Franklin Library System and Melinda Yates of the New York State Library for providing bibliographies.

The talent and spirit that were displayed at the Black History Month exhibits at two southern California shopping centers provided inspiration and impetus just when they were needed. They are the Baldwin Hills Crenshaw Plaza in the Crenshaw district of Los Angeles and the Fox Hills Mall in Culver City.

Much gratitude goes to all the men and women in this book who patiently answered questions about their lives and sent material, as well as to their helpful assistants. Many people made a special effort to supply us with information and photographs, including Geraldine Stepp of the Black American West Museum, Denver; Don Motley of the Negro Leagues Baseball Museum, Kansas City; Donna Wells of the Moorland-Spingarn Research Center, Howard University; Terry Geesken of New York's Museum of Modern Art film stills archives; Marty Silverstein of the CBS photo department; Reed Charington, director of the Old Stone House Museum, Orleans, Vermont; Esther Smith of the Institute of Jazz Studies at Rutgers University, New Jersey; Crystal Hyde and Andy Krausharr of the State

Historical Society of Wisconsin, Madison; and Mary Camilleri of IMG Artists in New York.

And the words could not have been transformed into an actual book without the expertise of Dale Schroeder, typographer and designer; and the creative and knowledgeable publisher, Roy Potter.

Note: Shirley Chisholm's quote in the chapter on Law & Government was taken from The Good Fight, *published by HarperCollins.*

FOREWORD

As a young person, educated in a small suburban school in Westchester County, I found myself, much of the time, the only African-American student in my class. In the 1940s and '50s little concern was given to the dissemination of information about the contributions of African-Americans to the growth of our country, not to mention the world.

During many class discussions Africans were described as living in the jungle, wearing loin cloths, leading white hunters to their prey. Descendants of Africans were said to have dark skin, kinky hair, and large lips. Rather than standing proud as a descendant of kings and queens, I was overcome with a feeling of shame as all eyes looked in my direction. The constant encouragement of my mother and the lessons taught at home and church helped combat that particular hurt. I found, however, there was much more to learn.

During those years of schooling, never once was reference made to Crispus Attucks during our study of the American Revolution. I never learned that Hiram Revels served as a U.S. senator from Mississippi after the Civil War or that Garrett Morgan invented the traffic light and the gas mask. I was twenty years old before I heard of Jan Matzeliger's automatic shoe lasting machine or that Dr. Daniel Hale Williams performed the first open heart surgery.

Perhaps on the class trip to Washington, D.C. my high school peers learned of Benjamin Banneker's role in designing that city. However, I did not go on the trip. I can only assume that in those days black children did not go to Washington because they couldn't stay at a hotel with the rest of the class.

When evaluating my options for the future I knew little of such African-Americans as Bessie Coleman, the first woman to earn an international pilot's license, or Mary McLeod Bethune, who started a school for African-American children in 1904 that later became a college.

When I attended a predominantly white college in the state university system of New York in the '50s, this same situation, with its paucity of references to any triumphs of African-Americans, was perpetuated. It was during those years, however, that I began the quest to get in touch with the history of my people. Freedom, black pride, civil rights, were the dominant thrust in that period.

A most dramatic turning point came when I became actively involved in the civil rights movement in the '60s. A growing relationship with Joan Potter was an integral part of that involvement. I was president of the local NAACP branch and she was the secretary. We spent much time together planning meetings, conducting tutoring sessions, protesting such issues as lack of minorities in the fire department or in the local school districts. Of special interest to us was testing housing discrimination. Whites and blacks would team up to find if landlords were discriminating against blacks. Joan would inquire as to the availability of a dwelling and receive a positive response. When I would arrive to inquire I would be told nothing was available. We would then file a complaint against the landlord.

We both learned a great deal in those years by our association with so many leaders and workers in the movement. Many went from branch presidents and delegates to high positions of authority in this country. We listened and learned and were proud of their accomplishments.

A lasting friendship prevailed, our children grew up together, and we were there for each other during milestones in one another's lives. Both families have remained lifelong friends. During our long discussions that often stretched into the night, I related to Joan the many frustrations I felt as a black woman in our society, one being a lack of knowledge of the history of my people.

This project is the culmination of many years of friendship, frustration, struggle, and accomplishment. This book is a must, not only for me but for all who would avail themselves of it. As a teacher I want to leave this work as a legacy to those youngsters who will read it with pride as well as those who will gain respect for these little-known feats by African-Americans. We want to help our readers discover the contributions made by African-Americans to this country's history and culture.

Thank you, Joan, for bringing your idea to me and for asking me to collaborate on this project. Thank you for helping me discover the many positive accomplishments of my people. We have merely scratched the surface.

—*Constance Claytor*

BUSINESS

WHAT WAS THE FIRST INSURANCE COMPANY OWNED BY AFRICAN-AMERICANS?

The Afro-American Insurance Company, the first known insurance firm to be owned and managed by African-Americans, was established in Philadelphia in 1810 by three businessmen, James Porter, William Coleman, and Joseph Randolph. The original purpose of the company, which stayed in business for thirty years, was to provide African-Americans with a proper burial.

WHO WAS THE COUNTRY'S FIRST AFRICAN-AMERICAN MILLIONAIRE?

In 1841 William A. Liedesdorff arrived in California from the Virgin Islands aboard his schooner; it was said that he was escaping an unhappy love affair. Already a wealthy man when he came to San Francisco, he bought land, built a home, and opened a store. He then proceeded to make a major impact on the city.

As a member of the city council, Liedesdorff was instrumental in setting up the first public school and organizing the first official horse race. He launched the first steamboat on San Francisco Bay and later opened the first hotel. He eventually owned an extensive amount of land in the city as well as a huge estate near Sutter's Mill, in gold rush country. Liedesdorff died at the age of thirty-eight from what was then called "brain fever." A short street in downtown San Francisco still bears his name.

WHO FOUNDED THE FIRST NATIONAL AFRICAN-AMERICAN LABOR UNION?

Born in Baltimore in 1835, Isaac Myers was apprenticed at the age of sixteen as a ship's caulker, an important job in the days of wooden-hulled ships. By 1860 Myers had become supervisor of one of the largest shipyards in Baltimore. After the Civil War, white caulkers in the city went on strike in an attempt to eliminate African-American shipyard workers. In response, Myers organized the caulkers and longshoremen who had been forced out of their jobs, raised money from the community, and established a black-owned cooperative shipyard.

The shipyard, the Chesapeake Marine Railway and Dry Dock Company, employed hundreds of African-Americans, won a number of government contracts, and provided the impetus for the establishment of the Colored Caulkers' Trade Union Society of Baltimore. Myers then organized the first national African-American labor union in United States history—the Colored National Labor Union—and became its first president.

WHO WAS THE FIRST WOMAN IN AMERICA TO BECOME A BANK PRESIDENT?

Maggie Lena Walker was born to a poor family in Richmond, Virginia, in 1867. A bright student, Walker graduated from high school and began a teaching career. After completing a course in business training in 1889 she took a job as executive secretary of the Independent Order of St. Luke Society, an African-American organization that assisted sick and elderly members and provided burial services.

Walker expanded the society into an insurance company, and in 1903 she added an independent bank, the St. Luke Penny Savings Bank, and became its president. Under her leadership it grew into a leading African-American bank, the St. Luke Bank and Trust Company.

She served as president until the bank merged with other African-American banks to form the Consolidated Bank and Trust Company, and chaired the board of Consolidated Bank until her death in 1934. Walker was active in many organizations, including the NAACP and the Urban League, and was the recipient of several honorary degrees. A high school in Richmond is named after this successful businesswoman.

WHO WAS THE COUNTRY'S FIRST AFRICAN-AMERICAN WOMAN MILLIONAIRE?

The woman who would become Madame C.J. Walker was born Sarah Breedlove in Delta, Louisiana, in 1867. Orphaned at seven, she was reared by an older sister until she was fourteen, when she left to get married. By the age of twenty she was a widow. She moved to St. Louis with her daughter A'Lelia and worked as a washerwoman until the early 1900s, when she created a formula to groom and condition hair. It was the first in a line of hair preparations, toiletries, and cosmetics that became immensely popular among African-American consumers.

Around 1905 she married a newspaperman named Charles Walker and began calling herself Madame C.J. Walker. She soon divorced her husband and in 1910 settled in Indianapolis, where she started manufacturing her products. She also established a line of beauty culture schools that reached throughout the United States and the Caribbean.

Walker came to New York just before World War I and built an Italianate mansion, Villa Lewaro, overlooking the Hudson River at Irvington. It was designed by Vertner Tandy, the first African-American architect registered in New York State. A millionaire and a generous philanthropist, Madame Walker made large donations to such institutions as Tuskegee Institute, Bethune-Cookman College, and the NAACP. After her death in 1919, her daughter A'Lelia constructed the Walker Building in Indianapolis, which housed the offices of Walker Enterprises and contained a theater built in an African-Egyptian style.

WHAT WAS THE FIRST AFRICAN-AMERICAN-OWNED RECORD COMPANY?

In 1921 Harry Pace formed the Pace Phonographic Corporation, which issued records on the Black Swan label. It was the first record company owned and operated by an African-American. Earlier, in 1908, Pace had organized a music publishing company in Memphis, Tennessee, with the blues composer W.C. Handy. The Pace and Handy Music Company moved to New York in 1918, but the partnership dissolved three years later when Pace formed his record business.

For his record company, Pace brought in Fletcher Henderson as recording manager and William Grant Still as arranger. His first releases featured performances of light classical music, blues, spirituals, and instrumental solos. Black Swan's first hit was a recording of "Down Home Blues" and "Oh, Daddy," sung by Ethel Waters. Although Pace recorded many outstanding artists, he was unable to withstand the competition from white-owned companies, and was forced to declare bankruptcy in December 1923. A few months later he sold the Black Swan label to Paramount Records.

WHO ORGANIZED AND SERVED AS FIRST PRESIDENT OF THE FIRST MAJOR AFRICAN-AMERICAN TRADE UNION?

A. Philip Randolph, born in Florida in 1889, was one of the country's leading spokesmen for the African-American worker. After moving to New York City to further his education, Randolph worked as a waiter and an elevator operator, and in both jobs he tried to organize his fellow workers to protest deplorable conditions.

In 1925 Randolph decided to organize the poorly paid men and women who worked on railroad sleeping cars. He founded the all-black International Brotherhood of Sleeping Car Porters and served as its first president, a position he held for forty-three years. In addition, he was the first African-American to serve as international vice-president of the AFL-CIO, a major labor organization formed in 1955.

Randolph also made history by proposing two major marches on Washington. The first, for which he set a date of July 1, 1941, was to be a march of African-Americans from all over the country to protest discrimination against black workers in the defense industry. President Franklin Roosevelt tried to dissuade him, but Randolph said the march would take place unless the president issued an order banning discrimination in defense plants. Roosevelt finally gave in and issued the executive order on June 25.

Randolph was also director of the 1963 March on Washington that called for civil rights for African-Americans and made Dr. Martin Luther King, Jr., a national figure. (The 1963 march was actually organized by Bayard Rustin, who could not be named as the director because he was known to be a conscientious objector, a socialist, and a homosexual.) In 1964 Randolph received the Presidential Medal of Freedom from President Lyndon Johnson.

WHEN DID THE FIRST AFRICAN-AMERICAN EARN A MASTER'S DEGREE FROM HARVARD BUSINESS SCHOOL?

H. Naylor Fitzhugh earned his master's degree from the Harvard Business School in 1933 and embarked upon a lengthy career as a professor of business at Howard University in Washington, D.C. He left Howard to join the Pepsi-Cola Company, where he became vice-president for special marketing. As a pioneer of target marketing—a technique in which a segment of the population is studied and sales techniques developed for that particular audience—Fitzhugh's target was the African-American consumer.

His expertise was much in demand by large corporations, and in 1974 he was called "the dean of black businessmen" by *Black Enterprise* magazine. A year later Fitzhugh was summoned to the White House and given a special black enterprise achievement award by Vice President Nelson Rockefeller. Fitzhugh died in 1992.

WHO WAS THE FIRST AFRICAN-AMERICAN WOMAN TO OPEN A TALENT AGENCY IN NEW YORK?

Ruth Bowen grew up in Virginia, where she was born in 1924, and moved to New York City to attend New York University. After two years of college, however, she met the singer Billy Bowen, one of the original Ink Spots, and left school to marry him. As she traveled to concerts with her husband, Bowen got to know many performers.

In 1945 she became a friend of the well-known vocalist Dinah Washington, and became her press secretary a year later. The singer convinced her new assistant to help manage her career, and by 1959 Bowen had gained enough experience working with entertainers to open her own company, the Queen Booking Corporation, with offices on Broadway in New York City. Bowen's clients included Sammy Davis Jr., Gladys Knight and the Pips, Aretha Franklin, Kool and the Gang, and the Mighty Clouds of Joy. Ten years after its inception, Queen Booking had become the largest black-owned entertainment agency in the world.

WHEN DID UNITED AIRLINES HIRE ITS FIRST AFRICAN-AMERICAN PILOT?

In 1965, William R. Norwood, a native of Centralia, Illinois, became the first African-American pilot to fly for United Airlines. Inspired by an elementary school teacher who had served in the all-black 99th Pursuit Squadron in World War II, Norwood maintained his interest in flying through high school and college, earning his private pilot's license in 1959 when he was a senior at Southern Illinois University. His first passengers were a fellow football player and the woman who was to become his wife.

Captain William R. Norwood

After graduating with a degree in chemistry, Norwood joined the air force and flew B-52s for six years until he left to apply for a pilot's job with United Airlines. After joining the airline in 1965, Norwood flew all cockpit positions in many different airplanes; in 1993 he became a captain on the DC-10.

Deciding to further his education, in 1974 Norwood earned an MBA from the University of Chicago. He served as president and board chairman of the Organization of Black Airline Pilots, was appointed to the Southern Illinois University Board of Trustees, and received many honors, including a flight operations special achievement award from United Airlines and membership in the Hall of Fame at Southern Illinois University, where he was the first African-American quarterback on the school's football team.

WHAT WAS THE FIRST AFRICAN-AMERICAN-OWNED COMPANY TO BE PUBLICLY OWNED AND TRADED ON THE STOCK MARKET?

Those who grew up in the 1950s and '60s can remember the sound of a child's voice on the radio making this plaintive demand: "More Parks sausages, Mom, please." The Parks Sausage Company, which made this famous product, was founded in 1951 in Baltimore by Henry G. Parks, Jr., a marketing graduate of Ohio State University with a varied background. Parks's work experience had included stints as a salesman for a beer manufacturer, an owner of a drug store, and a manufacturer of cinder blocks.

Parks was general manager of his new sausage company, where the sausage was made in the morning and sold in the afternoon. The sausage maker was also the production manager and the entire sales force. One of the two production workers doubled as clerk and demonstrated the sausages in supermarkets on weekends. Although the company grossed $30,000 three months after it opened, it had lost $10,000.

But the Parks Sausage Company expanded rapidly, and in 1952 Parks hired a new general manager, Raymond V. Haysbert. New products and sales areas were added, and in 1969 Parks Sausage become the first black-owned company to be publicly owned and traded on the stock market. In 1990 the company moved into a new 113,500-square-foot headquarters and meat-processing facility.

WHO WAS THE FIRST AFRICAN-AMERICAN ON THE NEW YORK STOCK EXCHANGE?

In 1970 Joseph L. Searles III became the first African-American proposed for a seat on the New York Stock Exchange. Leaving his position as an aide to New York City Mayor John Lindsay, Searles became a floor trader and general partner for Newburger, Loeb and Company.

WHAT WAS THE FIRST AFRICAN-AMERICAN-OWNED COMPANY LISTED ON THE AMERICAN STOCK EXCHANGE?

In 1954, George and Joan Johnson borrowed $250 to start a small cosmetics business. By the 1960s their organization, Johnson Products Company, based in Chicago, was leading the market for personal grooming and cosmetic products for African-Americans. In 1971 it became the first black-owned business to be listed on the American Stock Exchange.

In a 1989 divorce settlement, Joan Johnson acquired control of more than half the shares and became chief executive officer of the company, which until then had been run by her former husband, George. At that time the company was valued at $11 million. In June 1993 the Johnson Products Company was purchased for over $67 million by the IVAX Corporation, a Miami-based pharmaceutical company that already owned smaller cosmetics and hair care businesses.

After the deal, Mrs. Johnson, then sixty-four, stayed on as president of the company, which remained in its facilities on the south side of Chicago. Observers noted that the high-priced acquisition illustrated the importance of the African-American consumer market.

WHO WAS THE FIRST AFRICAN-AMERICAN DIRECTOR OF GENERAL MOTORS?

Leon Sullivan, born in Charleston, West Virginia, in 1922, was ordained a Baptist minister as a young man. He soon became involved in efforts to improve the economic situation of African-Americans, working with A. Philip Randolph in his successful effort in July 1941 to obtain jobs for black workers in the defense industry. Sullivan also served as an aide to New York's Rev. Adam Clayton Powell, Jr., in his 1944 Congressional campaign.

In 1951 Sullivan was named pastor of Zion Baptist Church in Philadelphia. It was there that he launched the Opportunities Industrial Center (IOC), one of the country's largest and most successful job training organizations. Founded in 1964, within five years the IOC had branches in seventy cities. In 1971, highly respected for his success as an economic development planner, Sullivan was chosen as the first African-American to serve on the board of directors of General Motors.

WHO WAS THE FIRST AFRICAN-AMERICAN DIRECTOR OF THE NEW YORK STOCK EXCHANGE?

Jerome Holland was born in Auburn, New York, in 1916 and earned bachelor's and master's degrees from Cornell University. Holland made a reputation as a star athlete on Cornell's football team; he was named an All-American for two seasons and he eventually was added to the roster of college football's Hall of Fame.

After receiving a Ph.D. from the University of Pennsylvania, Holland was appointed president of Delaware State College; in 1960 he took over the presidency of Hampton Institute. Ten years later Holland was made ambassador to Sweden, a position he held until 1972 when he returned to the United States to become the first African-American named to the board of directors of the New York Stock Exchange.

WHO WAS THE FIRST AFRICAN-AMERICAN WOMAN TO FLY FOR A COMMERCIAL AIRLINE?

At the age of seventeen, Jill Brown began piloting single-engine planes in her native Maryland when she and her parents took up flying as a hobby. Brown became a home economics teacher after graduating from the University of Maryland, but she couldn't turn her back on her love of flying.

In 1976 Brown read an article about Warren Wheeler, the African-American owner of a commuter airline in Raleigh, North Carolina. Wheeler hired her as an assistant and she eventually became a co-pilot. She handled everything—reservations, tickets, baggage, seating, and flying a fifteen-seat plane. By the time she left Wheeler, she had raised her flying time to 1,200 hours, enough to be accepted into the flight training program at Texas International Airline. In 1978, when she was twenty-eight years old, Texas International hired her as a pilot, a first for an African-American woman.

United Airlines, one of the country's largest airline companies, hired its first black woman pilot in 1987. A former flight attendant for United, Shirley Tyus entered flight school in 1977 and earned a commercial pilot's license two years later. Tyus also turned to Wheeler Airlines for a job, flying its commuter planes for several years until she was hired by United.

WHAT WAS THE FIRST AFRICAN-AMERICAN-OWNED COMPANY TO BE LISTED ON THE NEW YORK STOCK EXCHANGE?

Black Entertainment Television, one of the country's most successful cable television networks, was founded by Robert Johnson in 1980 with a $15,000 loan. Johnson, who grew up in Freeport, Illinois, with dreams of becoming an ambassador to Europe, majored in social studies at the University of Illinois and earned a master's degree at Princeton University in 1972.

In his job as a lobbyist for the National Cable Television Association, Johnson became increasingly aware of the scarcity of African-American programming. With the borrowed money he formed Black Entertainment Television, known as BET, which began broadcasting from Washington, D.C., for two hours a day. Within several years BET had become a full-time network carrying news, talk shows, music, and sports. In 1991 BET became the first African-American-owned company to be listed on the New York Stock Exchange.

WHO WAS THE FIRST AFRICAN-AMERICAN TO HEAD A FORTUNE 100 COMPANY?

Clifton R. Wharton, Jr.'s extensive list of accomplishments culminated with his appointment in December 1992 as a deputy secretary of state in the Clinton administration. Wharton, born in Boston in 1926, was the first African-American to earn a Ph.D. in economics from the University of Chicago, the first to be president of a major university that was predominantly white, the first to serve as chancellor of the State University of New York, the first to chair the board of a major foundation (the Rockefeller Foundation), and the first to head a Fortune 100 company.

Wharton, whose father, Clifton R. Wharton, Sr., was the country's first African-American career ambassador, also earned a bachelor's degree from Harvard and a master's from Johns Hopkins in Baltimore. He served as president of Michigan State University from 1970 to 1978 and chancellor of the State University of New York from 1978 to 1987. Before President Clinton named him deputy secretary of state he was chairman and chief executive of the country's largest private pension system, the Teachers Insurance and Annuity Association and College Retirement Equities Fund (TIAA-CREF).

WHO WAS THE FIRST AFRICAN-AMERICAN BUSINESSMAN TO MAKE THE FORBES MAGAZINE LIST OF THE NATION'S 400 WEALTHIEST PEOPLE?

When Reginald Lewis died in January 1993 of brain cancer at the age of fifty, he was one of the country's richest businessmen and a generous philanthropist. Lewis's business acumen began early in life. As a child in Baltimore, he started selling newspapers when he was nine years old; he said he earned about twenty dollars a week and saved eighteen.

After graduating from Virginia State University and Harvard Law School, Lewis worked for a prestigious New York City law firm for five years and then opened his own firm. In 1983, fifteen years after he began practicing law, Lewis moved into the world of finance when he established the TLC Group; four years later he bought Beatrice International, a giant food company, for $985 million. In 1992 he was included in Forbes magazine's list of the nation's 400 wealthiest people, with personal assets of $400 million. At the time of his death, his company, TLC Beatrice International, was the country's largest black-owned business.

Lewis donated millions of dollars to institutions ranging from homeless shelters and churches to universities such as Virginia State and Howard. His $3 million donation to Harvard Law School in 1992 was the largest from an individual in the school's 175-year history. In return, Harvard named its international law center in his honor, making it the first building at Harvard to be named for an African-American.

WHO WAS THE FIRST AFRICAN-AMERICAN TO BE NAMED CHIEF PILOT OF A MAJOR AIRLINE?

Louis Freeman is proud of achieving a list of "firsts" that began in his teens, when he and his older brother were two of the first students to integrate Woodrow Wilson High School in Dallas, Texas. Freeman was the first African-American cadet corps commander in his high school ROTC unit and filled the same position at East Texas State University, from which he graduated in 1974 with bachelor's degrees in sociology and psychology.

Captain Louis L. Freeman

Freeman earned his private pilot's license in college and enjoyed flying his friends around the local skies, but didn't imagine that someday he would fly planes as a career. He decided to take the U.S. Air Force qualifying test, and passed everything except the pilot's section. Studying hard and learning everything he could about airplanes, he took the test again and passed. After finishing pilot training at Reese Air Force Base in Texas,

Freeman was assigned to fly 737s in Sacramento, California. "A good airplane in a good location," he recalled.

In 1980 Freeman left the air force to become the first African-American pilot to fly for Southwest Airlines, which is based in Dallas. In August 1992 he was chosen to be chief pilot of Southwest's base in Chicago, making him the first black chief pilot for a major U.S. airline. He was responsible for overseeing all flight operations of the 150-pilot base and ensuring that all procedures exceeded F.A.A. requirements.

WHAT WAS THE FIRST AFRICAN-AMERICAN-OWNED COMPANY TO HAVE ITS OWN LINE OF SUPERHERO COMICS?

Only five months after DC Comics began distributing a line of comic books published by New York's Milestone Media, Inc., buyers snatched up more than three million copies of its first four titles, "Hardware," "Blood Syndicate," "Icon," and "Static," all featuring black superheroes. Milestone was started by four African-American men, Derek Dingle, Denys Cowan, Dwayne McDuffie, and Michael Davis. Their aim was to present colorful heroes battling in a realistic world. "We hope to help readers of all backgrounds to believe in the power they have as individuals that transcends racial and class lines," said the company's president, Derek Dingle.

Milestone's characters represent a variety of aspects of African-American life. Its first superhero, Hardware, is by day a brilliant scientist named Curtis Metcalf whose villainous boss is exploiting his talents. Icon, an alien being with superhuman powers, is actually Augustus Freeman IV, a conservative lawyer who promotes middle-class values. The daring superhero called Static is really Virgil Hawkins, a nerdy fifteen-year-old who suddenly acquires electrostatic powers. And Blood Syndicate is a superpowered street gang with the credo: Do or Die.

Expanding to include superheroes from other ethnic groups, Milestone created Xombi, a Korean-American hero with a perfect, indestructible body.

WHO WAS THE FIRST AFRICAN-AMERICAN PRESIDENT OF NATIONAL PUBLIC RADIO?

National Public Radio is a network that provides news, information, and cultural programs to about 480 member radio stations with a total audience of 14.5 million. Delano E. Lewis, the first African-American president of this influential, prize-winning organization, was appointed to his post in August 1993.

Delano E. Lewis

With degrees from the University of Kansas and the Washburn School of Law, Lewis has been an attorney for the U.S. Department of Justice and a Peace Corps director in Nigeria and Uganda. From 1969 to 1973 he worked on Capitol Hill, first as an assistant to Congressman Walter E. Fauntroy and then to Senator Edward Brooke.

Before joining National Public Radio, Lewis was president and chief executive officer of the Chesapeake & Potomac Telephone Company, an organization that he joined in 1973. Under his leadership, Chesapeake & Potomac, which serves the Washington, D.C., area, was one of the first telephone companies in the country to become involved in cable television.

EDUCATION

WHEN DID THE FIRST SCHOOL FOR AFRICAN-AMERICAN CHILDREN OPEN IN NEW YORK CITY?

In November 1787, the New York Manumission Society, one of the abolition societies that sprang up after the American Revolution, opened a school for African-American children. The African Free School, as it was called, started with a class of forty students.

WHO WAS THE FIRST AFRICAN-AMERICAN COLLEGE GRADUATE?

Alexander Lucius Twilight was born in 1795, the son of a farmer who had moved to Vermont from Plattsburgh, New York. As a youngster, Twilight was indentured to work on a neighboring farm, where he stayed until the age of twenty. He went on to attend Randolph Academy and in 1823 graduated from Middlebury College, in Middlebury, Vermont. Claiming Twilight as the country's first African-American college graduate, Middlebury later named a building in his honor.

Twilight was licensed as a preacher in 1827 and preached on Sundays in towns around Peru, New York, and Vergennes, Vermont, where he taught school during the week. In 1829 he arrived in Brownington, Vermont, to become minister of the Congregational Church and principal of the county secondary school, which was called Brownington Academy. It was a two-story frame schoolhouse with no dormitory; students boarded with neighboring families.

Somehow, Twilight managed to finance the construction of a huge stone building to serve as a dormitory and provide extra classroom space for the school. Legends say that he quarried the granite blocks from nearby fields and erected the building himself with only the help of an ox. The stone house, named Athenian Hall, had a kitchen, dining room, parlor, classrooms, and rooms for students to live in, all heated with fireplaces and stoves. In 1836, to prevent the state from reducing the funding for his school, Twilight got himself elected to the Vermont State Legislature for a two-year term, becoming the first African-American state legislator.

In 1847 Twilight resigned as headmaster to teach at other schools, but came back to Brownington Academy in 1852. He died five years later and both he and his wife were buried in the village cemetery overlooking the Academy campus. His students remembered him as a tough disciplinarian but an outstanding teacher with a vivid personality and a lively sense of humor. In 1916 the amazing stone house that Twilight built became the home of the Orleans County Historical Society.

Alexander Twilight and his Athenian Hall

WHAT WAS BOSTON'S FIRST SCHOOL FOR AFRICAN-AMERICAN CHILDREN?

In 1787 Prince Hall, an activist from Boston known as the founder of the first black Masonic lodge, petitioned the Massachusetts legislature to allow African-American children to attend public schools. His request was denied. Eleven years later, after more petitions were also rejected, African-American parents set up a community school in Prince Hall's home. The school was later moved to the African Meeting House, a church building.

In 1835 a brand new school was opened for Boston's African-American children. It was named the Abiel Smith School after a white businessman who had left an endowment of $2,000 for the education of black children. Soon a controversy erupted in the city over the issue of segregated schools, and William C. Nell, a lawyer who led a group called the Equal School Association, organized a boycott of the Abiel Smith School.

In 1848 a Boston resident, Benjamin Roberts, tried to enroll his young daughter Sarah in each of five white schools that stood between their house and the Abiel Smith School, but she was refused. Roberts sued the city, joined by abolitionists, and lost the case when the judge decided the Abiel Smith School was not inferior to the other public schools. But through the efforts of Nell and his organization, a bill outlawing school segregation in Massachusetts was passed in 1855. The Abiel Smith School was closed and the building was used for various purposes over the years, including housing the offices of the Museum of Afro-American History.

WHAT WAS THE FIRST UNIVERSITY FOR AFRICAN-AMERICAN STUDENTS?

The first college expressly intended for the education of African-American students was established in Chester County, Pennsylvania, in 1854. It was called Ashmun Institute, after the first president of Liberia, and in 1866 its name was changed to Lincoln University in honor of the slain president. Lincoln University's graduates include former U.S. Supreme Court Justice Thurgood Marshall, the poet Langston Hughes, and Kwame Nkrumah, the first president of Ghana.

Cheyney University in Pennsylvania is sometimes considered the first African-American college, but for many years it was actually a high school and preparatory school. It was started in 1837 by thirteen members of the Religious Society of Friends who were carrying out the terms of a will left by a Quaker named Richard Humphrey. Called the Institute for Colored Youth, the school was established on a farm about seven miles outside of Philadelphia.

In 1852 the Institute was moved into a three-story building in the city of Philadelphia, where it provided classes for both boys and girls. Fanny Jackson Coppin came to teach at the Institute in 1865 and eventually served as principal. The school was moved away from the city again in 1903, to the town of Cheyney, and in 1914 became the Cheyney Training School for Teachers. Cheyney became a fully accredited college in 1951 and in 1983 was given university status.

WHO WAS THE FIRST AFRICAN-AMERICAN TO TEACH WHITE STUDENTS IN MASSACHUSETTS?

Charlotte Forten Grimké was born in Philadelphia in 1837. Her grandfather, James Forten, Sr., was a wealthy sailmaker and abolitionist. But young Charlotte was not allowed to attend school because of her race and was tutored at home until she reached the age of sixteen. She then traveled to Salem, Massachusetts, to further her education, and graduated with honors from Salem Normal School when she was nineteen. She was hired to teach at a local grammar school, becoming the first African-American to teach white students in Massachusetts.

After the outbreak of the Civil War, a number of African-American women volunteered to teach former slaves in areas that were now under the Union flag. Charlotte joined them, becoming a schoolmistress in the Sea Islands of South Carolina. She stayed there until 1864, devoting herself to the education of hundreds of African-American children and adults. She remained a teacher until 1873, when she took a job as a clerk in the U.S. Treasury Department. Five years later she married the Rev. Francis J. Grimké, minister of the Fifteenth Street Presbyterian Church in Washington, D.C.

WHO WAS THE FIRST AFRICAN-AMERICAN WOMAN TO EARN A B.A. DEGREE?

About ten years after her birth in North Carolina in 1840, Mary Jane Patterson's father moved the family to Oberlin, Ohio, so his children could receive an education at Oberlin College, which was the first white college to accept black students. Patterson graduated from Oberlin in 1862, becoming the first African-American woman to earn a bachelor of arts degree, and devoted the rest of her life to the education of African-American children.

After receiving her degree from Oberlin, Patterson went to Philadelphia to teach at the Institute for Colored Youth. In 1869 she joined the faculty of the Preparatory High School for Colored Youth in Washington, D.C., later named Dunbar High School, and became its first African-American principal.

WHO WAS THE FIRST AFRICAN-AMERICAN COLLEGE PRESIDENT?

Born in Charleston, South Carolina, in 1811, Daniel A. Payne devoted his life to education. He attended school in Charleston and learned mathematics and several languages from private tutors. By the time he was eighteen he had established a school in Charleston for African-American children.

In 1834 the state passed a law making it a crime for African-Americans, either free or enslaved, to be educated. Payne closed his school and traveled north, entering a theological seminary in Pennsylvania. After two years he was made pastor of a Presbyterian Church in East Troy, New York, but soon returned to Pennsylvania and opened a school. In 1844 he became a minister in the African Methodist Episcopal Church and eight years later was elected a bishop.

In 1863 Payne encouraged the African Methodist Episcopal Church to purchase Wilberforce University in Xenia, Ohio, which had been founded eight years earlier for the education of African-American students. Wilberforce thus became the first institution of higher learning owned and operated by African-Americans, and Payne was named its first black president. Wilberforce was the first school to offer a work-study program and, under Payne's leadership, it became one of the country's leading African-American universities.

WHO WAS THE FIRST AFRICAN-AMERICAN TO EARN A PH.D.?

Patrick Francis Healy was born near Macon, Georgia, in 1834; his parents were an Irish planter and an African slave. Healy was one of eight children. His brother James Augustine was the country's first African-American Catholic bishop.

Healy studied at a Quaker school on Long Island, attended Holy Cross University, became ordained as a Catholic priest, and taught at Holy Cross for a time before traveling abroad for further study. In 1865 Healy received a Ph.D. from the University of Louvain in Belgium, and a year later became a philosophy professor at Georgetown University in Washington, D.C. In 1874 he was named president of Georgetown; he was the first African-American to head a primarily white university. Healy was buried on the school's campus after his death in 1910.

WHAT WAS THE FIRST AFRICAN-AMERICAN UNIVERSITY IN THE DEEP SOUTH?

Two of the country's most outstanding black educational institutions, Morehouse College and Spelman College, are offshoots of Atlanta University, which itself grew out of classes formed to educate freed slaves. Shortly after the end of the Civil War, the American Missionary Association began holding classes in collaboration with African-American residents of Atlanta. The classes developed into Atlanta University, which was established in 1866 with a young Yale graduate named Edmund Asa Ware as principal. James Weldon Johnson, the distinguished writer, diplomat, and teacher, graduated from Atlanta University in 1894, and W.E.B. DuBois taught there from 1897 to 1910.

In 1929 Atlanta University became the graduate school in a group that also included Morehouse College for men and Spelman College for women. Later, Clark College and Morris Brown College were added. Dr. Martin Luther King, Jr., graduated from Morehouse in 1948. And in 1988, just after Johnnetta Cole had become Spelman's first African-American woman president, comedian Bill Cosby gave the college a $20 million gift, the largest single donation to a black school at that time.

WHO WAS THE FIRST AFRICAN-AMERICAN WOMAN TO HEAD AN INSTITUTE OF HIGHER LEARNING?

Although she was born a slave, Fannie Coppin never wavered in her pursuit of education, and by the time she was in her early thirties she had been named principal of the Institute for Colored Youth in Philadelphia. She was the first African-American woman educator to hold such a high position. When Fannie was a child in Washington, D.C., her aunt worked for $6 a month until she had saved the $125 necessary to buy her young niece's freedom. Once free, Fannie went to live with another aunt in Massachusetts, and later worked for a family in Newport, Rhode Island, where she went to public school and then attended a state teachers college.

In 1860 Coppin enrolled in Oberlin College in Ohio, where she organized classes for freed slaves, gave music lessons, was named senior class poet, and served as the school's first African-American student teacher. When she graduated she became the second black woman to receive a bachelor's degree.

Coppin went to Philadelphia to teach Greek, Latin, and mathematics at the Institute for Colored Youth, where Ebenezer Bassett was principal. When Bassett was appointed United States Minister to Haiti in 1869, Coppin took his place as principal, remaining in that position for about thirty-five years.

WHO WAS THE FIRST AFRICAN-AMERICAN TO GRADUATE FROM HARVARD?

Richard Greener, born in Philadelphia in 1844 and raised in Boston, became the first African-American to graduate from Harvard, earning his degree in 1870 and winning top prizes in oratory and dissertation writing.

Greener had an outstanding career as an educator, administrator, and diplomat. He taught philosophy at the University of South Carolina until 1877, then earned a law degree and joined the faculty of the Howard University School of Law in Washington, D.C. He eventually left Howard and filled several government posts, including comptroller of the United States Treasury. In 1898 he was appointed United States Consul to Vladivostok, Russia.

WHAT WAS THE FIRST STATE-SUPPORTED SCHOOL FOR THE TRAINING OF AFRICAN-AMERICAN TEACHERS?

The institution that is now Alabama State University in Montgomery began in 1866 as Lincoln Normal School, a private school for African-American students in Marion, Alabama. In 1899 a new building was constructed; its cost was covered by a group of black citizens, the Freedmans Bureau (an agency formed by Congress in 1865 to provide aid to African-Americans and impoverished whites), and the American Missionary Association, whose teachers ran the school. In 1874 Lincoln Normal School was recognized as a state-supported institution for the education of black teachers.

The school was moved to Montgomery in 1887, its name was changed to Alabama Colored People's University, and the campus was expanded as new buildings were constructed over the years. As the school grew to a four-year college and then added a graduate school, its name was changed several times. In 1969 it received university status, and Alabama State University grew to include colleges of arts and sciences, business administration, education, music, and aerospace studies.

WHO WAS THE FIRST AFRICAN-AMERICAN TO EARN A PH.D. IN THE U.S.?

Edward Alexander Bouchet received a Ph.D. in physics from Yale University in 1876. He was the first African-American to earn a Ph.D. in the United States and he was also thought to be the first black college student elected to Phi Beta Kappa, the national scholastic fraternity. Bouchet devoted his life to teaching physics, chemistry, and mathematics to high school students.

WHO WAS THE FIRST AFRICAN-AMERICAN PHI BETA KAPPA AT HARVARD?

William Monroe Trotter, a native of Ohio, earned bachelor's and master's degrees from Harvard and was the first African-American student at that university to be elected to Phi Beta Kappa, the national scholastic organization. In 1901, when he was twenty-nine years old, Trotter founded the *Boston Guardian*, a crusading newspaper devoted to equal rights for African-Americans, which he edited until his death in 1934.

Trotter was a leader with W.E.B. DuBois of the Niagara Movement, an early protest organization, and was a founder and national secretary of the National Equal Rights League, an activist civil rights group. It is said that when he went to Paris to petition the World Peace Conference for equal rights for African-Americans, he was refused a passport and traveled abroad as a ship's cook. He continued his struggle for civil rights until his death in 1934.

WHO WAS THE FIRST AFRICAN-AMERICAN WOMAN TO SERVE ON A SCHOOL BOARD?

Mary Church Terrell was born in Memphis, Tennessee, in 1863 and studied at Oberlin College, earning a degree in 1884. For two years she taught at Wilberforce University in Ohio. She went on to teach Latin for a time at an African-American high school in Washington, D.C., and then traveled to Europe, where she studied for two years.

Returning to Washington, Terrell was appointed to the school board of the District of Columbia in 1895, the first African-American woman to hold that position. She was a founder of the National Association of Colored Women and served as its first president. She also was the first black woman to belong to the American Association of University Women, and was an active worker for women's suffrage.

Terrell published her autobiography, *A Colored Woman in a White World,* in 1940. In her late eighties this energetic woman was still going strong; she was a plaintiff in a lawsuit challenging discrimination in Washington restaurants that resulted in a 1953 Supreme Court decision ending segregation in public accommodations in the nation's capital.

WHO WAS THE FIRST AFRICAN-AMERICAN TO RECEIVE AN HONORARY DEGREE FROM HARVARD?

The most influential African-American of his time, Booker T. Washington was born in 1856 in Franklin County, Virginia. A studious youngster, he left home at fifteen and entered Hampton Institute in Virginia, earning his tuition as a janitor. He stayed to teach at Hampton, and when he was twenty-six years old he was chosen to head a newly established school for African-American students in Alabama called Tuskegee Institute.

Washington started at Tuskegee with thirty students, meeting in an abandoned church. He believed in the value of learning a trade; young men at Tuskegee were taught to be farmers, carpenters, painters, plumbers, and blacksmiths, and young women learned cooking, sewing, and nursing. Washington soon became the country's leading advocate of vocational education.

As president of the rapidly expanding Tuskegee Institute and a popular lecturer, Washington was an authoritative voice throughout the nation. He won the praise of three presidents, McKinley, Taft, and Theodore Roosevelt, even dining with Roosevelt at the White House, and was often called upon to recommend African-American candidates for political appointments.

Washington discouraged black Americans from fighting for social and political equality, a view that was rejected by newer leaders like W.E.B. DuBois, who also differed with Washington by promoting the importance of an academic education. Because of his philosophy of appeasement, Washington was popular with whites, and in 1896 he became the first African-American to be awarded an honorary degree at Harvard. He published his autobiography, *Up From Slavery*, in 1900, and in 1940 he became the first African-American to have his portrait on a postage stamp, a ten-cent stamp that was first placed on sale at Tuskegee Institute. Washington died in 1915 at the age of fifty-nine.

WHO WAS THE FIRST WOMAN TO ESTABLISH A SCHOOL THAT BECAME A FOUR-YEAR ACCREDITED COLLEGE?

Born in 1875 on a plantation in Mayesville, South Carolina, Mary McLeod Bethune was unable to begin her education until she was eleven years old, when a school opened five miles from her home. Eager to learn, the young Bethune walked back and forth every day. She went on to graduate from Scotia Seminary in Concord, North Carolina, and, aspiring to be a missionary, earned a degree from Moody Bible Institute in Chicago. But when her application to the Presbyterian Mission was rejected, she moved to Daytona Beach, Florida, and became a teacher.

Bethune soon decided to open her own school, the Daytona Normal and Industrial Institute, and got permission to use an old cottage near the city dump. With desks made from packing crates rescued from the dump, she started her first class in October 1904 with an enrollment of five little girls and her own son. When the rundown schoolhouse became crowded, Bethune offered to buy the nearby land. To help raise money for the purchase, she and her students baked sweet potato pies and sold them to railroad workers. On land that had once been the city dump, Bethune created the school that eventually became one of the most outstanding educational institutions in the South, Bethune-Cookman College, a fully accredited, four-year institution.

Bethune went on to found the National Council of Negro Women in 1935, and a year later she became the first African-American woman to be a presidential advisor when Franklin D. Roosevelt appointed her Director of Negro Affairs for the National Youth Administration. This inspiring educator and advisor to presidents died in Daytona Beach in 1955.

WHO WAS THE FIRST AFRICAN-AMERICAN TO BE SELECTED AS A RHODES SCHOLAR?

An educator, writer, historian, and social critic, Alain Locke has been called the dean of the African-American literary movement of the 1920s. Born in 1885 in Philadelphia, where his father was a schoolteacher, Locke graduated with honors from Harvard University. His brilliance was recognized in 1907 when he was chosen as the first African-American to win a Rhodes scholarship to study at Oxford in England.

After completing his education abroad, Locke returned to the United States and joined the faculty of Howard University, later becoming chairman of the philosophy department. He taught at Howard for thirty-six years. A scholar who focused on the achievements of African-Americans, Locke published a book in 1925, *The New Negro*, that made him a nationally known figure. He encouraged the work of black writers during the Harlem Renaissance, was an expert on African-American theater, and amassed a renowned collection of African art.

In 1945 Locke was elected the first African-American president of the American Association for Adult Education, a predominantly white organization. He was a popular lecturer and the recipient of many honors. In 1954 he suffered a fatal heart attack while working on a book, *The Negro in American Culture*, which was later completed by his collaborator, Margaret Just Butcher.

WHO CREATED THE FIRST BLACK HISTORY WEEK?

Carter G. Woodson, born in 1875, was known by many as the "Father of Black History." Forced to work in the coal mines of Virginia as a teenager, Woodson was unable to attend high school until he was twenty. A brilliant student, he went on to study at the University of Chicago, Harvard, and the Sorbonne in France.

Working as a public school teacher and principal in Washington, D.C., Woodson saw that his students had little knowledge of the contributions made by African-Americans to the country's history and culture. To help fill this void in American education, he founded the Association for the Study of Negro Life and Culture in 1915, and a year later he began publishing the *Journal of Negro History*, for which he wrote hundreds of articles and book reviews.

In 1926 Woodson created the first of what was to be an annual celebration of African-American achievement. In the beginning the celebration lasted for one week and was called Negro History Week. In 1976 it was extended to last for the entire month of February, and is now known as Black History Month.

Alain Locke

WHO WAS THE FIRST AFRICAN-AMERICAN PRESIDENT OF HOWARD UNIVERSITY?

In 1867 a new university for African-Americans was opened in Washington, D.C. It was named Howard University, after General O.O. Howard, the head of the Freedmen's Bureau. The university did not appoint its first African-American president until June 1926, when Mordecai Wyatt Johnson began his thirty-four-year tenure. Headlines in the *Washington Post* read: "Negro at Last Heads Howard University. Acquisition of Dr. Mordecai W. Johnson as President Places Local University as Capstone of Negro Education in America."

Mordecai Johnson was born in Paris, Tennessee, in 1890, and graduated from Atlanta Baptist College—later to become Morehouse College. He also earned degrees from the University of Chicago, Rochester Theological Seminary, and Harvard University, and served as pastor of a Baptist church in West Virginia before going to Howard.

During his university presidency, Johnson concentrated on attracting African-American scholars as administrators, deans, and heads of departments, but was also proud of the school's varied faculty and student body. A skilled orator and debater whose remarks sometimes made enemies, Johnson often said, "The Lord told me to speak, but He did not tell me when to stop."

WHO WAS THE FIRST AFRICAN-AMERICAN MEMBER OF THE NATIONAL INSTITUTE OF ARTS AND LETTERS?

By the time William Edward Burghardt DuBois was admitted to the National Institute of Arts and Letters in 1943, he had become a recognized sociologist, historian, writer, teacher, and civil rights leader. DuBois was born in Great Barrington, Massachusetts, in 1868, of African-American, French, Dutch, and Native American ancestry. He studied at Fisk University in Nashville, Tennessee, and earned three degrees from Harvard University, concluding with a Ph.D. in 1895.

DuBois came into conflict with the educator Booker T. Washington, disagreeing with Washington's opposition to academic education for African-Americans and his apparent acceptance of an inferior role for blacks. DuBois challenged Washington's beliefs in his collection of essays, *The Souls of Black Folk*, published in 1903.

Two years later DuBois convened a group of African-Americans in Niagara Falls, Canada, to examine ways to improve the social and political lives of black people. The members of the "Niagara Movement" called for civil rights for all African-Americans, and their effort was the forerunner of the National Association for the Advancement of Colored People (NAACP). W.E.B. DuBois became that organization's director of publications and research and started a magazine, *The Crisis*, which he edited until 1934. DuBois left America in 1961 and settled in Ghana, where he died two years later at the age of ninety-five.

WHEN DID FISK UNIVERSITY APPOINT ITS FIRST AFRICAN-AMERICAN PRESIDENT?

Although Fisk University in Nashville, Tennessee, was founded in 1865 to educate African-Americans, it didn't have a black president until Charles Spurgeon Johnson was appointed in 1946. Johnson, a specialist in African-American sociology, had headed Fisk's social science department since 1928. He was an expert on race relations and the author of countless books and articles about the life and role of African-Americans in the United States. In 1944 he established the Race Relations Institute at Fisk as an arena for an exchange of ideas among people with varied ethnic and racial backgrounds.

Johnson was born in Bristol, Virginia, in 1893, the son of a Baptist minister. After graduating from Virginia Union University and serving in World War I, he earned a degree from the University of Chicago, where he co-authored a 600-page report, *The Negro in Chicago*, a landmark study of the background of race riots in that city. From 1921 to 1928 he was director of research for the National Urban League, founding its magazine, *Opportunity*, which provided an outlet for many young African-American writers and scholars.

After his appointment as president of Fisk, Johnson remained in that position until 1956, when he died after suffering a heart attack in a railroad station in Louisville, Kentucky.

WHO WAS THE FIRST AFRICAN-AMERICAN STUDENT ADMITTED TO THE UNIVERSITY OF ALABAMA?

A courageous young African-American woman named Autherine Lucy braved a tradition of segregation and enrolled in the University of Alabama on February 1, 1956, after a federal court order forced the school to admit her. But five days later mobs of people rioted on campus, threw rotten eggs at Lucy as she hurried to class, and threatened to kill her. The university quickly suspended her.

The NAACP, which had been handling Lucy's case for three years, went to court to seek reinstatement. A federal judge revoked her suspension but, refusing to give in, the school's trustees expelled her permanently. Lucy finally abandoned her effort, and the University of Alabama remained segregated for another seven years. Thirty-two years later, Lucy received a letter from the University of Alabama telling her she was no longer expelled and encouraging her to enroll again.

WHO WAS THE FIRST AFRICAN-AMERICAN STUDENT TO GRADUATE FROM LITTLE ROCK HIGH SCHOOL?

In September 1957, three years after the U.S. Supreme Court's *Brown v. Board of Education* decision ended segregation in the nation's public schools, nine young African-Americans attempted to enroll in Little Rock High School in Little Rock, Arkansas. The state's governor, Orville Faubus, summoned the National Guard to surround the school and keep the students out. A federal court ordered Faubus to remove the troops, but when the students arrived to attend classes they were met by a vicious, shouting mob and were forced to turn back. The next day President Eisenhower sent troops to protect the area, and while soldiers with bayonets held back the crowds, the nine young African-American students walked into the school.

The first of the so-called "Little Rock Nine" to graduate from the high school was Ernest Green, who received his diploma on May 27, 1958. Green went on to earn undergraduate and graduate degrees from Michigan State University. He served as assistant secretary of labor for employment and training under President Carter, and later formed a consulting firm in Washington, D.C., that specialized in employment and training services for minority groups.

In 1987 Green joined Lehman Brothers, an investment banking firm, as a senior vice president, and by 1991 had become a managing director of the company, based in its Washington, D.C., office. Green was named to the board of directors of the NAACP, the Winthrop Rockefeller Foundation, the Eisenhower World Affairs Institute, and the Quality Education for Minorities Network. After the 1992 elections, he was appointed to President Bill Clinton's transition team.

WHO WAS THE FIRST AFRICAN-AMERICAN STUDENT AT THE UNIVERSITY OF MISSISSIPPI?

Fourteen months after air force veteran James Meredith applied for admission to the segregated University of Mississippi, the United States Supreme Court ruled on September 10, 1962, that the school had to accept him. But ten days later the Mississippi governor, Ross Barnett, physically blocked Meredith from entering the school. In response, a federal appeals court threatened the university with contempt and secured a promise that Meredith would be registered.

On September 25, Meredith, accompanied by the chief United States marshal, traveled to Jackson, Mississippi, to register; once again, Barnett rejected him. In a lengthy series of telephone calls, Attorney General Robert Kennedy warned the recalcitrant governor that he had to comply with the federal court order. The next day a *New York Times* headline read:

Ernest Green

"U.S. is Prepared to Send Troops as Mississippi Governor Defies Court and Bars Negro Student."

A day later Meredith and his escorts traveled to the university campus in Oxford. They were met by the state's lieutenant governor, backed by rows of state troopers and sheriffs, who denied him admission. Meredith tried to reach the university again the next day, but the attempt was called off when thousands of rowdy Mississippians gathered, some carrying rifles and other weapons.

When he came to the campus again on September 30, accompanied by a force of federal marshals, riots broke out among university students and adults from surrounding communities. Rocks, iron spikes, and fire bombs were thrown and about thirty marshals were hit by gunfire. In the end, two people were killed, including a reporter from London, and hundreds were injured. Finally, on October 1, Meredith was allowed to register and attended his first class.

WHO WAS THE FIRST AFRICAN-AMERICAN PRESIDENT OF THE NATIONAL EDUCATION ASSOCIATION?

In 1968 Elizabeth Duncan Koontz was elected president of the National Education Association and served in that position until 1969, when President Nixon appointed her director of the labor department's women's bureau. A native of North Carolina, where she was born in 1919, Koontz received degrees from Livingston College and Atlanta University. A special education teacher in North Carolina, Koontz was cited for her outstanding achievements in the teaching profession.

WHO WAS THE FIRST AFRICAN-AMERICAN PRESIDENT OF THE AMERICAN PSYCHOLOGICAL ASSOCIATION?

Born in Panama in 1914, Kenneth Bancroft Clark conducted groundbreaking research on the psychological harm to African-American children caused by segregation. His findings made a major contribution to the historic 1954 United States Supreme Court decision in *Brown v. Board of Education*, which outlawed segregation in public education.

A graduate of Columbia and Howard universities, Clark was a founder of Harlem Youth Opportunities Unlimited, an organization formed to provide job training for young people. In 1969 he was elected the first African-American president of the American Psychological Association. He later formed a consulting firm specializing in matters dealing with race relations, and published an important sociological study entitled *Dark Ghetto: Dilemmas of Social Power*, an overview of housing, schools, psychology, and politics in New York City's Harlem.

WHO WAS THE FIRST AFRICAN-AMERICAN PRESIDENT OF THE AMERICAN LIBRARY ASSOCIATION?

In 1976, the American Library Association named its first African-American president, Clara Stanton Jones, the creator of an innovative information and referral system for libraries. Born in St. Louis, Missouri, in 1913, Jones earned a bachelor's degree from Spelman College and a library science degree from the University of Michigan. Her library career began at Dillard University in New Orleans, and in 1944 she joined the staff of the Detroit Public Library. Starting as a children's librarian, she rose through the system until she was named the library's director in 1970.

WHO WAS THE FIRST WOMAN IN THE COUNTRY TO HEAD A MAJOR RESEARCH UNIVERSITY?

Mary Francis Berry, born in 1938 to a poor family in Nashville, Tennessee, graduated from high school with honors and worked her way through college and graduate school as a lab technician, earning bachelor's and master's degrees from Howard University and a Ph.D. from the University of Michigan. Berry taught college history while pursuing a law degree and

Mary Francis Berry

then joined the staff of the University of Maryland, where she was given positions of increasing administrative responsibility. All the while, she was an energetic participant in antiwar and civil rights activities.

In 1976 Berry was named chancellor of the University of Colorado at Boulder, making her the first woman in the country to head a major research university. The next year President Jimmy Carter asked her to join the Department of Health, Education and Welfare as assistant secretary of education, a position in which she administered an annual budget of almost $13 billion and supervised three national education organizations.

In 1980 Berry earned another honor when President Carter appointed her to the U.S. Commission on Civil Rights. But after Ronald Reagan became president, Berry found herself in conflict with his conservative policies. When Reagan tried to fire her from the commission, she sued him to retain her job and she won. In 1993 Berry, while serving the first year of her third six-year term on the commission, was appointed chairwoman.

WHO WAS THE FIRST AFRICAN-AMERICAN WOMAN GIVEN TENURE AT YALE?

Sylvia A. Boone, a specialist in African and women's art, joined the faculty of Yale University in 1979 and became a tenured, full professor there nine years later. She was an associate professor of Afro-American studies and art history, specializing in African art, women's art, and female imagery.

Born in Mt. Vernon, New York, Boone earned degrees from Brooklyn College and Columbia University. She went on to study at the University of Ghana, where she got to know such prominent African-Americans as W.E.B. DuBois, Maya Angelou, and Malcolm X. She made dozens of trips to Africa, and lived there for extended periods of time.

Returning to the United States, Boone became a visiting lecturer in Afro-American studies at Yale, teaching a course on black women and starting a black film festival. She joined the Yale faculty after earning master's and doctoral degrees in art history there.

Boone's books include Radiance from the Waters: Ideals of Feminine Beauty in Mende Art, and West African Travels: A Guide to People and Places. This outstanding scholar died of heart failure in 1993 when she was only fifty-two years old. She was buried in the historic Grove Street Cemetery in New Haven, the burial ground for Yale presidents and other prominent University officials and scholars.

ENTERTAINMENT

WHAT WAS THE FIRST MUSICAL PRODUCED ON BROADWAY WITH AN ALL-AFRICAN-AMERICAN CAST?

Oriental America, produced by John W. Isham in 1896, demonstrated for the first time that African-Americans could excel at material that previously had been reserved for whites. Rather than the usual minstrelsy and burlesque, the show ended with a medley of operatic arias performed by distinguished African-American singers, including J. Rosamond Johnson. The show had a short run on Broadway at Palmer's Theatre.

That same year, *Black Patti's Troubadours*, written by Bob Cole and featuring the popular concert singer Sissieretta Jones, opened at Proctor's 58th Street Theatre. A great success, the show toured throughout the North and South before traveling abroad.

WHAT WAS BROADWAY'S FIRST MUSICAL SKETCH WRITTEN AND PERFORMED BY AFRICAN-AMERICANS?

In June 1898, an hour-long musical called *Clorindy; or, the Origin of the Cakewalk*, opened at the Casino Theatre Roof Garden on New York City's Broadway. The songs were composed by Will Marion Cook with lyrics by the poet Paul Laurence Dunbar. Cook, who was trained as a classical violinist, came to New York to study composition and became fascinated by black vaudeville performers. He decided to write a musical that would explore the cakewalk, an African-American dance that had become a national craze.

It is said that when Cook's mother heard his songs, written in dialect, she burst into tears, fearing that he would never become the classical musician she had hoped for. Cook conducted the orchestra for the run of *Clorindy* and continued his career in musical theater, composing music for several shows and writing Broadway's first interracial musical, *The Southerners*, which opened in 1904.

WHAT WAS THE FIRST FULL-LENGTH BROADWAY MUSICAL WRITTEN AND PERFORMED BY AFRICAN-AMERICANS?

In 1903, comedian Bert Williams and his partner, George Walker, presented *In Dahomey* at the New York Theatre on Broadway. The show played to packed houses until it left New York for London, where it was presented at the Shaftesbury Theatre. Londoners gave the show only a mild response until it was chosen for a command performance at the birthday celebration of the young Prince of Wales.

After being presented to royalty, *In Dahomey* became the hit of London, where the theater was full night after night for months. Williams himself became immensely popular, and was invited to the homes and clubs of London's leading citizens.

WHO WAS THE FIRST AFRICAN-AMERICAN PERFORMER TO STAR ON BROADWAY?

Born Egbert Austin Williams in 1874 in Antigua, British West Indies, Bert Williams was a natural musician from early childhood, and as soon as he was old enough he joined a traveling troupe of entertainers. When he was about twenty years old and performing with the troupe in San Francisco, he teamed up with George Walker, another entertainer. The two made their way to New York City where they appeared in several small musical productions. But their fame began to spread in 1903 when they starred in wildly popular musical comedy, *In Dahomey*, the first full-length Broadway show to be written and performed by African-Americans.

Williams and Walker played in two more musicals, *In Abyssinia* and *Bandana Land*, before Walker became ill and was forced to retire. Williams then struck out on his own, starring in 1909 in another all-black show, *Mr. Lode of Koal*. In 1910 Williams's popularity grew even greater when he was featured in the *Ziegfield Follies*, becoming the first African-American performer to star in a white show. He received rave reviews, stopping the show every night with his rendition of the song that became his signature, "Nobody."

Williams performed with the *Follies* until 1919, appearing with such top comedians as W.C. Fields, who called Williams "the funniest man I ever saw." But despite the honors that were heaped upon him for his work in the theater, Williams suffered the pains of racism, unable to ride the elevator or eat in the dining room of hotels where he stayed when on the road. He had reached the top of his profession, he once said, "not because of what I am, but in spite of it." Williams died suddenly in 1922 at the age of forty-nine.

WHAT WAS THE FIRST AFRICAN-AMERICAN MUSICAL TO RUN MORE THAN FIVE HUNDRED PERFORMANCES?

The first all-black musical of the 1920s, *Shuffle Along*, was a model for all Broadway shows that followed, and its success was an inspiration for many African-American composers and songwriters. The show was written by Eubie Blake, a pianist and composer, and Noble Sissle, a singer and lyricist; the two had teamed up in 1915.

Shuffle Along opened in May 1921 at New York City's Sixty-Third Street Theatre. Blake led the orchestra, which included an oboist named William Grant Still, later to become a famous composer. Many members of the cast also reached stardom, such as Florence Mills, the singer, and Josephine Baker, who danced in the chorus. The show introduced a number of songs that became hits; "I'm Just Wild About Harry" and "Love Will Find a Way" were two of the favorites.

Soon after it opened, Shuffle Along became so popular that crowds gathered on the sidewalk waiting to buy tickets, and cars and taxicabs jammed the street. Finally the city's traffic department had to declare 63rd Street a one-way thoroughfare. After a record 504 performances on Broadway, Shuffle Along went on the road to play for two more years.

WHO WAS THE FIRST AFRICAN-AMERICAN WOMAN TO RECEIVE THE FRENCH LEGION OF HONOR?

Born in St. Louis, Missouri, in 1906, Josephine Baker began dancing in a local vaudeville house when she was only eight years old to help support her struggling family. By the time she was about fifteen, Baker was in Manhattan, dancing in the chorus of Shuffle Along, a hit show written by the African-American musical collaborators Noble Sissle and Eubie Blake. Her vivid features and energetic style won many admirers, and in 1925 she was offered a major role in La Revue Negre, an American production that opened in Paris. Baker became an international sensation, dancing the Charleston and the Black Bottom and sometimes wearing only a string of bananas around her waist. In 1930 Baker added singing to her act, and while she was appearing in the Folies Bergere, she is said to have received 40,000 love letters and 2,000 offers of marriage. Her film appearances attracted even more fans.

After World War II broke out, Baker served as a Red Cross volunteer and a spy for the French Underground, for which she was awarded the French Legion of Honor. In the 1950s she bought a spacious estate and adopted fourteen orphaned children of many nationalities, who became known as her Rainbow Tribe. Baker, who had always refused to perform wherever African-Americans were not allowed, participated in the 1963 March on Washington and gave a civil rights benefit in Carnegie Hall.

Baker died in Paris in April 1975. At her funeral she was honored with a twenty-one-gun salute, the first such tribute given to an American woman.

Josephine Baker

WHO WAS THE FIRST AFRICAN-AMERICAN ENTERTAINER TO BECOME AN INTERNATIONAL STAR?

Florence Mills was only four years old when she made her stage debut in the musical, *Sons of Ham*. The audience went wild when she warbled the tune "Hannah from Savannah." Known as Baby Florence Mills, she won medals in cakewalk contests, and as a teenager joined her sisters in a singing and dancing act called the Mills Trio.

Soon after she went out on her own, Mills became a star of the 1921 Broadway show, *Shuffle Along*, in which her rendition of "I'm Craving for That Kind of Love" was a show-stopper. She was featured in *Plantation Revue* in 1922 and toured Europe in *From Dover to Dixie*. Back in New York, Mills starred in *Dixie to Broadway*, in which her performance of "I'm Just a Little Blackbird Looking for a Bluebird" brought tears to the eyes of her audience and became her theme song. By the time she appeared in *Blackbirds of 1926* she had become an international star; when the show played in London the Prince of Wales is said to have seen it sixteen times.

Mills was set to star in *Blackbirds of 1928* but a few months before it was to open she was rushed to the hospital for an emergency appendectomy. Complications ensued and she died; she was only thirty-two years old. More than 100,000 people accompanied her funeral procession as it moved through Harlem. When it neared 145th Street, an airplane released a flock of blackbirds. On her grave in Woodlawn Cemetery there was a tower of red roses eight feet high with a card signed, "From a friend." Some believed it was a tribute from the Prince of Wales.

WHO WAS THE FIRST AFRICAN-AMERICAN COMEDIENNE TO BECOME A CELEBRITY?

Jackie "Moms" Mabley started her career as a singer when she was fourteen years old, appearing in clubs and theaters. Born in North Carolina and raised in Maryland, she changed her name from Lauretta Aiken because her family was opposed to her show business career. In 1947, while she was performing as a comedian in stage shows in the East, she appeared in her first film, *Killer Diller*. A year later she was featured in the movie *Boarding House Blues*, in which she played the operator of a boarding house for entertainers.

Mabley became a hit on television's "Ed Sullivan Show," and made her first comedy record album in 1960. In the 1974 movie *Amazing Grace* Mabley portrayed an elderly woman determined to remove political corruption from the city of Baltimore. She suffered a heart attack while making the movie and was forced to wear a pacemaker to complete the filming.

A year later Mabley, who was in her seventies, died at her home in Westchester County, New York.

WHAT WAS THE FIRST TELEVISION SERIES TO STAR AN AFRICAN-AMERICAN ACTRESS?

The weekly television sitcom "Beulah" made its debut on ABC in October 1950. The title character, portrayed at first by the distinguished actress Ethel Waters, was a congenial black maid working for a white family. Hattie McDaniel took over as Beulah the next season, and after she died in 1952 the role was played by Louise Beavers.

The show's run ended in 1953 and it remained in syndication for a time, but when African-American groups protested its stereotyped characters, "Beulah" was cancelled.

WHAT WAS THE FIRST PRIME TIME TV SHOW TO FEATURE AN AFRICAN-AMERICAN CAST?

"Amos 'n' Andy," a comedy series that began appearing on television in 1951, originated as a radio program in 1929. On radio, white actors were used to portray the characters, who were supposed to be African-American. On television, though, "Amos 'n' Andy" used an all-black cast.

Almost immediately after it began, the NAACP and other organizations denounced the television series as an affront to African-Americans, although it was said that some black viewers enjoyed the show. After two years CBS took it off the air, but the series was kept in syndication until 1966.

WHO WAS THE FIRST AFRICAN-AMERICAN TO HOST A NETWORK TELEVISION SHOW?

Nat King Cole began his career as a jazz pianist but gained fame as a masterful singer of romantic ballads, becoming so popular that he was given his own television series in 1956. Born Nathaniel Adams Coles in Montgomery, Alabama, in 1919, the singer grew up in Chicago. He started forming his own bands while still in high school, and after graduation he struggled for several years, playing the piano in bars and putting together small groups that soon disbanded. His career took off in the 1940s when he formed the King Cole Trio, which slowly but surely became successful as fans discovered Cole's original piano style.

In 1944 the King Cole Trio recorded its first hit song, "Straighten Up and Fly Right," with Cole singing. Four years later a record of Cole's rendition of the song "Nature Boy" was a huge success, and he became one of the first African-American male singers to succeed in the white market.

Nat King Cole

From that time on Cole concentrated on singing, becoming one of the most popular recording stars of his day and a frequent guest on television variety shows. In November 1956 he premiered on NBC as the host of his own weekly television program, "The Nat King Cole Show." But despite his enormous popularity the show was unable to find a regular sponsor, and it was cancelled after one year. Frustrated and bitter, Cole criticized the advertising industry for not trying hard enough to sell his show to sponsors. In 1965 he died of lung cancer at the age of forty-six.

WHO WAS THE FIRST AFRICAN-AMERICAN PERFORMER TO WIN AN EMMY?

Harry Belafonte appeared on the folk music scene in the early 1950s, singing traditional tunes in New York City clubs. After his album of calypso songs was released in 1956, his versions of "Day O" and "Jamaica Farewell" swept the country. And by 1960 the talented singer had been awarded an Emmy for his television variety special, "Tonight with Belafonte."

Born in New York City in 1927, Belafonte was sent to live in Jamaica, West Indies, at the age of five after his mother, a domestic worker, decided he and his brother would be safer there. He was twelve when he returned to New York, where his West Indian accent added to his alienation from his high school classmates. After a stint in the U.S. Navy he became a janitor's assistant in a New York apartment building. One day an actress who lived in the building gave him tickets to the American Negro Theater. Seeing African-American actors on stage opened a new world to him, and he wanted to be part of it.

Belafonte began theater studies at the New School for Social Research, and when his G.I. Bill tuition money ran out he began singing jazz and pop tunes at the Royal Roost, a Broadway club. After he and two friends opened a restaurant in Greenwich Village, he started spending time at a club called the Village Vanguard, where he discovered the folk music of singers such as Josh White and Leadbelly. He loved the music and developed his own repertoire of folk songs.

Belafonte's theater training paid off in the 1950s when he was given roles in such movies as *Odds Against Tomorrow* and *Carmen Jones,* in which he co-starred with Dorothy Dandridge. In the 1955 film *Bright Road* he portrayed a shy principal in a Southern school, with Dandridge playing a teacher. Two years later in *Island in the Sun* he starred as a labor leader attracted to a white socialite.

A longtime civil rights activist and international human rights advocate, Belafonte continued to perform in movies, both dramas and comedies, and to produce films and television shows. He did less singing as his voice became huskier with age, and in 1993 he made his first New York City appearance in almost thirty years when he performed in concert at Lincoln Center.

Still from Carmen Jones, *starring Harry Belafonte and Dorothy Dandridge*

WHO WAS THE FIRST AFRICAN-AMERICAN ACTOR TO STAR IN A DRAMATIC SERIES ON TELEVISION?

"**I** Spy," a weekly television show that went on the air in 1965, starred Bill Cosby and Robert Culp as partners in espionage, and earned Cosby three consecutive Emmy awards as the most outstanding actor in a continuing dramatic series. Born William Henry Cosby in 1937 in Germantown, Pennsylvania, he received a bachelor's degree from Temple University. He later earned a master's and doctorate from the University of Massachusetts.

Cosby began his comedy career performing in clubs throughout the East. He won six Grammy awards for Best Comedy Album, starting in 1964 for *Bill Cosby is a Very Funny Fellow...Right?* After "I Spy" ended in 1968, he starred in "The Bill Cosby Show," portraying Chet Kincaid, a high school track coach. In 1972 and 1976 he hosted two variety shows, both unsuccessful, but his Saturday morning animated series, "Fat Albert and the Cosby Kids," attracted an enthusiastic audience.

Cosby finally hit the television jackpot in 1984 as producer and star of "The Cosby Show," a weekly series about the Huxtable family in which he portrayed a doctor whose wife is a lawyer. Before the last episode aired in April 1992, "The Cosby Show" was watched by more people than any other situation comedy on television. Cosby was also an author; his 1986 book *Fatherhood* became a best-seller.

WHO WAS THE FIRST AFRICAN-AMERICAN ACTRESS TO HAVE HER OWN TV SERIES?

Diahann Carroll, whose weekly series "Julia" began in the fall of 1968, is considered the first African-American actress to star in her own weekly television show. (Although "Beulah," which made its debut in 1950, was the first television series starring a black actress, the title character was actually played by three different actresses over the show's three-year run.) In the title role of Julia, Carroll portrayed a war widow who worked as a nurse to support herself and her young son. The series ran until mid-1971.

Carroll, who began her career as a singer, was born in 1935 and grew up in New York's Harlem and the Bronx. At age ten, the talented youngster won a Metropolitan Opera scholarship, and at fourteen, while a student at the High School of Music and Art in New York City, she won first prize on "Arthur Godfrey's Talent Scouts."

Carroll gained fame in 1954 as the co-star of the Broadway musical *House of Flowers*, and eight years later she won a Tony award for her role in *No Strings*. In 1974 Carroll received another honor; the Academy Award committee gave her a Best Actress nomination for her touching performance as a single mother in the film *Claudine*. And in 1984, midway through the run of the hit television series "Dynasty," Carroll joined the show in the role of Dominique Deveraux, a glamorous, sophisticated, and unscrupulous singer.

WHAT WAS THE FIRST SUCCESSFUL TV VARIETY SHOW HOSTED BY AN AFRICAN-AMERICAN ENTERTAINER?

"The Flip Wilson Show," which aired on NBC television from 1970 to 1974, gained consistently high ratings and great popularity throughout its four-year run. Wilson and his collaborators won a 1970 Emmy for outstanding writing of a variety show.

On the show, comedian Flip Wilson played host to many African-American entertainers and performed in comedy sketches. His roles included the Reverend Leroy, pastor of the church of "What's Happening Now," and Geraldine, whose line, "The devil made me do it," became a national expression. But some African-American viewers criticized the show, believing that Wilson's extreme portrayals of black characters reinforced negative stereotypes.

WHO WAS THE FIRST AFRICAN-AMERICAN WOMAN TO COMPETE FOR MISS AMERICA?

In 1970 Cheryl Adrienne Browne became the first African-American contestant in the Miss America pageant. A native of Jamaica, New York, Browne was a sophomore at Luther College in Iowa when she was chosen to represent that state at the pageant in Atlantic City.

WHO WAS THE FIRST AFRICAN-AMERICAN MR. AMERICA?

Chris Dickerson earned a top bodybuilding honor in 1970 when he was crowned Mr. America. Dickerson, one of triplets born in Montgomery, Alabama, in 1939, was an outstanding athlete in school. Planning to pursue a singing career, he took up bodybuilding to strengthen his voice and develop his breath control. Dickerson's other titles include Mr. Junior USA, Mr. Eastern America, and Mr. California.

WHO WAS THE FIRST AFRICAN-AMERICAN TO HOST A TELEVISION GAME SHOW?

When Adam Wade was made host of the nationally televised game show "Musical Chairs" in 1975, he was the veteran of a successful singing career that had ended in disaster. Wade hit the peak of the popular music industry in the early 1960s. His first record, "Ruby," was a hit, and a year later, in 1961, he had three singles on the Top 10. But the singer, only in his mid-

Adam Wade

twenties, never learned how to manage his money, and soon found himself deeply in debt.

Refusing to be defeated, Wade pulled himself together, began managing his career, and eventually won the spot of the first African-American game show host on national television. Unfortunately, "Musical Chairs" was cancelled after just one season on CBS. Wade found work doing television commercials, for which he won two awards, and acted in TV dramas, on stage, and in movies.

WHEN WAS THE FIRST AFRICAN-AMERICAN WOMAN CROWNED MISS AMERICA?

Vanessa Williams, a twenty-one-year-old Syracuse University student from Westchester County, New York, was crowned the first black Miss America in September 1984. Ten months later, after revealing photographs of her were published in *Penthouse* magazine, her title was taken away and awarded to another African-American woman, runner-up Suzette Charles from New Jersey.

Williams started an acting career in 1987, appearing in movies and on television. After making her debut record album in 1988, she went on to become a successful pop singer.

WHO WAS THE FIRST AFRICAN-AMERICAN WOMAN TO HOST A NATIONAL TV TALK SHOW?

One of the wealthiest women in the entertainment industry, Oprah Winfrey has always worked hard to do her best. Born in Kosciusko, Mississippi, in 1954, Winfrey went to Nashville, Tennessee, when she was about eight to live with her father and stepmother. They encouraged her to read books and expand her vocabulary. After high school she entered Tennessee State University, earning a bachelor's degree.

In 1976 Winfrey was hired as a feature reporter by a Baltimore television station, and a year later was made host of the show "People are Talking," where she remained until she went to Chicago in 1984 as host of "A.M. Chicago." Her skills as a talk-show host attracted such a wide audience that one year later the program was renamed "The Oprah Winfrey Show." In 1986 the program was syndicated nationally, soon becoming the number one weekday talk show in the nation.

Winfrey has also pursued a parallel career as an actress; in 1985 she was nominated for an Academy Award for her role as Sophia in the film *The Color Purple*. And in 1988 Winfrey became the first African-American woman to own her own television and film production company, Harpo Studios, a $20 million dollar film and television complex in Chicago.

FILM

WHO WAS THE FIRST AFRICAN-AMERICAN FILMMAKER TO PRODUCE MOVIES WITH BLACK CASTS?

William Foster became interested in theater while living in New York City, where he settled in 1884. He first got a job working with horses, and became an authority on the performance records of race horses. Around 1900 Foster worked as a publicity manager for the early African-American musicals *In Dahomey* and *In Abyssinia.* In 1910 he moved to Chicago, started the Foster Photoplay Company, and began making short films with all-black casts. His first, *The Railroad Porter*, was a chase comedy. It was followed by *The Butler*, a detective story, and *The Grafter and the Maid,* a melodrama.

Foster wrote, directed, and filmed most of the movies himself, but his company had to rely on financing from white backers. Although his films were never successful, he continued to insist that African-American filmmakers should make movies with black actors for black audiences. He later became the circulation manager of the African-American weekly newspaper, the *Chicago Defender*, where he remained until 1925, when he established the Haitian Coffee Company. Three years later he left New York and went to Hollywood to launch a career as a director.

WHAT WAS THE FIRST MOVIE TO STAR AN AFRICAN-AMERICAN ACTOR?

In 1914 an independent black film company released a movie called *Darktown Jubilee*, starring the African-American comedian Bert Williams. A screening of the movie in Brooklyn produced shouts, catcalls, and a near race riot. Realizing that white audiences were not ready for African-American movie stars, the producers of *Darktown Jubilee* soon took their film out of circulation.

WHO WAS THE FIRST AFRICAN-AMERICAN ACTOR TO MAKE A CAREER IN FILMS?

Noble Johnson was one of Hollywood's most active and successful African-American actors, appearing in movies for thirty years after making his debut in 1914. Johnson spent his childhood in Colorado and at fifteen began traveling through the West.

In his first film, a western produced by the Lubin Film Production Company of Philadelphia, he played an Indian chief. In 1915 he moved to Los Angeles and became involved with the Lincoln Motion Picture Company, an African-American production company. He became president of Lincoln and starred in its first three films, *The Realization of a Negro's Ambition*, in which he played a successful engineer, *The Trooper of Company K*, and *The Law of Nature.*

Johnson then moved to the Universal Film Company, where he specialized in portraying characters of various races. He was a cannibal chief in *Little Robinson Crusoe*, Chief Sitting Bull in *The Flaming Frontier*, he drove a chariot in *King of Kings*, and in 1932 he played a Russian villain in Rodeo Pictures's *The Most Dangerous Game.*

WHAT WAS THE FIRST AFRICAN-AMERICAN-OWNED COMPANY TO PRODUCE SERIOUS FILMS?

The Lincoln Motion Picture Company was the first production company started by African-Americans to make serious films with black performers for black audiences. It was founded in 1915 in Los Angeles by the actors Noble Johnson and Clarence Brooks and a prosperous druggist, James T. Smith; Johnson's brother George soon joined the organization. The only white partner was the cameraman, Harry Gant, who filmed all of the company's productions.

Lincoln's first venture was *The Realization of a Negro's Ambition*, starring Noble Johnson as a Tuskegee Institute engineering graduate who leaves his sweetheart to travel to California, where he makes a fortune and then returns to marry the girl back home and live happily ever after. Lincoln's second film, *The Trooper of Company K*, also starring Noble Johnson, was about the African-American 10th Cavalry fighting in Mexico. Despite the high quality of its movies, Lincoln was often unable to persuade white theater owners to show them. And as an African-American company, it was unable to obtain financing in advance and had to rely on profits from finished films.

When Noble Johnson left Lincoln in 1918 to make movies for Universal, Clarence Brooks took over as leading man, starring in two well-received films, *A Man's Duty* and *By Right of Birth*. But by 1923, financial and distribution problems forced the company to dissolve.

WHO WAS THE FIRST AFRICAN-AMERICAN PERFORMER AWARDED A LONG-TERM MOVIE CONTRACT?

When Frederick Ernest Morrison was just an infant, his father, a cook for a movie producer, overheard his boss say that he was looking for a cute baby. The cook suggested his son. The tiny Morrison appeared in a number of comedy shorts and was eventually picked up by the producer Hal Roach. In 1919 Roach awarded the six-year-old Morrison a two-year studio contract, which was later renewed.

Billed as "Sunshine Sammy," the name of the character that he always played, Morrison appeared in more than 100 Hal Roach comedies. When the "Our Gang" series began in 1922, Morrison was one of the original group. By then, he was making $250 a week, an impressive amount for the time. As an adult, Morrison worked in vaudeville for a while and then left show business to join the aerospace industry.

WHO WAS THE FIRST SUCCESSFUL AFRICAN-AMERICAN FILMMAKER?

Oscar Micheaux was born on a farm in Illinois in 1884. He left home in his teens and worked as a bootblack and then a Pullman porter. When he was about twenty-five he settled in South Dakota, becoming one of the few African-American homesteaders in the state. After about four years of working the land, Micheaux used his own experiences to write a novel entitled *The Homesteader*, publishing it himself and selling it door-to-door around the region.

Micheaux moved on to Sioux City, Iowa, where he started his own publishing company and continued to produce and sell his own books. In 1918 the Lincoln Motion Picture Company, a black-owned company from Los Angeles, approached Micheaux with plans to make a movie of *The Homesteader*. But Micheaux decided to produce the movie himself. He established the Micheaux Film and Book Company and began to raise money around Sioux City.

Micheaux finished *The Homesteader* in 1919 and traveled from city to city with prints of the film, asking theater owners to show it and at the same time raising money from them for his next production. Using this technique, he produced thirty films with African-American themes over the next twenty years. His was the most successful black-owned film production company of its time. Micheaux made his last film, *The Betrayal*, in 1948, and died three years later.

WHAT WERE THE FIRST FEATURE-LENGTH AFRICAN-AMERICAN TALKIES?

The year 1929 marked the release of the first two talking pictures with African-American casts. The first to be released, *Hearts in Dixie*, produced by the William Fox Studio, featured the first all-black cast ever seen on the American movie screen (the only white role was that of a doctor). A musical about a farmer and his family on a southern plantation, the film abounded in stereotypes.

The role of the grandfather of the family was played by Clarence Muse, a lawyer, director, and producer with a background in theater. After starring in *Hearts in Dixie*, Muse had a successful career in films, making over

Still from Hallelujah! *starring Nina Mae McKinney*

Still from Hearts in Dixie *starring Stepin Fetchit*

fifty movies in twenty-five years. The movie also starred the actor Stepin Fetchit in one of his most prominent roles.

Several months later the director King Vidor released his first sound film, *Hallelujah!* The movie was a landmark in films about African-American families. Although the characters were stereotypical and the plot was melodramatic, the performances of the leads and the spirituals sung by the Dixie Jubilee Choir made it memorable. *Hallelujah!* told the story of a cotton farmer's son, played by Daniel Haynes, led astray by a cabaret dancer named Chick, portrayed by the beautiful young Nina Mae McKinney.

Hallelujah! was given a double premiere, one in the Lafayette Theater in Harlem and the other at a theater in midtown Manhattan. Although an attempt was made in the North to keep white and black movie audiences separate, in the South most theaters banned *Hallelujah* altogether.

WHO WAS THE FIRST AFRICAN-AMERICAN HOLLYWOOD STAR?

Lincoln Theodore Monroe Andrew Perry, better known as Stepin Fetchit, was born in 1902 in Key West, Florida, the son of a cigar maker. He was in his early teens when he left to seek his fortune in show business. He hooked up with a vaudeville partner, Ed Lee; they called their act "Step 'n' Fetchit: Two Dancing Fools from Dixie." The duo eventually broke up and he took the name with him to Hollywood.

Fetchit's first big break in the movies was the 1929 all-black talkie, *Hearts in Dixie.* He appeared in many films during the '20s and '30s, performing with such stars as Shirley Temple and Will Rogers. The first African-American movie star to receive feature billing, he always played the same role, a gawky, shuffling character who mumbled and muttered.

Offscreen, Fetchit's wild escapades made headlines, and he could be seen cruising the streets of Los Angeles in his expensive automobile. But by the late 1930s he had been released from his movie contract and, although he was said to have made millions, he ended up penniless.

WHO WAS THE FIRST AFRICAN-AMERICAN ACTRESS TO BECOME A WELL-KNOWN MOVIE STAR?

Nina Mae McKinney was born in 1913 in Lancaster, South Carolina, and was raised by her grandmother until the age of twelve, when her parents sent for her from New York City. When McKinney was fifteen she joined the chorus line of Lew Leslie's show, *Blackbirds of 1928*. A year later the Hollywood director King Vidor chose her to star in *Hallelujah!*, one of the first sound films with an all-black cast. She portrayed a seductive cabaret dancer named Chick.

Lincoln Theodore "Stepin Fetchit" Perry

After her successful appearance in *Hallelujah!*, MGM studios offered McKinney a five-year contract, but she discovered that there were few leading movie roles for African-American actresses. When her contract ended she left Hollywood, sang in theaters and clubs, and made a few minor movies. Her last screen appearance was a supporting role in the 1949 film *Pinky*.

WHO WAS THE FIRST AFRICAN-AMERICAN MOVIE ACTRESS TO ENTERTAIN AT THE WHITE HOUSE?

The lovely actress and singer Etta Moten captured the hearts of many filmgoers with her interpretation of the Depression-era song, "Remember My Forgotten Man," in the movie *Gold Diggers of 1933*, which starred the actor James Cagney.

In January 1934 President Franklin Roosevelt and his wife, Eleanor, invited Moten—a star of both stage and screen—to sing for their guests at a White House dinner. Moten had a lengthy career as a concert artist, and played the lead in an early production of the opera *Porgy and Bess*.

WHO WAS THE FIRST AFRICAN-AMERICAN MOVIE COWBOY?

During a 1933 stint as a singer with Earl Hines and his band, Herb Jeffries, a Detroit native, became one of the most popular singing emcees in the Midwest. Jeffries went to Los Angeles in 1937, where he again became a singer and emcee, gaining fame for his rendition of "Cocktails for Two."

The popular vocalist was discovered by Hollywood and soon became the star of a series of musical Westerns with all-black casts. Using the name Herbert Jeffrey, he was featured as a singing cowboy in such films as *Harlem on the Prairie*, released in 1937, and *The Bronze Buckaroo*, in 1938, which was advertised as a "roaring round-up of song-studded thrills!"

Jeffries left Hollywood to devote himself to music, joining Duke Ellington's orchestra and recording his signature tune, "Flamingo."

WHO WAS THE FIRST AFRICAN-AMERICAN ACTRESS TO STAR IN A MAJOR FILM?

One of the most talented performers in Hollywood, Louise Beavers made dozens of movies but suffered the plight of many fine African-American actresses—she could not avoid being cast as a servant. Born in Cincinnati in 1902, Beavers grew up in Pasadena, California, and was discovered by a movie studio agent when she performed in a talent show. She appeared in a number of films in the late 1920s and early '30s, usually playing a cheerful maid for the likes of Mae West and Jean Harlow.

Her great triumph was the 1934 film, *Imitation of Life*. She and the actress Claudette Colbert played two widows, black and white, each with a daughter to raise. The white widow, Miss Bea, becomes the breadwinner while the Beavers character, Aunt Delilah, cares for the house and children.

Etta Moten

The two eventually become rich by marketing Delilah's family pancake recipe, but their cold-hearted daughters cause them misery. Critics applauded Beavers's performance in *Imitation of Life* and many thought she should have been nominated for an Oscar.

Beavers continued to play her usual movie role throughout the 1940s and '50s; she was forced to gain weight and wear padding to maintain her plump appearance. Her other outstanding roles were in the 1939 film, *Made for Each Other*, and the 1948 Cary Grant movie, *Mr. Blandings Builds His Dream House*. In 1950 she played Robinson's mother in *The Jackie Robinson Story* and two years later she starred in the television series "Beulah." Her last movie was *Facts of Life* in 1961—playing a maid. She died a year later.

WHO WAS THE FIRST AFRICAN-AMERICAN TO WIN AN ACADEMY AWARD?

When Hattie McDaniel was seventeen years old she took the first step on the road to show business, singing on the radio with Professor George Morrison's orchestra. McDaniel, born in Wichita, Kansas, in 1898, soon became part of the vaudeville circuit and even starred in a radio show called "Hi-Hat Hattie." She eventually made her way to Hollywood where she worked as a maid until she started getting movie roles.

Even on the screen, McDaniel was limited to playing a maid, although she did give her portrayals a certain flair that made audiences remember her. In response to those who criticized her movie roles, she reportedly said, "It's better to play a maid than to be one." McDaniel's talent was rewarded when she was given an Academy Award as Best Supporting Actress for her performance as Mammy in the 1939 hit movie, *Gone With the Wind*. She was the first African-American to receive an Oscar.

McDaniel's many other movies include *The Little Colonel*, *Alice Adams*, *Saratoga*, *Babbitt*, and *Showboat*, in which she sang "I Still Suits Me" with Paul Robeson. She died of cancer at the age of fifty-four.

WHO WAS THE FIRST AFRICAN-AMERICAN WOMAN TO JOIN THE SCREEN WRITERS GUILD?

Mary Elizabeth Vroman was born in Buffalo, New York, in 1923 and raised in the British West Indies. She returned to the United States to attend Alabama State Teachers College. When she was in her twenties and employed as a schoolteacher she wrote a short story called "See How They Run," which was published in a 1952 issue of the *Ladies' Home Journal*.

Vroman's story was about a rural schoolteacher trying to help a troubled student. The story was bought by MGM studios and released in 1953 as the movie *Bright Road*, starring Dorothy Dandridge as the teacher and Harry Belafonte as the sensitive and devoted elementary school principal. Vroman wrote the screenplay for *Bright Road* and became the first African-American woman granted membership in the Screen Writers Guild. She went on to write two novels and one nonfiction book before she died in 1967.

WHO WAS THE FIRST AFRICAN-AMERICAN ACTRESS NOMINATED FOR AN OSCAR AS BEST ACTRESS?

Dorothy Dandridge started her performing career in Cleveland when she was only six years old, singing, dancing, doing acrobatics, and playing the violin with her sister, Vivian, in an act called Wonder Kids. In the 1930s the family moved to Los Angeles, where Dorothy, Vivian, and a young friend formed a singing group called the Dandridge Sisters that performed at the Cotton Club in New York and appeared in the Marx Brothers movie, *A Day at the Races*.

After the group disbanded, Dandridge sang in clubs and played a few bit parts in films. Her big break came in 1953 when she costarred with Harry Belafonte in *Bright Road*, and a year later she won an Academy Award nomination as Best Actress for her role in *Carmen Jones*, a first for an African-American actress. Dandridge's career, built on her image as a seductress, began a gradual decline. She failed at a comeback attempt in the 1960s, and met her tragic end at the age of forty-three when she was found dead in her Los Angeles apartment from an overdose of antidepressants.

WHO WAS THE FIRST AFRICAN-AMERICAN ACTOR TO WIN AN ACADEMY AWARD?

After Sidney Poitier made his way to New York from Miami, Florida, where he was born in 1927, he worked at any job he could find in an effort to survive. He labored as a dockhand, dishwasher, and chicken plucker before he applied for work as an actor at the American Negro Theater, which rejected him. Undeterred, he polished his speaking skills by listening to the radio and then reapplied. This time the theater group took him in.

He appeared in a few plays and then, in 1949, he captured a leading role in the movie *No Way Out*. After finishing a second film, *Cry, the Beloved Country*, he returned to New York to take the lead in a play, *Detective Story*, that was being produced at the Apollo Theatre in Harlem. The play had a short run, and Poitier decided to open a small barbecue restaurant called Ribs and Ruff to support himself. But before long he was called back to Hollywood for a major role in the groundbreaking film *Blackboard Jungle*.

Poitier went on to play other leading parts in such movies as the 1958 drama *The Defiant Ones* and the 1961 film version of Lorraine Hansberry's play *A Raisin in the Sun*, repeating the role he had played on Broadway two

Still from Bright Road, *starring Dorothy Dandridge*

years earlier. In 1963 he won an Oscar for his role in *Lilies in the Field*, becoming the first African-American actor to receive an Academy Award.

After making *Guess Who's Coming to Dinner* in 1967, Poitier concentrated more and more on directing. But this distinguished performer was once again honored in 1992 when he was given the American Film Institute Life

Achievement Award, the first time in the organization's twenty-year history that the award had been given to an African-American.

WHO WAS THE FIRST AFRICAN-AMERICAN TO PRODUCE AND DIRECT A FILM FOR A MAJOR STUDIO?

Gordon Parks, Sr., was born in 1912 in the small town of Fort Scott, Kansas, one of fifteen children. His mother died when he was a teenager and he set out on his own. To support himself he worked as a piano player, a bus boy, and a singer with a band. In 1933 he joined the Civilian Conservation Corps, a government program that gave work to impoverished young men. He then became a waiter on a cross-country train.

But Parks's fate was sealed when he bought a camera in a pawnshop for $7.50 and decided to become a photographer. His first exhibit of photographs was held in 1938 in the window of an Eastman Kodak store in Minneapolis. Before long his fashion photos were discovered by the boxer Joe Louis's wife, Marva, who encouraged him to move to Chicago, where he became a popular photographer of wealthy society women. In late 1941 he earned a fellowship that brought him to Washington, D.C., to take photographs for the Farm Security Administration and then the Office of War Information. Moving to New York City in 1944, he worked as a free-lance photographer for magazines and for the Standard Oil Company, and in 1949 he embarked on a lengthy career as a photographer for *Life* magazine.

In 1969 Parks turned to Hollywood, where he produced and directed *The Learning Tree* for Warner Brothers, making him the first African-American to produce and direct a major studio film. His other movie credits include *Shaft*, *Shaft's Big Score,* and a 1968 documentary, *Diary of a Harlem Family,* that won an Emmy award. A true Renaissance man, Parks has composed more than a dozen musical works and has written many books of poetry, fiction, and nonfiction, including his fourth volume of autobiography, *Voices in the Mirror.*

WHO WAS THE FIRST AFRICAN-AMERICAN WOMAN FILMMAKER TO PRODUCE A FULL-LENGTH FEATURE FILM?

In 1992 the movie *Daughters of the Dust,* directed by the African-American filmmaker Julie Dash, opened to critical acclaim. The film is an evocation of the West African culture that is preserved on the islands off the coast of Georgia and South Carolina, a background Dash inherited from her father. Dash, who grew up in a New York City housing project and studied filmmaking at the American Film Institute and the University of California at

Los Angeles, spent sixteen years making *Daughters of the Dust*. It was her eleventh film and first full-length feature.

WHO WAS THE FIRST AFRICAN-AMERICAN DIRECTOR NOMINATED FOR AN OSCAR?

John Singleton was only twenty-two years old when he made his 1991 film *Boyz N the Hood*, which earned him an Academy Award nomination as Best Director. He was the youngest person and the first African-American to be nominated for that award.

Singleton was born in 1968 in South-Central Los Angeles and grew up in the neighborhood. He wrote the script for *Boyz N the Hood* (which also gained an Oscar nomination for Best Screen Play) while he was a student in the film writing program at the University of Southern California. The story of young people trying to survive in a danger-ridden Los Angeles neighborhood, the film received rave reviews and attracted a wide audience. Singleton's second movie, *Poetic Justice*, released in 1993, starred singer Janet Jackson as a poetry-writing hairdresser from South-Central Los Angeles who falls in love with a postal worker.

HISTORY

WHO WAS THE FIRST MARTYR OF
THE AMERICAN REVOLUTION?

In the year 1770, at a time when people in the American colonies were growing increasingly weary of oppression under the British Empire, an African-American man named Crispus Attucks was shot and killed by a British soldier in an event that became known as the Boston Massacre. Attucks had run away twenty years earlier from his master in Framingham, Massachusetts, and had been living and working in Boston.

On the snowy night of March 5, Attucks stood at the front of a crowd of colonists who were protesting their British oppressors. One of the soldiers, struck by a chunk of ice, fired a shot, hitting Attucks in the chest. The tall, imposing man dropped to the ground and died. Four other men fell to their death at the hands of the British soldiers that night, but Attucks is remembered as the first colonist to die in the struggle for American independence.

WHO WAS THE FIRST AFRICAN-AMERICAN TO LEAD
A FIGHT FOR CIVIL RIGHTS IN MASSACHUSETTS?

Paul Cuffe was born in 1759 on the island of Cuttyhunk, near New Bedford, Massachusetts. He went to sea at sixteen, returned home after a few years, and settled on a farm. He began building his own sailing vessels and embarked on a highly successful career as a shipowner. When he was about twenty-one, Cuffe, his brother, and five other African-Americans petitioned the legislature, vowing they would not pay taxes until they were granted the same rights as white Massachusetts citizens. The lawmakers agreed and passed a law giving equal rights, including the right to vote, to Cuffe and all other African-Americans in Massachusetts.

As he grew older, Cuffe developed a plan to establish colonies for freed slaves in Africa. In 1815 he and thirty-eight African-Americans sailed to Sierra Leone to put his plan into action. He returned to America the next year, but died before he could further the cause of African resettlement.

WHAT WAS THE FIRST AFRICAN-AMERICAN
MUTUAL AID SOCIETY?

The Free African Society, the first mutual aid organization for African-Americans, was founded in Philadelphia in 1787 by Richard Allen and Absalom Jones, who later became prominent religious leaders. Members of the Free African Society promised to lead orderly, sober lives characterized by decorum and marital fidelity, and to contribute to the assistance of those who became widowed, orphaned, or ill.

One of the society's most remarkable public services took place during the great plague of 1793, when a yellow fever epidemic raced through the entire population of the city. The organization offered to help all citizens who were stricken with the disease, and its members stepped forward to nurse the sick and carry away the bodies.

WHO FOUNDED THE FIRST AFRICAN-AMERICAN MASONIC LODGE?

Prince Hall, an African-American patriot who fought in the Battle of Bunker Hill during the American Revolution, was born in Barbados around 1748 and migrated to Massachusetts in 1765. A few weeks before the outbreak of the Revolution, Hall and several other African-Americans were initiated into the Masons, an international mutual aid society, by a British military lodge then stationed in Boston.

In July 1776 Hall and his fellow Masons were granted a license and became established as African Lodge No. 1, the first organized group of African-American Masons in the country. The group finally received a charter from the Grand Lodge in England in 1787, and Hall, who had become an affluent soapmaker and an activist for the rights of African-Americans, was named the master. Four years later Hall was made grand master of the African Grand Lodge, which was renamed the Prince Hall Grand Lodge after Hall died of pneumonia in 1807,

WHO WAS THE FIRST SETTLER OF THE CITY OF CHICAGO?

When Jean Baptist Pointe DuSable arrived at the mouth of the Chicago River sometime in the late 1700s and established a trading post, he was known as a tall, handsome, cultured, Paris-educated fur trader who had friendly relationships with both Native Americans and whites. DuSable was born in Haiti around 1745; his mother was an African slave and his father a French seaman. When DuSable's mother died, his father sent him to France for an education and then put him to work as a sailor on one of his ships.

But when DuSable's ship was wrecked near New Orleans, he was afraid that he might become enslaved. He was hidden by Jesuits until he managed to leave the South for the Northwest, where he became a fur trapper. DuSable eventually reached the mouth of the Chicago River and set up his trading post, creating the first permanent settlement in what is now the city of Chicago. It was there that he built a comfortable five-room home that he shared with his wife, Catherine, a Potawatomi Indian, and their son and daughter.

His trading post gradually expanded and became a major supply center for traders, trappers, and Native Americans. Despite his success, DuSable sold his property around 1800 and left Chicago forever. No one knows why he left or where he ended his days.

WHO WAS THE FIRST TO EXPLORE THE DEPTHS OF THE LONGEST CAVE IN THE WORLD?

Mammoth Cave in Kentucky is the longest cave in the world, with more than 335 miles of passageways. There is evidence that Native Americans discovered entrances to Mammoth Cave about 4,000 years ago. Guided by the light of torches made from dried weeds and canes, they explored about twenty miles of underground corridors. White men came to the cave in the 1790s to dig for saltpeter, which was used in making gunpowder, and adventurers arrived to investigate its subterranean wonders. But the most famous name connected with Mammoth Cave was that of Stephen Bishop, a slave.

In 1838 a Kentucky attorney, Franklin Gorin, bought Mammoth Cave. He brought his slave, seventeen-year-old Stephen Bishop, to learn the passageways and become a guide. Bishop was fascinated by the underground twists and turns and fearlessly explored the deepest sections of the cave, discovering rivers, bottomless pits, and dramatic chambers. Visitors were attracted to the handsome, knowledgeable Bishop, and he was in great demand. He guided many famous people, including painters, writers, and even a Norwegian violinist, who played a concerto in an underground hall.

Bishop gained his freedom in 1856, as his master had decreed before he died. Although Bishop had talked of taking his wife and son to Liberia when he became free, he remained at Mammoth Cave. He died in the summer of 1857 and was buried on a hill near the cave's entrance, his grave marked by a cedar tree.

WHO WAS THE FIRST AFRICAN-AMERICAN WOMAN TO LECTURE AGAINST SLAVERY?

Born Isabella Baumfree near Kingston, New York, around 1797, Sojourner Truth changed her name some fifteen years after she was freed by the New York State Emancipation Act of 1827. She took the name Sojourner because of her wanderings and Truth because she was to speak the truth about the evils of slavery. After years of being a slave, a wife and mother, a domestic worker in New York City, and an evangelist, Sojourner Truth spent much of the rest of her life traveling around the country, lecturing against slavery and in support of voting rights for women.

Nearly six feet tall with a deep voice and impressive features, she wore a satin banner across her chest that read: "Proclaim liberty throughout the land unto all the inhabitants thereof." She was a compelling lecturer, drawing crowds wherever she spoke. She visited President Lincoln in the White

House several times, urging him to allow African-American troops to fight with the Union forces in the Civil War. In Washington, she nursed wounded soldiers and helped resettle newly freed slaves.

After the war she continued to lecture for women's suffrage and on behalf of her people. She died in 1883 at her home in Battle Creek, Michigan.

WHO WAS THE FIRST TO SETTLE THE BUSH PRAIRIE AREA OF WASHINGTON STATE?

George Washington Bush was born a free citizen in Pennsylvania in the late 1700s, fought under Andrew Jackson in the Battle of New Orleans during the War of 1812, and made extensive journeys to the Pacific Coast in the 1820s while working for the Hudson's Bay Company. He bought a farm and raised cattle in Missouri, but because of a new law denying residency to African-Americans, he and his family joined a wagon train heading west.

Arriving in the Oregon territory in 1844, Bush found to his dismay that African-Americans were prohibited from owning property. Still seeking a place where he and his family could live peacefully, he crossed the Columbia River into Washington, where he staked a claim to 640 acres in an area south of what is now the state capital of Olympia. The area came to be known as Bush Prairie. Bush became a prosperous farmer and a generous neighbor, supplying produce and grains to new settlers, and lending them tools and supplies.

WHO WAS THE FIRST AFRICAN-AMERICAN WOMAN TO BE HONORED WITH HER PICTURE ON A POSTAGE STAMP?

Harriet Tubman, referred to as "Moses" because she led hundreds of her people out of slavery, was born around 1820. Growing up as a slave on a Maryland plantation, she was forced to perform hard labor. When she was thirteen an overseer hit her on the head with a two-pound weight, causing a fractured skull that resulted in frequent seizures.

When her master died she decided to escape, and in 1849 she left her husband and children and made her way north to Canada. Recalling her escape for her biographer, Tubman said, "When I found I had crossed that line, I looked at my hands to see if I was the same person. There was such a glory over everything."

Starting in 1850, Tubman became a "conductor" on the Underground Railroad, leading slaves to freedom. Large rewards were offered for her capture, but she was never caught and she never lost a passenger. In a ten-year period before the Civil War she made nineteen trips down South,

Harriet Tubman

bringing back three hundred slaves, including her children, her brothers and their families, and her elderly parents. Her husband had married another woman during her absence.

After serving in the Civil War as a scout, spy, and nurse, she settled on a small farm in Auburn, New York, later turning her house into a home for poor and elderly African-Americans. After she died of pneumonia in 1913, the residents of Auburn installed a plaque in her honor in the town square. She was commemorated by a postage stamp issued on February 1, 1978, the first to picture an African-American woman.

WHO FIRST DISCOVERED THE LOWEST PASS THROUGH THE SIERRA NEVADA MOUNTAINS?

The son of a Revolutionary War officer and a slave, James Beckwourth became a famous Indian fighter and frontiersman who discovered a pass through the northern Sierra Nevadas, between what is now Reno and Sacramento. Beckwourth, born in Virginia in 1798, escaped from slavery at nineteen and headed west, joining Colonel Ashley's Rocky Mountain Fur Company, where he became adept at handling a gun, hatchet, and Bowie knife. Adopted by the Crow Indians in 1824, he led the tribe in several battles against its enemies.

Beckwourth went on to make many expeditions throughout the West, serving as an Army scout and a mail carrier and prospecting for gold. In 1850 he made the discovery that put his name on the map; he found the lowest pass through the Sierra Nevadas and led the first wagon train of settlers along the new trail. This pass and a nearby California town still bear his name. After settling for a time in Plumas County, California, Beckwourth returned to the Southwest, and died in 1866 while living with his old comrades, the Crow Indians.

WHO WAS THE FIRST TO SETTLE CENTRALIA, WASHINGTON?

Born in Virginia in 1817 to a white mother and a father who was a slave, George Washington was raised by a white family who eventually settled in Missouri. Unable to attend school, Washington was taught reading, writing, and mathematics at home and learned the skills of a marksman, miller, tanner, cook, and weaver. He ran a sawmill in Missouri for a time, and in 1850 joined a wagon train traveling to the Oregon territory. Locating a spread of land on the Chehalis River, he settled down as a homesteader in an area that later became part of Washington State.

In 1872, when the Northern Pacific Railway made plans to run its tracks across his land, he decided to establish a town midway between the Columbia River and Puget Sound. He named it Centerville, sold lots to settlers for five dollars each, built a church and a school, and gave food and clothing to townspeople who were going through hard times. The town's name was later changed to Centralia, and Washington remained there as an honored resident. In 1905, after he was killed in a horse-and-buggy accident, the mayor proclaimed a day of mourning.

WHO WAS THE FIRST AFRICAN-AMERICAN WOMAN TO DRIVE A U.S. MAIL COACH?

Mary Fields was born in 1832 in a slave cabin in Tennessee. Little is known about her early life, but she eventually headed West, ending up at about the age of fifty in Montana, where she worked for the Ursuline nuns at their mission in Cascade. Standing six feet tall and weighing about 200 pounds, Fields was an impressive sight in the long dress and apron she wore over a pair of men's pants to protect herself from the cold. The nuns helped her set up a restaurant in Cascade but it is said that the business failed because Fields gave away too many free meals.

In 1895 Fields got a job carrying the U.S. mail. Known as "Stagecoach Mary," she delivered the mail sitting on the coach smoking a big cigar, sometimes having to fight her way through blizzards and fend off attacks by wolves. She was past seventy when she decided to retire from the mail delivery job and open a laundry. Although this career was less arduous, Fields didn't lose her spirit. Legend has it that she once punched a man and knocked him onto the street because he neglected to pay his laundry bill.

WHO FOUNDED THE FIRST AFRICAN-AMERICAN TOWN IN CALIFORNIA?

After serving with the Union forces during the Civil War, Allen Allensworth, who earlier had escaped from slavery, settled in St. Louis, Missouri, where he and his brother ran two successful restaurants. Allensworth continued his education and in 1871 he became a minister. Fifteen years later he returned to the military as the chaplain of an all-black army unit. By the time Allensworth retired in 1906 he held the rank of lieutenant colonel, making him the highest ranking chaplain and highest ranking African-American officer of the time.

After his retirement, Colonel Allensworth moved to Los Angeles with his wife and daughters. Committed to furthering the cause of black Americans, he decided to establish a town where African-Americans could govern themselves, own property, and reach their economic potential without being hampered by discriminatory laws and practices. In 1908 Allensworth and four colleagues located a site for the town in Tulare County, near the Santa Fe railroad line and midway between Los Angeles and San Francisco.

The town, which was named Allensworth, grew quickly as African-American men and women representing a range of occupations moved in and built homes, schools, churches, shops, and a hotel. Travelers who used the railroad depot provided business for the town, and it soon became a lively center of activity. But in 1914 Colonel Allensworth was killed in an

Colonel Allen Allensworth

accident. The townspeople were despondent, but other leaders tried to keep things going. Over the years, however, the town's water supply gradually diminished and use of the railroad declined. Residents began to move away, and by the early 1990s only about thirty families remained.

Today, the town has been transformed into Colonel Allensworth State Historic Park, with restored buildings and special events commemorating this visionary leader.

WHO WAS THE FIRST PERSON TO REACH THE NORTH POLE?

In 1866, one year after General Lee surrendered at Appomattox, Matthew Henson was born in Charles County, Maryland, on a farm that was an old slave market site. At thirteen he went to sea on a sailing ship bound for China, signing on as cabin boy. After that adventure he made many world voyages, becoming an able-bodied seaman in the process.

Henson met Commander Robert R. Peary in 1888 and joined him on an expedition to Nicaragua. Impressed with Henson's seamanship, Peary recruited him as a colleague, not a servant, as had been recommended. For years they made many trips together including Arctic voyages in which Henson traded with the Eskimos and mastered their language, built sleds, and trained dog teams—all talents that made him ideally suited for polar exploration.

In April of 1909 Peary mounted his third attempt to reach the North Pole, selecting Henson to be one of the team of six who would make the final run to the Pole. Before the goal was reached Peary could no longer continue on foot and rode in a dog sled. Various accounts say he was ill, exhausted, or had frozen toes. In any case he sent Henson on ahead as a scout. In a newspaper interview Henson said: "I was in the lead that had overshot the mark a couple of miles. We went back then and I could see that my footprints were the first at the spot." Matthew Henson then proceeded to plant the American flag, becoming the first man to reach the North Pole.

Although Admiral Peary received many honors, Henson was largely ignored, and spent most of the next thirty years working as a clerk in a federal customs house in New York. But in 1945 Congress awarded him a duplicate of the silver medal given to Peary. Presidents Truman and Eisenhower both honored him before he died in 1955.

Finally, in 1988, years of effort and petitions by a Harvard history professor were successful in having Matthew Henson's body moved from a shared grave in New York to Arlington National Cemetery where, with full military honors, it was placed in the ground next to Admiral Peary.

WHO WAS THE FIRST TO RECORD THE HISTORY OF AFRICAN-AMERICANS IN CALIFORNIA?

A tireless researcher and journalist, Delilah Beasley wrote a landmark book on the history of African-Americans in the State of California and became the first to record the contributions of these black pioneers. Beasley was born in Cincinnati in 1871. Orphaned while still young, she was forced to become a maid for the family of a judge. Her writing career began early; by the age of twelve she was selling short stories to a Cleveland newspaper, and at fifteen she was writing a regular column for the *Cincinnati Inquirer*.

Beasley became a physical therapist and in 1910 settled in Berkeley, California, as a nurse for a former patient. She had developed an interest in African-American history, and began a study of California's black pioneers, which a friend encouraged her to expand into a book. After eight and a half years of research, Beasley's book was published in 1919. The 317-page volume, *The Negro Trailblazers of California*, received critical acclaim.

For twenty-five years Beasley wrote a column for the *Oakland Tribune* called "Activities Among Negroes." Increasingly involved in civil rights issues, she mounted a campaign to end the use of insulting racial terms in newspapers. In 1933 she played a major role in the passage of civil rights legislation in the state. When Beasley died at the age of seventy-three, her book was all but forgotten. She would have been proud to know that *The Negro Trailblazers of California* was reprinted in 1968.

WHO WAS THE FIRST AFRICAN-AMERICAN WOMAN TO EARN AN INTERNATIONAL PILOT'S LICENSE?

As a child in Amarillo, Texas, where she was born in 1893, Bessie Coleman was a hard worker, picking cotton and doing laundry to help her mother meet family expenses. After high school the ambitious young woman joined her brother in Chicago, attended beauty school, and got a job as a manicurist. Intrigued by flying, she read everything she could find on aviation, but when she applied to flying school she was denied admission because of her race and sex. Taking the advice of a friend, she saved her money and made two trips to Europe, learning to fly from French and German aviators. In 1921 she became the first African-American woman in the world to earn an international pilot's license.

Returning to the United States, Coleman embarked on tours of air shows throughout the country, astounding audiences with her daring maneuvers. Her goal was to earn enough money to open a flying school for African-Americans. But during a test flight in 1926 in Jacksonville, Florida, Coleman was thrown from the cockpit of her plane when it went into a nose dive and was hurled to the ground, dying before her dream could be realized.

Bessie Coleman

WHO WAS THE FIRST WOMAN TO RECEIVE THE SPINGARN MEDAL?

The Spingarn Medal was instituted by the NAACP in 1914 to be awarded annually for the highest achievement during the year by an African-American. In 1922 the medal was awarded to Mary B. Talbert, the first woman to be honored. Talbert, a founder and president of the National

Association of Colored Women, was chosen "for service to the women of her race and the restoration of the Frederick Douglass home."

Talbert was born in 1866 in Oberlin, Ohio, where her family had settled to take advantage of educational opportunities there. She earned a bachelor's degree from Oberlin College in 1894 and taught school in Little Rock, Arkansas, later becoming principal of a high school and a small university. Under her leadership the National Association of Colored Women led projects to improve educational opportunities for African-American children and to protect them from the harsh juvenile justice system in the South. During World War I Talbert served for several months as a Red Cross nurse in France, and after the war she joined the fight for passage of an anti-lynching bill. A strong advocate for African-American women leaders and a fighter for civil rights in the United States and human rights throughout the world, Talbert died in 1923 at the age of fifty-seven.

WHOSE ACT SPARKED THE FIRST MAJOR BOYCOTT OF THE CIVIL RIGHTS MOVEMENT?

In 1955, Rosa Parks, a resident of Montgomery, Alabama, was working as a tailor's assistant at a downtown department store. A quiet but determined woman, Parks, forty-three years old, had been secretary of the Montgomery NAACP for several years before becoming the organization's youth advisor. On December 1, exhausted after a long day of work, she boarded a city bus for the ride home. Although more than three-quarters of Montgomery's bus passengers at that time were African-Americans, they were forced to sit in the back of the bus and surrender their seats to whites if asked. When some white passengers boarded Rosa Parks's bus that December day, the driver ordered her to give up her seat and she refused. She was arrested, taken to the city jail, and later convicted and fined.

In response to the arrest of Rosa Parks, Montgomery's black ministers and civil rights leaders met to organize a boycott of the city's buses by African-Americans. The new minister of the Dexter Avenue Baptist Church, the Rev. Martin Luther King, Jr., only twenty-six years old, was chosen president of the Montgomery Improvement Association, which led the boycott. In an emotional speech to a large, enthusiastic gathering, King said, "We will not retreat one inch in our fight to secure and hold onto our American citizenship."

Thirteen months later the U.S. Supreme Court outlawed segregation on Alabama's buses, the boycott ended, and African-American passengers once again rode on city buses in Montgomery. The courageous Rosa Parks, who had been fired from her tailoring job, moved to Detroit, where she was a special assistant to Congressman John Conyers for twenty-five years.

WHO WAS THE FIRST TO POPULARIZE
THE SLOGAN "BLACK POWER"?

In the 1960s, civil rights activist Stokely Carmichael adopted the term "black power" as a rallying cry for African-Americans who were fighting injustice. Carmichael was born in the British West Indies in 1941 and moved to New York City's Harlem when he was eleven years old. He graduated from the prestigious Bronx High School of Science and entered Howard University. While majoring in philosophy there he became involved in the civil rights movement as a Freedom Rider in Mississippi.

In 1964 Carmichael went to work full time for the Student Nonviolent Coordinating Committee (SNCC), an organization that focussed on voter registration and other civil rights issues in the South, and became chairman two years later. He left SNCC in 1967 to join the Black Panther Party, and in 1969 moved to West Africa, where he changed his name to Kwame Touré and lived in self-imposed exile.

In the 1967 book that Carmichael wrote with African-American political scientist Charles V. Hamilton, *Black Power: The Politics of Liberation in America,* they said: "Black Power is a call for black people of this country to unite, to recognize their heritage, to build a sense of community."

WHO WAS THE FIRST AFRICAN-AMERICAN
TO HEAD A MAJOR FOUNDATION?

In 1979 Franklin A. Thomas was named president of the Ford Foundation, the country's largest philanthropic organization. Born in Brooklyn, New York, Thomas earned a bachelor's degree in 1956 from Columbia College. After four years as a navigator in the United States Air Force's Strategic Air Command, Thomas entered Columbia University Law School, receiving a degree in 1963.

His career after law school included such positions as assistant U.S. attorney, deputy police commissioner for the New York City Police Department, and president of the Bedford Stuyvesant Restoration Company, a community development organization. Thomas joined the board of trustees of the Ford Foundation in 1977 and two years later was elected president.

Thomas has received a number of awards, including Columbia Law School's James Kent Medal for distinguished professional achievements and Columbia University's Medal of Excellence. He also has been granted several honorary law degrees.

Franklin A. Thomas

WHO WAS THE FIRST AFRICAN-AMERICAN IN SPACE?

On August 30, 1983, Guion S. Bluford, Jr., became the first African-American astronaut in space when he flew aboard the space shuttle *Challenger* on its night launch from the Kennedy Space Center in Florida.

Born in 1942 in Philadelphia, Bluford showed an early interest in engineering—his father's profession—and in airplanes. He received his air force wings in 1965 and served as a pilot in Vietnam, flying 144 combat missions. Two years after his first space flight, Bluford spent seven days in space aboard the *Orbiter Challenger* on the nation's first spacelab mission.

Another black astronaut, Robert H. Lawrence, Jr., became the first African-American to be appointed to the manned orbiting laboratory program in June, 1967, but he never made it into space. He was killed six months after his appointment when his fighter jet crashed on the runway at an air force base in California.

Guion S. Bluford, Jr.

WHO WAS THE FIRST AFRICAN-AMERICAN TO BE HONORED WITH A NATIONAL HOLIDAY?

On January 20, 1986, eighteen years after this renowned civil rights leader was assassinated, the birthday of the Rev. Martin Luther King, Jr., became a national holiday. Born in Atlanta, Georgia, in 1929, King graduated from Morehouse College when he was only nineteen. He went on to earn a bachelor of divinity degree and a doctorate. When he was just twenty-five, he was named pastor of the Dexter Avenue Baptist Church in Montgomery, Alabama.

On December 1, 1955, when Montgomery resident Rosa Parks was arrested for refusing to give up her bus seat to a white man, King responded by leading a year-long bus boycott that put an end to segregated seating on Montgomery's buses. Returning to Atlanta, King became an associate pastor of his father's church, Ebenezer Baptist.

In 1957 King was named the first president of the Southern Christian Leadership Conference, an organization dedicated to gaining full rights for African-Americans through nonviolent action such as boycotts and sit-ins. Although his home was bombed and he was arrested and jailed, King never backed down in his struggle to gain civil rights for black Americans. He was a leader of the 1963 March on Washington, where he made his famous "I have a dream..." speech, and a year later he was awarded the Nobel Peace Prize.

On April 4, 1968, King was shot and killed while standing on a motel balcony in Memphis, Tennessee, where he was supporting a strike by garbage collectors. In 1986 when President Reagan signed a bill making King's birthday a national holiday, his widow, Coretta Scott King, said: "His memory is engraved in the hearts and minds of his fellow Americans, and it is appropriate...to remember and honor the principles for which he stood."

WHO WAS THE FIRST AFRICAN-AMERICAN WOMAN ASTRONAUT?

When the space shuttle *Endeavor* left its launching pad at Cape Canaveral, Florida, on September 12, 1992, its crew of seven included Dr. Mae Jemison, the first African-American woman to travel into space. A physician and a space engineer, the thirty-five-year-old Jemison was responsible during the seven-day flight for conducting experiments involving weightlessness and motion sickness.

As a young girl growing up in Chicago, Jemison had dreams of someday traveling in space. Her parents, a maintenance supervisor and an elementary school teacher, encouraged her interest in astronomy and other sciences. She was only sixteen when she entered California's Stanford University, where she received bachelor's degrees in 1977 in chemical engineering and African and Afro-American Studies.

Jemison earned an M.D. from Cornell University Medical College and then served for several years as a doctor in the Peace Corps, working mainly in Liberia and Sierra Leone. In 1985 she opened a private medical practice in Los Angeles, began taking graduate engineering courses, and

Mae Jemison

applied to the astronaut program. In 1987, out of nearly 2,000 applicants, she was one of fifteen chosen for NASA's astronaut training program.

On her space flight Jemison carried several small art objects from West African countries, which, she said, symbolized her belief that space belongs to all nations.

JOURNALISM

WHAT WAS THE FIRST AFRICAN-AMERICAN NEWSPAPER?

On March 16, 1827, *Freedom's Journal* began publication in New York City. The opening editorial in the first issue of the first African-American newspaper in the United States announced, "We wish to plead our own cause. Too long have others spoken for us..."

The paper was started by John Russworm and Samuel Cornish. Russworm, who graduated from Bowdoin College in Maine in 1826, was one of the first African-Americans to receive a college degree. Cornish, a Presbyterian minister, left the paper during its first year of publication but returned two years later after Russworm was forced to resign because of his strong opinions on resettling black Americans in Africa.

WHO PUBLISHED THE FIRST AFRICAN-AMERICAN MAGAZINE?

David Ruggles, a renowned abolitionist, was editor and publisher of the first African-American periodical, *The Mirror of Liberty*. The first issue of this quarterly magazine appeared in July 1838. Its articles promoted the rights of African-Americans.

Ruggles also opened an African-American bookstore on Lispenard Street in New York City, as well as a reading room nearby for use by African-Americans, who were not allowed to enter the city's libraries.

WHO WAS THE FIRST AFRICAN-AMERICAN NEWSPAPERWOMAN?

Mary Ann Shadd Cary was born in 1823 in Wilmington, Delaware, and grew up in a home where escaped slaves were given refuge. Unable to receive an education in Delaware, she was enrolled in a Quaker school in Pennsylvania. When she returned to Wilmington she opened a school for African-American children. After the Fugitive Slave Law was passed in 1850, giving slave owners sanction to retrieve their runaway slaves, Cary and her brother fled to Windsor, Canada, and were soon joined by the rest of the family.

Shortly after her arrival, Cary wrote and distributed a pamphlet listing opportunities for black Americans in Canada. Seeing the need for a newspaper for African-Americans, especially fugitive slaves, she began publishing a weekly paper, *The Provincial Freeman*. Its motto was: "Self-reliance is the true road to independence."

Cary was an eloquent speaker against slavery, and when President Lincoln called for men to fight with the Union Army in the Civil War, she returned to the United States and became an army recruiting officer. She eventually moved to Washington, D.C., enrolled in the Howard University Law Department, and, in 1883, became the second African-American woman in the United States to earn a law degree.

WHO STARTED THE FIRST FAMILY-OWNED AFRICAN-AMERICAN NEWSPAPER?

In 1864 a young African-American, John H. Murphy, enlisted to fight in the Civil War and was assigned to the 30th Regiment, U.S. Colored Maryland Volunteers, where he was eventually promoted to sergeant. In a letter he wrote in 1920 recalling his Civil War experiences, Murphy said: "That was a real war for liberty. I went in a slave and came out a freedman. I went in a chattel and came out as a man with the blue uniform of my country as a guarantee of freedom..."

Murphy went home to Baltimore and began looking for ways to make a living. Over the years he was a whitewasher, porter, janitor, postal employee, and printer. By the time he founded a newspaper, the *Afro-American*, in 1892, he had a wife and ten children to support. The weekly paper's coverage of black social issues attracted a growing number of readers, and by 1922 the older Murphy was ready to turn its operation over to his son Carl.

The *Afro-American* focused on stories that were overlooked by the white press. In a December 1912 edition, for example, a front-page headline read: "Discrimination Charged in Uncle Sam's Navy." In October 1940 another headline announced: "Roosevelt, as Commander-in-Chief, permits Jim Crow in U.S. Navy." And a 1945 article about the atomic bomb plant in Oak Ridge, Tennessee, said the 7,000 African-American workers there were "plagued by Jim Crow at work, in housing and other facilities."

When Carl Murphy died in 1967, a grandson of the founder, John Murphy 3rd, became publisher. By the early 1990s, the paper, with editions in Baltimore, Washington, and Richmond, Virginia, was being run by two fourth-generation members of the Murphy family, John J. Oliver, Jr., and Frances Murphy Draper. Five direct descendants of the founder were on staff and two more were contributing writers.

WHO WAS THE FIRST WRITER TO DOCUMENT THE LYNCHING OF AFRICAN-AMERICANS?

Ida B. Wells was born in Mississippi in 1862 and orphaned at sixteen when her parents both died in a yellow fever epidemic. Although she had to care for her brothers and sisters, she managed to further her education, attending Rust College and Fisk University. After settling in Memphis, Tennessee, where she taught school, Wells began writing articles for a local church paper. Soon, under the name "Iola," she started contributing to several

Baptist newspapers in the South. In 1889 she became editor of a Baptist weekly in Memphis, *Free Speech and Headlight.*

In March 1892, when three African-American grocery store owners were lynched, she wrote a series of editorials urging that the murderers be punished and encouraging black residents to leave the city. After the newspaper printed a particularly vehement editorial attacking the motives of southern white men, the *Free Speech* office was vandalized, equipment was destroyed, and Wells, who was visiting in New York at the time, was warned not to return to Memphis.

Wells settled in New York City and became a writer for *New York Age,* where she continued to publish crusading articles exposing the horrifying crimes of lynch mobs. Her articles were collected in two pamphlets, *Southern Horrors* and *A Red Record.* She set out on a lecture tour of England and the United States, helping to set up anti-lynching societies. After marrying Chicago newpaper owner Ferdinand Barnett in 1895, she used his paper as a means to carry on her campaign to end injustice toward African-Americans.

WHO WAS THE FIRST AFRICAN-AMERICAN WAR CORRESPONDENT?

After the start of World War I, bowing to pressure from black newspapers, the United States government appointed an African-American reporter, Ralph W. Tyler, to cover war news of special interest to black readers. Tyler was the only accredited African-American war correspondent during World War I.

WHO WAS THE FIRST AFRICAN-AMERICAN REPORTER GIVEN ACCESS TO THE WHITE HOUSE?

A native of St. Louis, Missouri, Harry McAlpin studied journalism at the University of Wisconsin and attended Robert E. Terrell Law School in Washington, D.C. In 1942 he was hired as a Washington correspondent for the *Chicago Defender*, and two years later he became the first African-American journalist to be accredited as a White House correspondent. His reports appeared in fifty-one newspapers.

In 1945, as the first accredited African-American Navy correspondent, McAlpin reported on the war from the Pacific. And during the Korean War, he was an information specialist with the Office of War Information. He then entered private practice as an attorney in Louisville, Kentucky, and eventually became a federal judge.

WHO WAS THE FIRST AFRICAN-AMERICAN WOMAN TO GAIN WHITE HOUSE AND CONGRESSIONAL PRESS CREDENTIALS?

Alice Dunnigan didn't start out to be a journalist. She was born in 1906 in Kentucky, where her parents were a sharecropper and a laundress. An outstanding student, Dunnigan graduated first in her class in her segregated high school. She attended Kentucky State College and embarked on a teaching career, but eventually decided to try for a more lucrative field. She took a federal civil service exam in 1942 and went to Washington, D.C., working during World War II in various office jobs.

After the war Dunnigan moved into journalism, starting in 1946 as a free-lance reporter for Associated Negro Press and succeeding in winning access to the White House as well as the House and Senate. A high point of her career was in 1948 when she accompanied Harry Truman on his campaign train from Washington to California. Dunnigan left the Associated Negro Press in 1960 to work for the Kennedy-Johnson campaign, and later held jobs with the Equal Employment Opportunity Commission and the Department of Labor.

WHAT JOURNALIST WAS THE FIRST AFRICAN-AMERICAN WOMAN TO BE A VICE-PRESIDENTIAL CANDIDATE?

Charlotta Bass, a pioneering California journalist, was named the Progressive Party candidate for vice-president of the United States in 1952, when she was seventy-eight years old. Forty-two years earlier, the young Charlotta Spears had arrived in Los Angeles and found a job as a newspaper girl, selling subscriptions to a small black newspaper called the *Advocate*. She soon was promoted to an office job and within two years had become editor. When the newspaper's owner suddenly died, the paper went on the auction block, but Spears couldn't afford to bid on it. Anxious to help her, a neighboring second-hand dealer bought the paper for fifty dollars and handed Spears the deed.

With assets of ten dollars and a printing press, Spears took over and changed the paper's name to the *California Eagle*. That same year she married Joseph B. Bass, a founder of the Topeka *Plaindealer*, who had journeyed West. The energetic couple began a campaign to end segregation and discrimination in Los Angeles. In 1914, Bass tried to halt the making of D.W. Griffith's film, *The Birth of a Nation*, which glorified the Ku Klux Klan. Her effort failed, but she forced the director to cut some especially offensive scenes.

Bass tangled with the KKK again in 1925, when she exposed plans for a Klan takeover of the Watts neighborhood of Los Angeles. She was sued and threatened but she did not back down. Later, just before the beginning of World War II, Bass and her newspaper started a campaign for fair housing for African-Americans.

By 1951, when Bass sold the *Eagle*, she had already served as the first African-American on the Los Angeles County grand jury and had lost her first political campaign, a City Council race, in 1945. She left the Republican Party and joined the new Progressive Party, losing a bid for a congressional seat in 1950. Bass made her last stab at politics when she ran as the Progressive Party's candidate for vice-president in 1952; she died in 1969 at the age of ninety-five.

WHAT JOURNALIST WAS THE FIRST AFRICAN-AMERICAN WOMAN TO INTEGRATE THE UNIVERSITY OF GEORGIA?

In 1961, Charlayne Hunter-Gault and her fellow student, Hamilton Holmes, ended segregation at the University of Georgia when they enrolled as the school's first black students. Because of her desire to become a journalist, Hunter-Gault agreed to be a test case in the integration of the university, which was the only school in the state with a journalism school.

She and Holmes were met by cross burnings, screaming mobs of white students, and a riot outside the dormitory. Claiming it was trying to keep the peace, the school suspended the two students, but the action was overruled by a federal court and they returned to classes. Before graduating, the two succeeded in desegregating the swimming pool, cafeteria, and other university facilities.

Holmes was elected to Phi Beta Kappa and, after graduation, continued his education at Emory Medical School. Hunter-Gault's first job after college was at the *New Yorker* magazine. She then won a fellowship to study at Washington University, where she served on the staff of *Trans-Action* magazine, and later joined the news team at WRC-TV in Washington. In 1968 Hunter-Gault began a ten-year stint as a metropolitan reporter for the *New York Times*, covering the urban African-American community. In 1978 she became a national correspondent for the public television program, "The MacNeil/Lehrer Newshour," where she won many awards for her outstanding reporting. Her memoir, *In My Place*, was published in 1992.

WHO WAS THE FIRST AFRICAN-AMERICAN TV NEWS COMMENTATOR?

After Mal Goode was hired by ABC in 1962 as the first African-American news commentator on television, he was assigned to cover the United Nations. Two months later he found himself reporting on lengthy UN

Charlayne Hunter-Gault

debates over one of the country's most critical events—the Cuban missile crisis.

Born in White Plains, Virginia, Goode attended the University of Pittsburgh. During high school and college he worked as a laborer in the steel mills, a job he kept for five years after graduation. He started his journalism career in 1948 when he joined the *Pittsburgh Courier,* and a year later he started doing a fifteen-minute radio news show twice a week.

In 1950 Goode became a news reporter for radio station WHOD in Pittsburgh, and was named news director two years later. He and his sister, Mary Dee, were the only brother-and-sister team on radio for six years. Goode was the first African-American member of the National Association of Radio and Television News Directors.

WHAT JOURNALIST WAS THE FIRST AFRICAN-AMERICAN TO SIT ON THE NATIONAL SECURITY COUNCIL?

Carl T. Rowan, who has been called the dean of the country's African-American journalists, was born in 1926 in a small Tennessee town and grew up in a house without electricity or running water. He left home to serve in the navy in World War II and went on to attend Oberlin College. After graduate school at the University of Minnesota, Rowan joined the staff of the *Minneapolis Tribune,* becoming one of the first African-American reporters in the mainstream press. His first book, *South of Freedom,* a collection of articles about conditions in the South, was published in 1952.

Rowan had published three other books by 1961, when President Kennedy made him spokesman for the state department. Two years later he was appointed ambassador to Finland. In 1964 President Johnson named him director of the United States Information Agency and he became the first African-American to sit on the National Security Council.

Rowan returned to journalism in 1965, writing more books, articles, and syndicated columns and appearing on television and radio. His memoir, *Breaking Barriers,* came out in 1991 and two years later he published a biography of an old friend entitled *Dream Makers, Dream Breakers: The World of Thurgood Marshall.*

WHO WAS THE FIRST AFRICAN-AMERICAN ANCHOR OF A TV MORNING NEWS SHOW?

Bryant Gumbel made his debut as an anchor of the NBC news program "Today" on January 4, 1982, and anchored this national early-morning television show longer than anyone in its history. Gumbel was born in New Orleans in 1948 and raised in Chicago. He earned a liberal arts degree from Bates College in Lewiston, Maine, in 1970 and two years later began his television career as a sportscaster for KNBC in Los Angeles. By 1982 he had become the host of almost all of NBC's sports programs.

During his career on "Today" Gumbel anchored broadcasts from all over the world, including China, Saudi Arabia, Cuba, and sub-Saharan Africa. For his telecasts from Moscow in 1984, Gumbel received the Ed-

Carl T. Rowan

ward R. Murrow Award for Outstanding Foreign Affairs Work from the Overseas Press Club. His other professional awards include Emmys in news and sports. He also won the Frederick D. Patterson Award, the highest honor bestowed by the United Negro College Fund, an organization that benefits from an annual celebrity golf tournament that Gumbel sponsors.

WHO WAS THE FIRST AFRICAN-AMERICAN EDITOR AND OWNER OF A MAJOR DAILY NEWSPAPER?

A trailblazing newspaperman who won praise for his efforts to help young African-Americans follow him into journalism, Robert C. Maynard was the editor, publisher, and owner of the *Oakland Tribune* for a decade. Maynard was born in Brooklyn, New York, in 1937 to parents who came from Barbados. He was so fascinated by journalism as a youngster that he cut classes to watch courtroom reporters and finally dropped out of high school.

Maynard got his first newspaper job when he was still a teenager, working for the *New York Age*, a Brooklyn weekly. He also worked for the *Afro-American* in Baltimore and the *York Gazette and Daily* in Pennsylvania. After studying at Harvard under a Nieman fellowship in 1966, Maynard joined the staff of the *Washington Post*, where he was a White House correspondent, national correspondent, and editorial writer.

Maynard left the *Post* to form, with his wife, Nancy, the Institute for Journalism Education at Berkeley, California, which trained hundreds of minority students. Maynard was an outspoken advocate for the hiring and promotion of minority employees by news organizations.

In 1979 Maynard returned to newspapers when he became editor of the *Oakland Tribune* in California. Four years later he bought the paper, and became increasingly prominent in the journalism field, writing a syndicated column, appearing as a news commentator on television, and serving on the boards of newspaper organizations and on the Pulitzer Prize board. Maynard died of cancer in August 1993 at the age of fifty-six.

WHO WAS THE FIRST AFRICAN-AMERICAN WOMAN EDITOR OF A MAJOR DAILY NEWSPAPER?

In 1992 the 188-year-old *Oakland Tribune* in California named Pearl Stewart as editor, making her the first African-American woman to edit a metropolitan daily newspaper. At the time of her appointment Stewart had been a journalist in the San Francisco Bay area for more than twenty years, starting as a reporter for United Press International.

A native of Camden, Alabama, Stewart moved with her family to Rochester, New York, when she was five years old. She graduated from Howard University in 1971 and a year later earned a master's degree in communication from American University in Washington D.C. A winner of numerous journalism prizes, Stewart first joined the *Oakland Tribune* in 1976, starting as a reporter and later becoming a features editor. She left the

Pearl Stewart

Tribune in 1982 to become a reporter for the *San Francisco Chronicle*, where she covered Oakland government, education, and community planning. In her history-making job as editor of the *Tribune*, she was given responsibility for the direction of the paper's news and editorial staff.

LAW
&
GOVERNMENT

WHO WAS THE FIRST AFRICAN-AMERICAN FEDERAL EMPLOYEE?

William Cooper Nell, a lawyer, author, and prominent abolitionist from Boston, refused to take an oath that would admit him to the bar because he didn't want to uphold a Constitution that allowed slavery. As founder of the Equal School Association, he led a campaign that in 1855 brought an end to segregated schools for black children in Massachusetts.

In 1861 this courageous African-American mounted an attack against discrimination in federal employment and was appointed a clerk in the Boston post office, making him the first black American to hold a federal civilian job. Also an historian, Nell wrote a book called *The Colored Patriots of the American Revolution.*

WHEN DID THE FIRST AFRICAN-AMERICAN LAWYER PRACTICE BEFORE THE SUPREME COURT?

By 1865, when John S. Rock was admitted to practice before the United States Supreme Court, he had already been a teacher, doctor, and dentist. Rock, born in 1825 in New Jersey, taught for a time in a one-room schoolhouse before he decided to study medicine. Because of his race he was denied admission to medical school, so he became a dentist. Around 1852 he was allowed to earn a medical degree, one of the first African-Americans in the country to do so. He practiced both medicine and dentistry in Boston, where he had settled.

An abolitionist, Rock participated in an effort to desegregate Boston's schools and challenged discrimination in jobs and public accommodations. His activities prompted him to earn a law degree, and in 1865 he became the first African-American lawyer allowed to argue cases before the Supreme Court.

WHO WAS THE FIRST DEAN OF HOWARD UNIVERSITY LAW SCHOOL?

John Mercer Langston was born in Virginia in 1829 and left the South after his parents died. He attended school in Cincinnati and then enrolled in Oberlin College, graduating with honors in 1849. After studying law and being admitted to the bar, he settled in the nearby town of Brownhelm, where he became active in the abolitionist movement and was elected town clerk. When the Civil War began, Langston served as a recruiting agent for African-American regiments. After the war, in 1867, a new university for African-Americans, named after General O.O. Howard, the head of the Freedmen's Bureau, opened in Washington, D.C. Langston set up the law department a year later and became its dean. In 1877 he was named minister to Haiti and twelve years later was elected a Virginia delegate to the U.S. House of Representatives.

WHO WAS THE FIRST AFRICAN-AMERICAN DIPLOMAT?

Born in Connecticut in 1833 and educated at Yale and the University of Pennsylvania, Ebenezer Don Carlos Bassett was principal of the Institute for Colored Youth in Philadelphia when President Ulysses S. Grant named him minister to Haiti in 1869. The appointment marked the first time a diplomatic assignment outside the United States was given to an African-American.

After he had served in Haiti for eight years, the Haitians named Bassett their consul general to the United States. When he retired from the post after ten years, he returned to Haiti and wrote a book about the island entitled *Handbook of Haiti*.

WHO WAS THE FIRST AFRICAN-AMERICAN SENATOR?

Hiram Rhoades Revels was born in 1822 in Fayetteville, North Carolina, the son of an African-American Baptist minister and a Scottish mother. Revels himself was ordained a minister in the African Methodist Episcopal Church in Baltimore, Maryland, in 1845. After the Civil War began in 1861, Revels helped organize the first two African-American army regiments from Maryland. When the war was over he held pastorates in Kansas and New Orleans before settling in Natchez, Mississippi.

In January 1870 the Mississippi legislature chose Revels to represent the state in the U.S. Senate; he was to fill the unexpired term of Confederate President Jefferson Davis. Withstanding the insults of those who were opposed to an African-American Senator, Revels was finally sworn in. In his first speech on the Senate floor, he argued that Georgia not be readmitted to Congress unless an effort were made to protect the rights of black citizens. Although his speech was praised, it had little effect, but he became a popular lecturer in northern cities. Revels left the Senate in 1870 to accept the presidency of Alcorn, a new African-American college in Mississippi.

WHO WAS THE FIRST AFRICAN-AMERICAN IN THE U.S. HOUSE OF REPRESENTATIVES?

Until the Civil War began, Joseph H. Rainey worked alongside his father as a barber in Charleston, South Carolina. When the war started Rainey and his wife escaped to Bermuda, where he continued his trade; on their return in 1866 they settled in Georgetown, South Carolina. Attracted to politics, Rainey became involved in the state Republican party, and was eventually elected to the state senate. He served until July 1870, when he was elected to fill a vacancy in the United States House of Representatives.

As a congressman, Rainey fought for legislation to prevent individuals and groups like the Ku Klux Klan from terrorizing African-Americans and whites and pushed for a bill that would grant equal treatment to African-Americans in public places. Rainey, an effective, hard-working congressman, was regularly returned to his seat until 1878 when, largely due to the mudslinging campaign of his opponents, he was not reelected. For the next two years he worked as an agent for the Internal Revenue Service, then resigned and ran for the position of House clerk, which he lost. After failing in the banking and brokerage business, Rainey returned to Georgetown. He died in 1887 at the age of fifty-five. A local newspaper claimed that Rainey's stressful years in Washington had ruined his health.

WHO WAS THE FIRST AFRICAN-AMERICAN VOTER?

On March 30, 1870, the Fifteenth Amendment to the United States Constitution went into effect. The amendment gave citizens the right to vote regardless of "race, color, or previous condition of servitude."

On March 31 Thomas M. Peterson of Perth Amboy, New Jersey, cast his vote in a special election to revise that city's charter, making him the first African-American to exercise his vote under the new amendment. Peterson, a school custodian, was later appointed to serve on the commission set up to revise the charter.

WHO WAS THE FIRST AFRICAN-AMERICAN TO SERVE AS A GOVERNOR?

When he was twelve years old, Pinckney Benton Stewart Pinchback took a job as a cabin boy on a river boat. He worked on the Mississippi and Missouri rivers until he was twenty-five, when he went to Louisiana, served in the army for a time, and then settled in New Orleans.

Pinchback became involved in politics and was serving as lieutenant governor of the state of Louisiana in December 1872 when the governor was impeached and forced to resign. Pinchback took his place for a month, stepping down in January 1873. The next day the state legislature elected him to the United States Senate.

WHO WAS THE FIRST AFRICAN-AMERICAN WOMAN LAWYER?

When Charlotte Ray decided she wanted to go to law school—unheard of for an African-American woman in the 1800s—she applied as C.E. Ray. But when the Howard University School of Law found out that she was a woman, they admitted her anyway. Ray, who was born in New York City in 1850, was such an outstanding student at Howard that she was inducted into Phi Beta Kappa, the national scholastic organization.

After graduating in 1872 with a specialty in commercial law, Ray looked forward to a bright future. But because of her race, she was unable to attract enough clients and finally had to give up her practice. She closed her Washington, D.C., law office and returned to New York City, where she worked in the Brooklyn school system. She died in 1911, leaving little information about how she spent her life after ending her legal career.

WHO WAS THE FIRST AFRICAN-AMERICAN JUDGE IN U.S. HISTORY?

Mifflin W. Gibbs made history twice—he started the first black newspaper in California and he was the first African-American elected a judge. Gibbs was born in Philadelphia in 1828 and grew up to be an antislavery activist, working for the Underground Railroad and lecturing on behalf of abolition. In 1850, intrigued by reports of the California gold rush, Gibbs headed West. Once there, he shined shoes, started a successful clothing store, and became involved in politics. In 1855 he began publishing *Mirror of the Times*, the state's first African-American newspaper.

Three years later, the restless Gibbs journeyed to British Columbia looking for gold. He opened a store and was elected a local councilman. Back in the United States, Gibbs attended Oberlin College, graduating in 1869. Four years later he was elected a city judge in Little Rock, Arkansas, making him the country's first African-American judge. He went on to earn several presidential appointments and toward the end of his life was named consul to Madagascar. Gibbs died in Little Rock in 1915.

WHO WAS THE FIRST AFRICAN-AMERICAN TO SERVE A FULL TERM IN THE U.S. SENATE?

In 1875, when he was thirty-four years old, Blanche Kelso Bruce was appointed a United States Senator from Mississippi, and served in that post until 1881. Bruce had been born into slavery on a Virginia plantation, eventually moving with his family to Missouri. He taught school there and in Lawrence, Kansas, and then worked as a porter on a steamer until settling in Floreyville, Mississippi. It wasn't long before he had established himself as a successful planter and become a respected politician. In 1974 the state legislature named him to represent Mississippi in the U.S. Senate for the term starting the following year.

During his years in the Senate, Bruce vigorously defended the rights of minority groups, including African-Americans, Native Americans, and Chinese immigrants. Soon after he left his Senate seat in 1881, President

Garfield named him Register of the Treasury, making him the first African-American to sign his name on the country's currency.

WHO WAS THE FIRST AFRICAN-AMERICAN U.S. MARSHAL?

In 1877 Frederick Douglass, the noted abolitionist, orator, editor, and activist, was appointed United States marshal for the District of Columbia by President Rutherford B. Hayes. Douglass was born in 1817 on a farm in Maryland, where he lived with his enslaved mother and grandparents. At the age of eight, a year after his mother's death, the boy was sent to Baltimore to work for a family named Auld. There he learned to read and write, but he was eventually returned to a plantation where he suffered years of brutal treatment.

When he was twenty-one years old Douglass escaped to Massachusetts and became an ardent abolitionist. He was hired as a traveling orator by the Massachusetts Anti-Slavery Society for $450 a year, and in 1845 he published his autobiography, *Narrative of the Life of Frederick Douglass, An American Slave*. Because he admitted in his book that he was a runaway slave, Douglass was forced to flee to England, where he stayed until British admirers bought his freedom.

Upon his return, Douglass set up a printing plant in Rochester, New York, and in 1847 began publishing a newspaper, the *North Star*. He continued to crusade against slavery, and when the Civil War began he recruited African-American troops for the Army. Two of the first volunteers were his sons, Lewis and Charles. When the war ended Douglass focused his efforts on gaining civil rights for freed slaves, and after he was named U.S. marshal he fought against segregationist policies in Washington. In 1881 Douglass was appointed Recorder of Deeds and he later served as minister to Haiti for three years, returning to Washington to write and struggle against racism until he died in 1895.

WHO WAS THE FIRST AFRICAN-AMERICAN TO PRESIDE OVER A NATIONAL POLITICAL CONVENTION?

Although born a slave, John Roy Lynch managed to gain an education; it is said that he sat outside the windows of a white schoolhouse and listened to the teachers. He then settled in Natchez, Mississippi, where he opened a photography shop. He was soon named to the state legislature, becoming speaker of the house of representatives.

In 1872, when he was only twenty-five years old, Lynch was elected to the U.S. Congress, serving for four years. In 1884 he was made temporary chairman of the Republican National Convention, where he gave a keynote address. Said to be the most respected black congressman of his time, Lynch later became paymaster of the regular army, retiring with the rank of major.

WHO WERE NEW YORK CITY'S FIRST AFRICAN-AMERICAN POLICE OFFICERS?

Before 1898, when all of New York's boroughs were consolidated into one city, each borough had its own separate police department. The first documentation of an African-American police officer in any of the departments was in March 1891 when Wiley G. Overton was appointed to the police force in Brooklyn and assigned to a foot patrol in a black neighborhood. Overton was met with hostility by the white officers; they gave him no assistance and refused to speak to him unless absolutely necessary. Less than two years after his arrival, Overton resigned.

The second African-American officer hired in Brooklyn, Moses P. Cobb, was treated no better but decided to stick it out. He continued to serve in the New York City Police Department after consolidation and remained on the force until his retirement in 1917.

In 1911 Samuel J. Battle, a former baggage porter at Grand Central Station, became the first African-American hired to be an officer in the New York City Police Department. For more than two years he was totally ostracized by the white officers. But Battle ignored them and concentrated on his work; eventually the other officers learned to respect him. Battle rose through the ranks to become a lieutenant, and in 1941 he was named the city's parole commissioner, a post he held until his retirement ten years later.

WHO WAS THE FIRST AFRICAN-AMERICAN U.S. ASSISTANT ATTORNEY GENERAL?

William H. Lewis originally gained fame as a football star—he was the first African-American player to be chosen for an All-American team. Lewis was born in Virginia in 1868 and attended school there until his father, a Baptist minister, moved the family to New England. Saving the money he earned working in hotels and restaurants, Lewis eventually was able to enroll in Amherst College in Massachusetts. An outstanding scholar and athlete, he played on Amherst's football team for four years and was captain in 1891. He continued playing while at Harvard Law School and was chosen an All-American in 1892 and '93.

After graduating from Harvard, Lewis became a lawyer in Massachusetts, and in 1911 President Taft appointed him to be the first African-American assistant attorney general of the United States.

WHO WAS THE FIRST AFRICAN-AMERICAN JUDGE IN NEW YORK STATE?

Well before he became a distinguished New York City judge, James S. Watson, fresh from his hometown in the British West Indies, supported himself as a bellhop in New York City. Born in Spanish Town, Jamaica, in 1882, Watson was twenty-six years old when he found a job with a New York law firm. While there he studied at New York Law School. Admitted to the bar in 1914, he handled tax and corporate matters for the firm.

Watson's public life began in 1922 when he was appointed a special counsel to the Corporation Counsel of the City of New York. Nine years later he was named a justice of the New York City Municipal Court, becoming the state's first African-American judge. He remained on the bench until 1950, when he resigned to become president of the Municipal Civil Service Commission of New York. His dedication to the people of New York brought him many honors, and shortly before his death his work on behalf of the welfare of West Indians was recognized when he was cited on the Birthday Honors List of King George VI of England for appointment as a Commander of the Most Excellent Order of the British Empire.

Watson's children also served with distinction in their professions. His daughter Barbara was the country's first African-American assistant secretary of state, his son Douglas was the nation's first black aeronautical engineer, and his son James L. became senior judge of the United States Court of International Trade.

WHO WAS THE FIRST AFRICAN-AMERICAN LAWYER TO WIN A SUPREME COURT CASE FOR THE NAACP?

A grandson of slaves, Charles Hamilton Houston was born in Washington, D.C., in 1895. In 1915 he graduated magna cum laude and Phi Beta Kappa from Amherst College in Massachusetts, and earned an LL.B. from Harvard Law School in 1922 and his doctorate a year later. While at Harvard, he became the first African-American member of the Harvard Law Review.

For the next twelve years Houston taught at Howard University Law School, becoming its dean and reorganizing the school into an institution that would train African-American lawyers to use the law to effect social change. In 1935 Houston successfully argued a Supreme Court case for the NAACP. In *Hollins v. State of Oklahoma*, he convinced the Court to overturn the conviction of a black man on the grounds that African-Americans had been illegally excluded from the jury panel.

Soon afterward Houston joined the NAACP as special counsel, directing his energies to exposing the unsoundness of the *Plessy v. Ferguson* Supreme Court ruling of 1896 that sanctioned segregation. To show that separate facilities for blacks and whites were inherently unequal, Houston argued and won the *Gaines v. Missouri* case in 1938, upsetting the University of Missouri's policy of providing a law school for whites but not African-Americans. He later won decisions in *Hurd v. Hodge* and *Shelley v. Kraemer* that prevented the enforcement of racially restrictive covenants in housing.

Houston's ultimate victory was the creation of the legal strategy that finally struck down educational segregation when the Supreme Court declared it unconstitutional in the landmark 1954 *Brown v. Board of Education* decision. Although Thurgood Marshall argued the case, he gave the credit to Houston, who had died four years earlier. "Charlie Houston," said Marshall, was the "engineer of it all."

WHO WAS THE FIRST AFRICAN-AMERICAN TO BECOME A FEDERAL JUDGE?

A Phi Beta Kappa at Amherst College, William H. Hastie graduated at the head of his class in 1925. He was a top student at Harvard Law School, earning a degree in 1930. He went to Washington, D.C., to practice law and joined the faculty of the Howard University School of Law where his cousin, Charles Houston, was dean. In 1933 Hastie became a lawyer in the Department of the Interior under President Franklin Roosevelt. Four years later Roosevelt named him a judge of the federal district court of the Virgin Islands, a territory of the United States, making him the first African-American federal judge.

After two years Hastie returned to Howard to become dean of the law school. In 1940 he was named a civilian aide to the secretary of the army, but later resigned in protest against segregation in the military. He ended his tenure as dean of Howard Law School in 1946 when President Harry Truman appointed him the first African-American governor of the Virgin Islands. Three years later Truman named Hastie to the United States Court of Appeals, Third District, making him the first African-American to serve on a federal appeals court.

WHEN WAS AN AFRICAN-AMERICAN WOMAN FIRST ELECTED TO A STATE LEGISLATURE?

Crystal Byrd Fauset, a former teacher and social worker with a background in politics, was elected to the Pennsylvania House of Representatives in 1938, the first time an African-American woman had been elected to a state legislature. Fauset was born in Maryland in 1894 and raised by her aunt in Boston, where she excelled in school. She went on to earn a bachelor's degree at Columbia University Teachers College.

Fauset entered the world of politics in 1934 when she became director of African-American women's activities for the Democratic National Committee. In 1936 she became assistant personnel director in the Philadelphia office of the Works Progress Administration (WPA). After finishing her term in the state legislature, Fauset held several other important posts until her death in 1965.

WHO WAS THE FIRST AFRICAN-AMERICAN WOMAN JUDGE?

In 1939, Jane M. Bolin, then a thirty-one-year-old lawyer in the office of New York City's Corporation Counsel, was summoned to meet with Mayor Fiorello LaGuardia. After conferring briefly with Bolin's husband, also a lawyer, LaGuardia asked the startled young woman to raise her right hand. He then proceeded to swear her in as a judge of the Domestic Relations Court of the City of New York, making Bolin the first African-American woman judge in the United States.

When she decided to become a lawyer, Bolin was following in the footsteps of her father, Gaius Bolin, the first black graduate of Williams College, who practiced law in Poughkeepsie, New York. She graduated from Wellesley College and entered Yale Law School, where she was the only African-American in her class and one of three women. With law degree in hand, Bolin was received coolly by New York law firms. She practiced law with her husband for five years, then joined the corporation counsel's office as the first African-American on the staff. She was also the first black woman to join the New York City Bar Association.

Bolin remained on the Domestic Relations Court, which was renamed New York Family Court, for nearly forty years, leaving at the mandatory retirement age of seventy. She always enjoyed the work of the court, she said, and loved being able to help children and families.

WHO WAS THE FIRST AFRICAN-AMERICAN CONGRESSMAN FROM AN EASTERN STATE?

Adam Clayton Powell, Jr., arrived in New York City as a twelve-year-old when his father, a Yale graduate, became minister of the Abyssinian Baptist Church in Harlem. After graduating from Colgate University in upstate New York in 1930, Powell joined his father as assistant minister of the church, which grew to attract the largest congregation of any African-American church in the country. During the Depression of the 1930s, Powell led efforts to give financial aid to Harlem residents and to demand that white businessmen hire African-American workers.

In 1941 Powell was elected to the New York City Council, becoming its first black member. Three years later he was elected to the U.S. Congress, the first African-American congressman from an eastern state. He was responsible for desegregating press galleries, restaurants, and barber shops on Capitol Hill, and he introduced legislation to desegregate the armed forces.

He often gained attention for his flamboyant behavior, and in a 1960 television interview he claimed that a certain New York City woman was a "bag woman for the police department." She later sued him and in 1963 he was ordered to pay damages. He refused and was cited for contempt of court. Despite his legal problems Powell won reelection to Congress, and in 1966 President Lyndon Johnson praised him for his "brilliant record of accomplishment" as chairman of the House Education and Labor Committee.

But Powell's financial problems continued, resulting in his 1967 expulsion from Congress, yet a year later his loyal constituents reelected him by a margin of nearly thirty thousand votes. In 1969 the Supreme Court ruled that his suspension was unconstitutional, but by that time Powell was spending most of his time in the Bahamas. The next year he was defeated in the Democratic primary by Charles Rangel, and he died in 1972. The length of Seventh Avenue running through Harlem was named Adam Clayton Powell, Jr., Boulevard, in his honor.

WHO WAS THE FIRST AFRICAN-AMERICAN SUPREME COURT CLERK?

In 1949 William Thaddeus Coleman, a graduate of both Harvard Law School and Harvard Business School, was appointed a clerk to U.S. Supreme Court Justice Felix Frankfurter. He was the first African-American ever to serve as a law clerk to a Supreme Court justice.

After the 1949 Supreme Court term, unable to find a job in his hometown of Philadelphia, Coleman went to work for a law firm in New York City. He later was made a partner in Philadelphia's most powerful law firm, was named the first African-American director of Pan American World Airways, and served as president of the NAACP Legal Defense and Educational Fund. In 1975 Coleman was named Secretary of Transportation by President Gerald Ford, becoming the second African-American in history to hold a cabinet post.

WHO WAS THE FIRST AFRICAN-AMERICAN TO WIN THE NOBEL PEACE PRIZE?

After studying at the University of California and Harvard University, Ralph Bunche embarked on a diplomatic career. He went first to the U.S. State Department and then to the United Nations, where he negotiated an armstice in the Arab-Israeli conflict, earning a Nobel Peace Prize in 1950.

Born in Detroit, the grandson of a slave, Bunche worked as a janitor to help pay his expenses at the University of California at Los Angeles, where he played football, baseball, and basketball, and graduated with high honors in 1927. He received a master's and a doctorate from Harvard, and in 1944 became the first African-American official in the State Department. Two years later he joined the United Nations.

After winning the Nobel Prize in 1950, Bunche went on to negotiate peace-keeping efforts in the Congo, Yemen, Cyprus, India, Pakistan, and the Suez, and in 1963 President John Kennedy awarded him the Medal of Freedom. Bunche became undersecretary general of the United Nations in 1967, a post he held until ill health forced him to retire in 1971. He died in September of that year in New York City.

WHO WAS THE FIRST AFRICAN-AMERICAN WOMAN TO PRACTICE LAW IN MARYLAND?

A native of Baltimore, Juanita J. Mitchell graduated from the University of Pennsylvania and earned her law degree from the University of Maryland. Her mother, Lillie Carroll Jackson, was an early leader of the NAACP, and her husband, Clarence Mitchell, Jr., was the organization's chief lobbyist. Admitted to the bar in 1950, Mitchell also became involved in the NAACP, serving as a lawyer for the local chapter. In that role, she succeeded in requiring Baltimore to hire more African-American social workers, police officers, and librarians.

During the 1950s she was involved in a series of legal actions that helped open schools and public accommodations to African-Americans, and that forced schools and colleges to hire black staff members. Mitchell and Thurgood Marshall, another Baltimore native, filed lawsuits that resulted in a 1955 decision by the Supreme Court to integrate parks in Baltimore and Annapolis. Mitchell died in July 1992 at the age of seventy-nine.

WHO WAS THE FIRST AFRICAN-AMERICAN WOMAN TO REPRESENT THE U.S. AT THE UNITED NATIONS?

Edith Spurlock Sampson was appointed in August 1950 as an alternate delegate to the United Nations, becoming the first African-American to represent the United States at the United Nations.

The first woman to earn a law degree from Loyola University, in 1927, Sampson later entered the judiciary. In November 1962 she was elected associate judge of the Municipal Court of Chicago, and two years later she became an associate judge of the Circuit Court of Cook County.

WHO WAS THE FIRST AFRICAN-AMERICAN CAREER AMBASSADOR?

When Clifton R. Wharton, Sr., was appointed U.S. Minister to Romania in 1958, he became the first African-American diplomat to be the leading representative of the United States in a foreign country. A native of Baltimore, Wharton earned bachelor's and master's degrees from Boston University. He practiced law in Boston for three years and then went to Washington, D.C, where in 1925 he joined the Foreign Service, a corps of diplomats that had been established a year earlier.

For twenty years Wharton was the only African-American career diplomat in the Foreign Service. He advanced steadily through the ranks, and in 1958 President Eisenhower appointed him minister to Romania. Three years later President John F. Kennedy named him ambassador to Norway, a post he held until he retired in 1964.

WHO WAS THE FIRST AFRICAN-AMERICAN FEDERAL DISTRICT COURT JUDGE IN THE CONTINENTAL UNITED STATES?

Early one morning in August 1961, James Benton Parsons was vacationing at his summer home in Lakeside, Michigan, when he got a telephone call from President John F. Kennedy, saying he intended to appoint him federal district judge for the Northern District of Illinois. In earlier years several African-Americans had served as federal district judges in the Virgin Islands, but Parsons became the first black district judge in the continental United States.

Parsons was born in Kansas City, Missouri, the son of a minister. He worked his way through Milliken University in Decatur, Illinois, earning a bachelor's degree in 1934. After teaching for several years and serving in the navy during World War II, Parsons received a law degree in 1949 from the University of Chicago. Before being appointed to the federal district bench, he was a partner in a Chicago law firm, an assistant U.S. attorney, and a superior court judge. Parsons retired from trial work in 1992 and died a year later at the age of ninety-one.

WHEN WAS THE FIRST AFRICAN-AMERICAN WOMAN ADMITTED TO THE MISSISSIPPI BAR?

Marian Wright Edelman, a graduate of Spelman College and Yale Law School, was admitted to the Mississippi bar in 1965, one year after she was named director of that state's office of the NAACP Legal Defense and Educational Fund. Born in South Carolina in 1939, the daughter of a Baptist minister, Edelman was an early civil rights activist. In 1960, while a senior in college, she participated in a sit-in and was arrested along with thirteen other students.

In 1968 Edelman founded the Washington Research Project, which five years later had evolved into the Children's Defense Fund. As president of the Children's Defense Fund, she devoted herself to such issues as health care and education for children, youth employment, child welfare and mental health, adolescent pregnancy prevention, and family support systems. Her books include *Families in Peril: An Agenda for Social Change* and *The Measure of Our Success: A Legacy to My Children and Yours.*

WHEN WAS THE FIRST AFRICAN-AMERICAN POPULARLY ELECTED TO THE U.S. SENATE?

In 1966, Edward Brooke became the first African-American to be elected to the U.S. Senate by popular vote. (Hiram Revels, the first black senator, was chosen by the Mississippi legislature in 1870 to fill the unexpired term of Jefferson Davis, who had become the Confederate president. Blanche Kelso Bruce, the second African-American senator, also from Mississippi, was chosen by the legislature in 1875 and served a full term.)

Brooke also made history in 1962 when he became the first African-American to be elected a state attorney general. He served in that post for two terms until his election to the Senate. Brooke, born in 1919 in Washington, D.C., was a graduate of Howard University and Boston University Law School. He served as a U.S. Senator until 1979.

WHO WAS THE FIRST AFRICAN-AMERICAN TO BE ELECTED SHERIFF?

In 1966 the citizens of Macon County, Alabama, elected a Tuskegee resident named Lucius Amerson to be their sheriff, making him the first African-American sheriff in United States history. Born in Eutaw, Alabama, in 1933, Amerson earned a degree in political science from Tuskegee University, served in the army, and then attended Jones Law School in Montgomery. Before becoming sheriff, he worked for the United States Postal Service.

Amerson served as sheriff for twenty years, deciding in 1986 to leave law enforcement. During his entire tenure as sheriff, he said, he suffered constant harassment from some of his opponents. "I figured they were trying to run me away," he said, "that's why I stayed."

WHO WAS THE FIRST AFRICAN-AMERICAN WOMAN TO BE A FEDERAL JUDGE?

Constance Baker Motley made history for the first time in 1962 when, as a lawyer for the NAACP Legal Defense and Educational Fund, she won the right for James Meredith, an African-American, to attend the segregated University of Mississippi.

Motley was born and grew up in New Haven, Connecticut, where her parents had immigrated from the Caribbean island of Nevis. After she finished high school, a local businessman, impressed by her spirit, offered to pay her college tuition. She attended Fisk and New York universities and graduated from Columbia Law School in 1946. In her senior year of law school she worked as a clerk for Thurgood Marshall, then head of the NAACP Legal Defense and Educational Fund. Motley remained with the Legal Defense Fund for twenty years, eventually becoming an associate counsel. She argued a number of cases before the United States Supreme Court, and was involved in many civil rights victories.

Motley left the Fund to enter politics, and in 1964, at the age of forty-two, became the first African-American woman elected to the New York State Senate. A year later she was the first woman and first African-American to be elected Manhattan Borough President. In 1966 President Lyndon Johnson appointed her to the United States District Court, making her the first African-American woman to serve on the federal bench. In 1982 Motley was named chief judge of the Southern District of New York, becoming a senior judge four years later.

WHO WAS THE FIRST AFRICAN-AMERICAN TO SERVE IN A PRESIDENT'S CABINET?

When Robert C. Weaver became a cabinet member in 1966, he could claim a lengthy history in government service. In the 1930s he had held a responsible position in the Department of Interior under President Franklin Roosevelt, and in 1961 he became the first African-American to head a major government agency when he was named administrator of the Housing and Home Finance Agency.

Born in Washington, D.C., in 1908 and trained as an economist and educator, Weaver served in New York City and State governments and in 1946 directed foreign assistance to the Soviet Union for the United Nations Relief and Rehabilitation Administration. In 1966 he became the first African-American to attain cabinet rank when President Lyndon Johnson named him Secretary of Housing and Urban Development.

WHO WAS THE FIRST AFRICAN-AMERICAN SUPREME COURT JUSTICE?

When Thurgood Marshall died of heart failure in January 1993 at the age of eighty-four, the country lost one of its most illustrious legal scholars. In 1967, when Marshall was named the first African-American on the United

States Supreme Court, it was the culmination of a career that had resulted in many historic legal victories.

Born in Baltimore, Maryland, in 1908, Marshall described himself as a "hell-raiser" in high school. It was there that he was exposed to the U.S. Constitution when, as punishment, the teacher made students learn parts of it. "I made my way through every paragraph," he said. He graduated from Lincoln University, a predominantly black college in Pennsylvania, waiting on tables to help pay tuition. Excluded from the all-white law school at the University of Maryland, he attended Howard University Law School, where he graduated first in his class in 1933. His mother had pawned her wedding and engagement rings to pay the school's entrance fee. He subsequently brought successful lawsuits that integrated the University of Maryland and other state university systems, and years later the University of Maryland named its law library after him.

At Howard, Marshall met the man who would become his mentor, Charles Houston, a law professor and dean who later became special counsel to the NAACP. In fact, he credited Houston with helping shape the strategy that resulted in Marshall's greatest legal victory, the Supreme Court's 1954 decision in *Brown v. Board of Education* that declared an end to racial segregation in public schools. Marshall won that case while he was director-counsel of the NAACP Legal Defense and Educational Fund, a position he held for more than twenty years.

In 1961 Marshall was appointed a federal appeals court judge by President Kennedy, and from 1965 to 1967 he served as Solicitor General of the United States. By the time President Johnson made him a Supreme Court justice in 1967, Marshall had argued thirty-two cases before the Supreme Court, winning twenty-nine. During his twenty-four years on the Supreme Court, he voted against every death sentence presented to him, believing that capital punishment was inherently unfair and permeated with racism. In 1991 Marshall was forced to step down as a Supreme Court justice because of his failing health.

WHEN DID A MAJOR U.S. CITY ELECT ITS FIRST AFRICAN-AMERICAN MAYOR?

In November 1967, the city of Cleveland, Ohio, elected Carl Stokes to the mayor's office. A Democrat, lawyer, and former state legislator, Stokes won ninety-six percent of the city's African-American vote and nineteen percent of the white vote.

Richard Hatcher, also an African-American, was elected mayor of Gary, Indiana, that same month, but Stokes was inaugurated first, making him the first African-American to become mayor of a large American city.

WHO WAS THE FIRST MAYOR OF WASHINGTON, D.C.?

In 1967 President Johnson reorganized the government of the District of Columbia and appointed Walter Washington as the chief executive of Washington, D.C. Seven years later, when the residents of the District of Columbia were given the right to elect their own mayor, they chose Walter Washington, making him the first elected head of the nation's capital.

Walter Washington was born in 1915 in Georgia and earned a law degree from Howard University. Before becoming mayor he held various administrative positions, including five years as executive director of the New York Housing Authority and a year as its chairman.

WHO WAS THE COUNTRY'S FIRST AFRICAN-AMERICAN ASSISTANT SECRETARY OF STATE?

Born in New York City in 1918, Barbara Watson was a member of an illustrious family. Her father, James S. Watson, was the first African-American judge in New York State and her brother, Douglas, was to become the country's first black aeronautical engineer.

After earning a bachelor's degree from Barnard College in 1943, Watson embarked upon a series of diverse occupations. She was an interviewer for the United Seamen's Service, she managed her own modeling agency, and she was coordinator of student activities at Hampton Institute in Virginia. She then decided to enter New York Law School, graduating third in her class in 1962. A group of outstanding jurists selected her as the most outstanding law student in New York City.

With her law degree, Watson held a number of governmental positions, including Assistant Corporation Counsel for the City of New York, and executive director of the New York City Commission to the United Nations, in which she served as liaison between the city and various U.N. missions. In 1966 her background and talent attracted President Lyndon Johnson, who appointed her to the Bureau of Security and Consular Affairs, U.S. State Department. In 1968 she was appointed Assistant Secretary of State for Consular Affairs. The first woman and the first African-American to achieve the rank of assistant secretary of state, she served in that position under Presidents Johnson, Nixon, Ford, and Carter.

In 1980 President Carter named her United States Ambassador to Malaysia, where she negotiated several important trade agreements on behalf of the United States. Her lifelong commitment to African and Caribbean countries brought her many honors, including a designation as Commander of the National Order of the Republic of the Ivory Coast. At her funeral in Washington in 1983, the ninety-three honorary pallbearers included ambassadors, senators, congressmen, mayors, and heads of educational and political organizations.

WHO WAS THE FIRST AFRICAN-AMERICAN WOMAN TO SERVE IN THE U.S. CONGRESS?

Born in Brooklyn in 1924, Shirley Chisholm spent her early childhood in Barbados. After returning to New York she attended Brooklyn College and Columbia University to prepare for a teaching career. In her autobiography, *Unbought and Unbossed,* she said that there was no other road open to a young black woman, since law, medicine and nursing were too expensive, "and few schools would admit black men, much less a woman."

After college Chisholm became involved in politics, and was elected to the New York State Assembly in 1964. Four years later, running as a Democrat from the Bedford-Stuyvesant section of Brooklyn, she became the first African-American woman to be elected to the U.S. Congress.

In 1972 Chisholm broke another barrier, becoming the first black woman to actively run for the presidential nomination of a major party. Although she did not win the nomination, her compelling voice was heard on the issues of better education for minority groups, programs for the poor, and equality for minorities and women. In her book *The Good Fight* she explained why she ran for the presidency, saying: "The next time a woman of whatever color, or a dark-skinned person of whatever sex aspires to be President, the way should be a little smoother because I helped pave it."

After a fourteen-year career in Congress, Chisholm returned to education, becoming a professor at Mt. Holyoke College in Massachusetts.

WHO WAS THE FIRST AFRICAN-AMERICAN MEMBER OF THE F.C.C.?

Best known as the executive director of the NAACP, Benjamin Hooks first made national headlines in June 1972 when he was appointed the first African-American member of the seven-person Federal Communications Commission, a government body that oversees the operation of the broadcast industry.

Born in Memphis, Tennessee, in 1925, Hooks graduated from Howard University and received a law degree from DePaul University. He practiced law in Memphis, was the first African-American public defender in that city, and served for several years as a county court judge. As an F.C.C. commissioner, Hooks worked to improve the portrayal of blacks on television and to increase the employment and ownership opportunities for African-Americans in the electronic media. He served as the executive director of the NAACP from 1977 until he resigned in 1993.

WHO WAS THE FIRST TO DISCOVER THE WATERGATE BREAK-IN?

On June 17, 1972, an African-American security guard at the Watergate Hotel in Washington, D.C., made a discovery that changed history. The guard, twenty-four-year-old Frank Wills, was patrolling the building in the early morning hours when he noticed a piece of tape over a door lock at the garage level. Wills removed the tape, but when he returned about an hour later a new piece of tape had been placed over the lock.

Wills called the police and they in turn were able to capture five men who had broken into the headquarters of the Democratic National Committee. The burglars turned out to be connected with the re-election campaign of President Richard Nixon, a Republican. The ramifications of Wills's discovery led to an effort to impeach Nixon and to the president's eventual resignation in 1974.

WHO WAS THE FIRST AFRICAN-AMERICAN WOMAN ELECTED TO THE HOUSE OF REPRESENTATIVES FROM CALIFORNIA?

Yvonne Brathwaite Burke's political career in California has been marked by three notable achievements—she was the first African-American woman elected to the state assembly, the first African-American woman elected by Californians to serve in the U.S. House of Representatives, and the first African-American to be elected supervisor in the history of Los Angeles County.

Born in 1932 in South-Central Los Angeles, Burke earned a degree in political science from UCLA and a law degree from the University of Southern California. She was elected to the state assembly in 1966 and served until 1972, when she won election to the House of Representatives. She gave up her seat in the House in 1978 in an unsuccessful race for state attorney general.

After sitting on the Los Angeles County Board of Supervisors in 1979 and 1980 as the appointed successor to a supervisor who had died in office, she returned to the private sector. In 1992, then a partner in a prestigious law firm, Burke stepped back into politics. She ran for county supervisor and won, making her the first African-American ever elected to the Board of Supervisors in Los Angeles County.

WHO WAS THE FIRST AFRICAN-AMERICAN MAYOR OF LOS ANGELES?

In 1973, when Thomas Bradley was elected mayor of Los Angeles, he—along with Coleman Young of Detroit—became the first African-American elected to head a city with a population greater than one million.

Born in 1917 in Calvert, Texas, Bradley attended the University of California at Los Angeles and received a law degree from Southwestern University. The son of a sharecropper, Bradley devoted fifty years of his life to public service—two decades as a police officer, a decade as the first black city councilman in Los Angeles, and five terms as mayor.

WHO WAS THE FIRST AFRICAN-AMERICAN TO HOLD A DEMOCRATIC LEADERSHIP POSITION IN THE HOUSE OF REPRESENTATIVES?

In 1972 Cardiss Collins's husband, George, a Democratic congressman from Illinois, was killed in a plane crash while returning to Chicago from Washington. Elected to fill her husband's unexpired term, Collins took office in 1973.

Collins's tenure in Congress was filled with firsts. She was the first African-American woman to chair the Congressional Black Congress and the first African-American and the first woman to chair the Manpower and Housing subcommittee of the House Government Operations Committee. A fighter for women's health rights, Medicare reform, environmental issues, and airline safety, Collins became the first African-American and the first woman to hold a Democratic leadership position in the House of Representatives when she was named whip-at-large.

WHO WAS THE FIRST AFRICAN-AMERICAN TO GIVE A KEYNOTE SPEECH BEFORE A DEMOCRATIC NATIONAL CONVENTION?

Barbara Jordan, born in Houston, Texas, in 1936, earned a bachelor's degree from Texas Southern University, where she was forced to take segregated buses to attend class. In 1959, after receiving a law degree from Boston University, Jordan returned to Houston, and seven years later was elected to the Texas Senate. She was the first African-American to serve in that body in eighty-three years.

In November 1972 Jordan was elected a United States Representative, the first African-American woman from the South to win a seat in Congress. During her three terms as a congresswoman, she sponsored bills advocating the causes of the poor and disadvantaged. During the impeachment hearings of President Nixon, her eloquence drew national attention. In July 1976 she became the first African-American and the first woman to give a keynote address at a Democratic National Convention. Two years later she retired from public office and became a professor at the University of Texas.

WHEN WAS THE FIRST AFRICAN-AMERICAN WOMAN ELECTED A MAYOR IN MISSISSIPPI?

After graduating from high school, Unita Blackwell, born in 1933 on a plantation in Lula, Mississippi, began working in the cotton fields. By the 1960s she had become a civil rights activist, involved in voter registration drives. Because of her tenacity she was terrorized by members of the Ku Klux Klan, which burned a cross in her yard, and she was arrested about seventy-five times. But Blackwell would not be defeated. In 1964 she was one of the organizers of the Mississippi Freedom Democratic Party, which challenged the all-white delegation to the Democratic Convention.

She eventually settled in Mayersville, Mississippi, a river settlement with about 500 residents. In 1976 Blackwell was elected the first mayor of Mayersville, which she incorporated, and became the first African-American woman mayor in the state. Her interest in international affairs led her to travel abroad dozens of times, and from 1976 to 1983 she was national president of the U.S.-China People's Friendship Association. She earned a master's degree in regional planning from the University of Massachusetts in 1983, has twice been president of the National Conference of Black Mayors, has received several honorary doctorates, was a Harvard Fellow in 1991, and in 1992 was a winner of the prestigious MacArthur Foundation "genius" award.

For seventeen years Blackwell operated out of her office in the one-room city hall that was once a Baptist church, until retiring in July 1993 to write and lecture. But even after she left office her phone kept ringing with reports of crises and requests for help. "I'm the only mayor this town has ever had," she said two months after her retirement. "For seventeen years all they saw was me."

WHO WAS THE FIRST AFRICAN-AMERICAN WOMAN TO SERVE IN A PRESIDENT'S CABINET?

Patricia Roberts Harris, born in Illinois in 1924, earned a bachelor's degree from Howard University and a law degree from George Washington University School of Law, where she graduated first in a class of ninety-four. While still an undergraduate, Harris took part in a student sit-in in an effort to integrate a local cafeteria.

After law school Harris worked for the U.S. Justice Department for a time and then joined the faculty of Howard University Law School. In 1965 she became the first African-American woman ambassador when President Lyndon Johnson appointed her ambassador to Luxembourg, a post she held for two years. In 1977 President Jimmy Carter gave Harris a position in his cabinet, naming her Secretary of Housing and Urban Development. Just two years later he appointed her Secretary of Health, Educa-

Unita Blackwell

tion and Welfare, a position she held until Ronald Reagan was elected president.

Harris left government service and in 1982 became a professor at George Washington Law School, where she remained until her death from cancer three years later.

WHO WAS THE FIRST AFRICAN-AMERICAN AMBASSADOR TO THE UNITED NATIONS?

After graduating from Howard University in 1951 at the age of nineteen, Andrew Young decided to study for the ministry. He earned a divinity degree in 1955, was ordained a Congregational minister, and served as a pastor in rural churches in Georgia and Alabama.

In the early 1960s Young became active in the civil rights movement in the South, joining the Southern Christian Leadership Conference and eventually becoming its executive director. A close associate of the Rev. Martin Luther King, Jr., he organized citizen education programs and voter registration drives and helped draft the Civil Rights Act of 1964 and the Voting Rights Act of 1965. In 1972 Young was elected to the U.S. House of Representatives, becoming the first African-American congressman from Georgia in 101 years.

Young served in Congress until 1977, when he was named the first African-American ambassador to the United Nations, where he stayed until 1979. In 1982 he was elected mayor of Atlanta, Georgia, serving for eight years.

WHO WAS THE FIRST WOMAN TO CHAIR THE EQUAL EMPLOYMENT OPPORTUNITY COMMISSION?

Eleanor Holmes Norton, an African-American woman of many accomplishments, was born in Washington, D.C., in 1937. The oldest of three girls, Norton earned a bachelor's degree from Antioch College and then entered Yale, where she received a master's in American history and a law degree. She worked with the American Civil Liberties Union for five years and in 1970 was appointed chairperson of the New York City Commission on Human Rights, where she fought against discrimination in housing and the workplace.

Aware of her outstanding work in New York, in 1977 President Jimmy Carter made Norton the chairperson of the Equal Opportunity Employment Commission, a federal agency created to end discrimination in hiring practices. The first woman to chair that commission, she stayed until Ronald Reagan became president in 1981. She then became a professor at Georgetown University Law Center and in November 1990 was the first woman elected to represent the District of Columbia in the House of Representatives.

WHO WAS THE FIRST AFRICAN-AMERICAN MAYOR OF CHICAGO?

Born in Chicago in 1922, Harold Washington earned a law degree from Northwestern University in Evanston, Illinois. In 1954 he became an assistant city prosecutor in Chicago, a post he held for four years. He was elected to the Illinois House of Representatives in 1964, serving six terms.

In 1976 Washington was elected to the Illinois State Senate, but lost a bid for mayor a year later. In 1980 he won election to the United States House of Representatives, and in 1983 he was elected Chicago's first African-American mayor. In November 1987 his constituents chose him to serve a second term, but before the month was over he suffered a heart attack in his office and died.

WHO WAS THE FIRST AFRICAN-AMERICAN POLICE COMMISSIONER OF NEW YORK CITY?

In January 1984, Benjamin Ward was sworn in as New York City's 34th police commissioner—the first African-American appointed to the job. Ward's appointment as head of the police department of the country's largest city was the culmination of almost forty years in the criminal justice field.

Born in 1926, Ward served as a military police officer and a criminal investigator with the army in World War II. He joined the New York City Police Department in 1951 and was the first black officer assigned to the precinct that covered Crown Heights, Brooklyn. Recalling that assignment, Ward said, "I think my Irish named confused them."

By the time he left the department Ward had filled a number of important positions: he was the first African-American in the department to act as a prosecutor, an administrative law judge, and a deputy commissioner for community affairs. He also earned degrees from Brooklyn College and Brooklyn Law School, where he was in the top one percent of his class.

After serving as the first black traffic commissioner of New York City and first black director of the Pretrial Services Agency, Ward was appointed the first African-American commissioner of the New York State Department of Correctional Services, one of the largest prison systems in the world.

Ward retired as New York City Police Commissioner in October 1989 and became a professor at Brooklyn Law School.

WHO WAS THE FIRST AFRICAN-AMERICAN APPOINTED TO A FULL TERM ON NEW YORK'S HIGHEST COURT?

In 1985, New York Governor Mario Cuomo made Fritz Alexander a judge on the Court of Appeals, the state's highest court. Born in Florida in 1926, Alexander studied at Dartmouth and New York City Law School, and was admitted to the New York bar in 1952. After seven years on the high court, he resigned to become New York City's Deputy Mayor for Public Safety.

Benjamin Ward

WHO WAS THE FIRST AFRICAN-AMERICAN WOMAN MAYOR OF A LARGE U.S. CITY?

A lifelong resident of Hartford, the capital of Connecticut, Carrie Saxon Perry was elected mayor in 1987. Perry was educated in Hartford's public schools and attended Howard University. Before entering politics she was a social worker, an anti-poverty program administrator, and the director of a group home for adolescent girls.

In 1980 Perry was elected to the Connecticut General Assembly, where she served four terms. As mayor, Perry led efforts for adequate and afford-able housing, job training, education, and health care for underprivileged and needy Hartford residents.

WHO WAS THE FIRST AFRICAN-AMERICAN WOMAN TO SERVE ON A STATE'S HIGHEST COURT?

On March 3, 1988, Juanita Kidd Stout was inducted into office as a justice of the Pennsylvania Supreme Court, making her the first African-American woman in the country to serve on a state's highest court. Earlier, in 1959, when she was elected to the Philadelphia Municipal Court, she became the first black woman in America to be elected to a court of record. She was later elected twice to the Common Pleas Court of Pennsylvania.

Stout, a native of Oklahoma, earned a bachelor's degree in music from the University of Iowa and two law degrees from the Indiana University School of Law. Earlier in her career, she was administrative secretary to William H. Hastie when he was a judge of the U.S. Court of Appeals.

The recipient of twelve honorary doctorates and many awards, in 1988 Stout was named Justice of the Year by the National Association of Woman Judges and a Distinguished Daughter of Pennsylvania by the governor. Stout left the supreme court bench in 1989 when she reached the manda-tory retirement age of seventy, and became a senior judge in the court of common pleas.

WHEN DID NEW YORK CITY ELECT ITS FIRST AFRICAN-AMERICAN MAYOR?

In November 1989 David Dinkins was elected the 106th mayor and the first African-American mayor in New York City's 365-year history. Born in Trenton, New Jersey, in 1927 and educated at Howard University and Brooklyn Law School, Dinkins served in the U.S. Marine Corps. He entered politics in 1966 as a state legislator. He was president of the New York Board of Elections from 1972 to 1973, city clerk from 1975 to 1985, and Manhattan Borough President from 1986 to 1989.

David Dinkins

As he took the oath of office as mayor of the largest city in the United States, Dinkins said, "I stand before you today as the elected leader of the greatest city of a great nation, to which my ancestors were brought, chained and whipped in the hold of a slave ship. We have not finished the journey toward liberty and justice, but surely we have come a long way."

WHO WAS THE FIRST AFRICAN-AMERICAN TO BE ELECTED GOVERNOR?

On January 13, 1990, Lawrence Douglas Wilder was sworn in as governor of Virginia, the first African-American to be elected governor in United States history. Wilder, born in 1931 in Richmond, Virginia, was the grandson of slaves. His parents named him after Frederick Douglass, the abolitionist, and the poet Paul Lawrence Dunbar. In 1951, just after Wilder earned a bachelor's degree from Virginia Union University in Richmond, he was drafted into the army and sent to Korea. While serving his country he distinguished himself by earning a Bronze Star for rescuing fellow soldiers and capturing enemy troops.

Back home, Wilder decided to take advantage of the GI Bill to study law, but he had to leave the state because Virginia barred African-Americans from attending its law schools. He enrolled in Howard University School

Lawrence Douglas Wilder

of Law, earning a degree in 1959, and returned to Richmond to establish a law firm.

Wilder entered politics in 1969 and was elected the first African-American state senator in Virginia since Reconstruction. He served five terms in the state senate and made history again in 1985 when he was elected Virginia's first African-American lieutenant governor. Four years later he was elected governor. In September 1991 Wilder declared his candidacy for the U.S. Presidency, but withdrew from the race four months later.

WHO WAS THE FIRST WOMAN MAYOR OF THE NATION'S CAPITAL?

In November 1990, Sharon Pratt Kelly was elected mayor of Washington, D.C., making her the first woman to lead the nation's capital and the first African-American woman mayor of a major city. In her campaign, Kelly had promised to "clean house with a shovel, not a broom."

A Washington native, born in 1944, Kelly attended local schools and entered Howard University, where she earned a bachelor's degree with honors and a juris doctorate from the law school. In 1972 Kelly became an instructor at Antioch Law School, and was appointed vice-chairperson of the D.C. Law Revision Commission. In the mid-70s she joined the general counsel's office of the Potomac Electric Power Company and, in 1983, was made the first African-American woman vice-president of the company.

Starting in 1977, Kelly was elected to four terms as the Democratic National Committeewoman from the District of Columbia, and in 1985 she was elected the first African-American and first woman to serve as treasurer of the committee. An active community member, Kelly received awards from such organizations as the District of Columbia chapter of the NAACP, the United Negro College Fund, and the Association of Black Women Attorneys.

WHO WAS THE FIRST AFRICAN-AMERICAN POLICE CHIEF OF LOS ANGELES?

In 1992 Willie Williams took over the police department in a city that was still reeling from the effects of devastating riots set off by the acquittal of four white Los Angeles police officers charged with the brutal beating of a black man, Rodney King. Williams followed on the heels of a recalcitrant chief, Daryl Gates, who had finally resigned after protests of his handling of the unrest that followed the acquittals.

A law enforcement veteran, Williams became a police officer in Philadelphia in 1964 at the age of twenty. He received regular promotions and in 1988 was appointed Police Commissioner of the City of Philadelphia, a position he held until he was named chief of the police department in Los Angeles, the nation's second largest city.

Willie Williams

WHO WAS THE FIRST AFRICAN-AMERICAN MAYOR IN ALASKA?

In 1955, when James Hayes was a seven-year-old living in Sacramento, California, his mother made up her mind to start a new life. Accompanying the family of a Baptist minister, she and young James headed for Fairbanks, Alaska. Once settled, his mother worked as a domestic and a cook and he helped out by shining shoes and selling newspapers.

After graduating from high school in Fairbanks, Hayes earned a degree in education from the University of Alaska. He began his political career in 1973 when he was elected to a local school board, and went on to win two terms on the Fairbanks City Council. He was elected mayor of the city of Fairbanks in October 1992.

One of Hayes's special challenges as mayor of an Alaskan city was dealing with the harsh winters. During his first year on the job he had to supervise the removal of 141 inches of snow. In addition to his job as mayor, Hayes was an investigator in the state attorney general's office and an assistant pastor at Lily of the Valley Church of God in Christ.

WHO WAS THE FIRST WOMAN TO SERVE ON THE GEORGIA SUPREME COURT?

Leah Sears-Collins set more than one record in the state of Georgia. When she was elected to the Superior Court of Fulton County in 1988, she was the first woman and the youngest person, at age thirty-two, to run for and be elected to a superior court in Georgia. And in 1992 Sears-Collins became the first woman and the youngest person in the history of the state appointed to serve on the Supreme Court of Georgia.

Sears-Collins is the daughter of Onnye J. Sears, a teacher, and Colonel Thomas E. Sears, a retired army aviator who earned two silver stars in the Korean and Vietnam wars. She graduated from Cornell University and Emory University School of Law and earned a Doctor of Laws Degree from Morehouse College. She received numerous awards and honors and, among her many activities, she served as chair of the Atlanta Bar Association's Judicial Section and was founding president of the Georgia Association of Black Women Attorneys.

WHO WAS THE FIRST FORMER BLACK PANTHER PARTY MEMBER TO BE ELECTED TO CONGRESS?

Bobby L. Rush of Chicago, a founder of the Illinois Black Panther Party, was elected in November 1992 to represent Illinois's first congressional district in the United States House of Representatives. Rush grew up in Chicago, graduating from high school there and then enlisting in the army. After completing his military service, he graduated with honors from Roosevelt University and at the time of his election to Congress was completing a master's program in political science at the University of Illinois in Chicago.

Leah Sears-Collins

An active participant in the civil rights movement of the 1960s, Rush was a member of the Student Nonviolent Coordinating Committee (SNCC). As founder of the Black Panther Party in Illinois, he coordinated the party's free breakfast program for children and its free medical clinic,

Bobby L. Rush

which developed the first mass sickle cell anemia testing program in the country.

Rush was elected to Chicago's city council in 1983, the same year that Harold Washington became that city's first African-American mayor. He was reelected twice, and during his years as alderman he fought for environmental protection, equal housing, and job development. Soon after his election to Congress, he was chosen to serve on several important committees and national Democratic policy groups.

WHO WAS THE FIRST AFRICAN-AMERICAN WOMAN SHERIFF IN THE U.S.?

Jacquelyn Barrett was elected sheriff of Fulton County, Georgia, in November 1992, making her the first African-American woman sheriff in the United States. Barrett, forty-two years old when she took office, had been director of the Fulton County Public Safety Training Center. A graduate of Beaver College in Pennsylvania with a master's degree from Atlanta University, Barrett had sixteen years of law enforcement experience when she became head of the Fulton County Sheriff's Department, where she became responsible for the largest county jail operation in the state of Georgia with a staff of more than 700 employees.

After her election, in response to letters she received from other women, Sheriff Barrett said, "if I'm brave enough to run for office, maybe they can too."

WHEN WAS THE FIRST AFRICAN-AMERICAN WOMAN ELECTED TO THE U.S. SENATE?

Carol Moseley-Braun made headlines as well as history in November 1992 when she became the first African-American woman elected to the United States Senate. The daughter of a police officer and a medical worker, Moseley-Braun grew up in Hyde Park, an integrated area of Chicago. A University of Chicago Law School graduate, Moseley-Braun worked for three years in the U.S. Attorney's office and spent ten years in the Illinois state legislature, where she was a chief sponsor of bills to improve education and increase school funding in the city of Chicago. She was Cook County Recorder of Deeds at the time of her election to the Senate.

Forty-five years old when she was elected, Moseley-Braun became the only black member of the Senate and the fourth African-American to serve in that body in its history. She was named to the important Senate Judiciary Committee, which up to that time had been all-male and all-white.

WHAT AFRICAN-AMERICAN WOMAN WAS THE FIRST TO BE ELECTED A STATE ATTORNEY GENERAL?

In November 1992, Pamela Fanning Carter was elected attorney general of the state of Indiana. She was the first woman and the first African-

Jacquelyn Barrett

American to be attorney general of that state, and the first African-American woman in the United States to be elected to that position.

After her victory, Carter gave credit to her parents, a former teacher and a businessman, and to her paternal grandfather, who lived to be 101 and enjoyed reading law books and quoting legal principles to her when she

Carol Moseley-Braun

was a youngster. She also credited a short conversation she had with Dr. Martin Luther King, Jr., at a fair housing march in Chicago, when the civil rights leader told the fifteen-year-old Carter to be "courageous in any pursuit."

Pamela Carter

A native of Indianapolis, Carter received a bachelor's degree from the University of Detroit, a master's from the University of Michigan, and a law degree from Indiana University School of Law. She worked as a Vista volunteer, a social worker, and a litigation lawyer for the United Auto Workers.

In 1987 she became an enforcement attorney for the secretary of state, fighting white-collar crime, and in 1988 she joined Governor Evan Bayh's office as executive assistant for health and human services, rising to deputy chief of staff. Governor Bayh supported Carter in her run for attorney general.

During her campaign, Carter's opponent carried a life-size cardboard cutout of her to all his appearances, causing one rural voter to call her on the telephone. "That guy comes here with that cutout and assumes because we're rednecks we're also racists," he said. "Well, I'm a redneck but I'm not a racist, and I'm voting for you."

WHO WAS THE FIRST AFRICAN-AMERICAN TO BE NAMED SECRETARY OF COMMERCE?

In December 1992, the newly elected president, Bill Clinton, named Ronald H. Brown to his Cabinet as head of the Commerce Department. Brown had been the first African-American chairman of the Democratic National Committee, a position he had held since 1989, and the first black partner in the Washington law firm of Patton, Boggs & Blow.

Born in Washington, D.C., in August 1941, Brown spent most of his childhood in New York City's Harlem, where his father was manager of the Hotel Theresa on 125th Street. He attended private schools in Manhattan and went on to Middlebury College in Vermont, where he became the first African-American to join a fraternity. The fraternity, Sigma Phi Epsilon, had a whites-only charter and was expelled by its national office when Brown was admitted.

After a stint in the Army, Brown attended St. John's Law School in Queens, New York, and then joined the staff of the National Urban League, where he remained for twelve years. He later served as chief counsel of the Senate Judiciary Committee. In 1988, Brown was head campaign aide to Jesse Jackson in his attempt to win the Presidential nomination.

WHO WAS THE FIRST AFRICAN-AMERICAN TO BE APPOINTED SECRETARY OF AGRICULTURE?

On Christmas Eve 1992, President-elect Bill Clinton announced his choice for Secretary of Agriculture—Mike Espy, a thirty-nine-year-old congressman from Mississippi. The first African-American to represent Mississippi in Congress since Reconstruction, Espy belonged to a distinguished family. His grandfather, T.J. Huddleston, Sr., opened the Afro-American Sons and Daughters Hospital in Yazoo City in 1921, the first black hospital in Mississippi, and started a chain of funeral homes that is now operated by Espy's brother.

Mike Espy

Espy, who was one of four students to integrate the Yazoo City high school, earned degrees from Howard University and Santa Clara Law School in California. In 1978 he returned home to take the job of managing attorney of Central Mississippi Legal Services. He became the state's first

African-American assistant attorney general and, in 1986, its first black congressman since Reconstruction.

In Congress, Espy was a strong voice on behalf of rural concerns, serving on the House Agriculture Committee, and was an outspoken promoter of catfish farming, a major industry in the South. As secretary of agriculture, he became head of one of the biggest federal agencies, responsible for programs that benefit farmers; social programs such as food stamps, school lunches, and nutrition assistance to mothers and children; and the management of federal lands.

WHO WAS THE FIRST AFRICAN-AMERICAN AND FIRST WOMAN TO BE MADE SECRETARY OF ENERGY?

When she was sworn into office on January 22, 1993, Hazel Rollins O'Leary became the first woman and first African-American to serve as Secretary of Energy. In taking over direction of the Energy Department, O'Leary was able to draw upon almost twenty years of experience in energy issues.

A graduate of Fisk University and Rutgers University Law School, O'Leary, who was fifty-five at the time of her appointment, served as a regulator of the petroleum, natural gas, and electric industries under presidents Ford and Carter. From 1981 to 1989, she and her husband, John O'Leary, a former deputy energy secretary under President Carter, ran their own international energy, economics, and strategic planning firm in Washington, D.C.

Just before joining President Clinton's cabinet, O'Leary had been made president of the gas utility of Northern States Power Company, a Minnesota company she joined in 1989. A former assistant attorney general for the state of New Jersey, O'Leary was also a board member of the Executive Leadership Council, which is composed of leading African-American corporate executives.

WHO WAS THE FIRST AFRICAN-AMERICAN TO BE NAMED SECRETARY OF VETERANS AFFAIRS?

Jesse Brown, a former Marine, was appointed by President Clinton as the first Secretary of Veterans Affairs to be both an African-American and a member of a veterans' advocacy group. Brown, born in Detroit in 1945, lost the partial use of his right arm after it was shattered by sniper fire in Vietnam. When Clinton announced the nomination, he noted that the combat-disabled Brown "knows first-hand that those who have given of themselves to fight for our country deserve the best we can offer."

After returning from Vietnam in 1967, Brown, an honor graduate of Chicago City College, joined the staff of the Disabled American Veterans and in 1988 became the agency's first African-American director, guiding its advocacy and lobbying efforts. This work, along with his experience in Vietnam, made him an outstanding choice to head the federal veterans affairs agency, which administers benefit programs for the nation's 27 million veterans and their families.

WHO WAS THE FIRST AFRICAN-AMERICAN CHAIRMAN OF THE HOUSE ARMED SERVICES COMMITTEE?

In January 1993, Representative Ronald V. Dellums, a Democratic Congressman from Berkeley, California, and a longtime peace advocate, was named chairman of the House Armed Services Committee. When Dellums was first suggested for a seat on the committee twenty years earlier, many opposed his membership because of his opposition to armed conflict.

A congressman since 1970, Dellums, a former Marine, opposed the war in Vietnam as well as other foreign military intervention by the United States and espoused diplomacy as the best way to settle international disputes. He also voted against expensive defense systems and advocated cuts in the defense budget as a way to fund social programs.

At a news conference after his colleagues in the House voted to make him Armed Services Committee chairman, Dellums said, "I came here as an advocate of peace and I am going to continue to do so."

WHO WAS THE FIRST WOMAN TO HEAD THE NAACP LEGAL DEFENSE AND EDUCATIONAL FUND?

The NAACP Legal Defense and Educational Fund, Inc., with headquarters in New York City, was founded in 1940 to fight for racial and social justice. Its lawyers provide legal assistance in cases involving discrimination in housing, employment, voting, education, health care, the environment, and the administration of criminal justice. The organization became nationally known in 1954 when Thurgood Marshall, then its director-counsel, argued and won the *Brown v. Board of Education* case that outlawed segregation in public schools.

In February 1993 Elaine R. Jones became the first woman to be named director-counsel of the Legal Defense and Educational Fund. The appointment was a culmination of her twenty-six-year career as a litigator and civil rights activist. Born in Norfolk, Virginia, in 1944, Jones, the daughter of a teacher and a Pullman porter, was the first African-American woman to graduate from the University of Virginia Law School.

142

Ronald V. Dellums

After earning her law degree she became an attorney with the Legal Defense Fund, where she served as a counsel of record in *Furman v. Georgia*, a landmark U.S. Supreme Court case that abolished the death penalty in

Elaine R. Jones

thirty-seven states. In 1975 she left the Fund to become a special assistant to Secretary of Transportation William Coleman. Two years later she returned to the Fund to head its Washington, D.C., office, where her efforts helped pass scores of civil rights laws. In 1989 Jones became the first African-American elected to the board of the American Bar Association.

WHO WAS THE FIRST AFRICAN-AMERICAN TO WRITE A POEM THAT WAS LATER PUBLISHED?

Lucy Terry came to America on a slave ship and was brought to Deerfield, Massachusetts, when she was about five years old. At the age of sixteen Terry wrote a poem about a battle between Native Americans and whites at the Bars, an area outside of Deerfield. Her poem, "Bars Fight," was written in 1746 but not published until 1893.

Although "Bars Fight" was her only published work, Terry was known as a talented storyteller. When she was in her mid-20s she married a man named Abijah Prince. They settled in Vermont where they raised six children. Two of their sons fought in the American Revolution. Terry, who lived to be ninety-one, was an ardent fighter for equal rights for her family.

WHAT WAS THE FIRST PUBLISHED PROSE WRITTEN BY AN AFRICAN-AMERICAN?

According to a narrative written and published by Briton Hammon, he was given permission by his master in 1747 to sail from his Massachusetts home on a sloop bound for the West Indies. It is unclear whether Hammon was a servant or a slave. On his way back home, Hammon's ship was caught on a reef, he was captured by Native Americans, he escaped, and he eventually reached England. When he signed on for a ship headed for Boston, he discovered to his delight that his master was on board.

After his return to Massachusetts, Hammon wrote an autobiographical piece entitled *A Narrative of the Uncommon Sufferings and Surprising Deliverance of Briton Hammon, a Negro Man*. The narrative was published as a fourteen-page pamphlet in Boston in 1760.

WHAT WAS THE FIRST PUBLISHED POEM BY AN AFRICAN-AMERICAN MAN?

Jupiter Hammon was born a slave on Long Island in 1711. It is known that his owners were named Lloyd, that he learned to read in the Queen's Village school (now Lloyd's Neck in the town of Huntington), and that he had the use of his master's library. He was not related to Briton Hammon, who was the first African-American to publish a work of prose.

On Christmas Day 1760 his eighty-eight-line poem, *An Evening Thought*, was printed; it was the first poem published by an African-American man. The poem was printed on a broadside—one large sheet of paper. His second broadside, published in 1778, was a poem about Phillis Wheatley, the first African-American woman to publish a volume of verse. It was entitled *An Address to Miss Phillis Wheatley, Ethiopian Poetess, in Boston*.

In addition to poetry, Hammon wrote some notable prose, including, at the age of seventy-five, *An Address to the Negroes in the State of New York*. In it he describes a heaven where blacks and whites are judged as equals, and he calls attention to the irony of the American Revolution where whites were passionately concerned with defending their own liberty, yet ignored the subjugation of black Americans.

WHO WAS THE FIRST AFRICAN-AMERICAN TO PUBLISH A VOLUME OF POETRY?

Born in Africa around 1753, Phillis Wheatley arrived in Boston on a slave ship when she was about eight years old. She was bought by an affluent tailor and merchant named John Wheatley. A bright child, Phillis was provided a broad education by the Wheatley family, who encouraged her talent for poetry.

She was just a teenager when she wrote an elegy on the death of the Reverend George Whitefield, a noted evangelist; it was published in 1770. Two years later, when the Wheatleys tried to publish a volume of her poems, the publishers refused to believe that Phillis was the poet. A group of eighteen prominent Bostonians questioned her and then wrote a two-paragraph introduction attesting to her ability.

Accompanied by her master's son Nathaniel, Wheatley sailed to England. She met a number of prominent citizens, and it was there in 1773 that her book *Poems on Various Subjects, Religious and Moral* was published. It was the first book of writings of any kind to be published by an African-American.

After her return to America, Wheatley continued to write poetry. When George Washington was named commander-in-chief of the military forces in 1775, she wrote him a poem of congratulations and he invited her to visit him at his headquarters. Phillis's life began a downward spiral as one by one the members of the Wheatley family died, and she was left alone. She finally married, but her husband mistreated her. She had two children who died, and her third baby perished in December 1784, on the same day that Wheatley herself passed away.

WHO WAS THE FIRST AFRICAN-AMERICAN WOMAN TO PUBLISH A BOOK OF ESSAYS?

Little is known about the life of Ann Plato except that she was born in Hartford, Connecticut, around 1820, and was a teacher of young children when she was about fifteen. Plato's name has gone down in history as the author of the first book of essays published by an African-American woman. The volume, published in 1841, was entitled *Essays; Including Biographies and Miscellaneous Pieces, in Prose and Poetry*.

Plato's book, only the second published by a black woman, contained sixteen essays on such subjects as religion, education, death, and the seasons. It also included twenty poems, eleven of which had death as their subject.

WHO WAS THE FIRST AFRICAN-AMERICAN TO PUBLISH A NOVEL?

Clotel, or The President's Daughter: a Narrative of Slave Life in the United States, was written by William Wells Brown and published in London in 1853. It was the story of a child born to President Thomas Jefferson's African-American housekeeper. The book was finally published in the United States in 1864 with a different title—*Clotelle: A Tale of the Southern States*—and with no reference to the President. Brown also wrote a play, *The Escape; or, A Leap for Freedom,* that was published in 1858 and performed by the author in readings to audiences sympathetic to his anti-slavery sentiments.

After he himself escaped slavery by fleeing to the North, Brown, an ardent abolitionist, wrote about the evils of slavery not only in his book and play, but also in the autobiographical *Narrative of William Wells Brown, a Fugitive Slave,* and in many articles. He lectured widely on slavery in America and Europe, and lived abroad for several years.

WHAT WAS THE FIRST NOVEL PUBLISHED BY AN AFRICAN-AMERICAN WOMAN?

Harriet Wilson's 1859 novel, *Our Nig: Sketches from the Life of a Free Black,* was the first published novel by an African-American woman and the first novel by a black writer to be published in the United States. The recollection of a free African-American woman's experience as a servant for a white family in Massachusetts, *Our Nig* provides a picture of life in the antebellum North.

Virtually unnoticed when it was published, the book's manuscript was discovered in 1983 by the African-American scholar Henry Louis Gates, and the novel was reissued.

WHO WAS THE FIRST AFRICAN-AMERICAN POET TO RECEIVE NATIONAL RECOGNITION?

Paul Laurence Dunbar was born in 1872 in Dayton, Ohio, the child of former slaves. In high school, where he was the only African-American student in his class, Dunbar was editor of the school paper, president of the literary society, and writer of the class song, which was sung at his graduation in 1891. Before he finished high school he had already published a poem in a local newspaper. Dunbar's widowed mother could not afford to send him to college, so he found a job as an elevator operator for four dollars a week.

Devoting as much time as possible to his writing, Dunbar published his first collection of poems, *Oak and Ivy*, written in an African-American dialect. His second collection of dialect poems, *Majors and Minors*, was published in 1894 and received an excellent review from the prominent critic William Dean Howells in *Harper's* magazine. Howells wrote the introduction to Dunbar's next book, *Lyrics of Lowly Life*, which became one of the most popular poetry collections of the time. Dunbar went on to produce novels, short stories, and articles, and wrote the libretto and lyrics for Will Marion Cook's 1898 musical, *Clorindy, the Origin of the Cakewalk*.

But the public showed little interest in Dunbar's work unless it was written in dialect, and he was forced to produce writing that he felt was not his best. He contracted tuberculosis and after his doctor prescribed whiskey for his cough he developed a drinking problem. When he was only thirty-four years old, Dunbar died of pneumonia in his hometown of Dayton.

WHO WAS THE FIRST AFRICAN-AMERICAN POET TO TEACH WRITING AT A BLACK UNIVERSITY?

Poet, teacher, civil rights leader, diplomat—James Weldon Johnson, born in 1871 in Jacksonville, Florida, made his mark in an amazing number of undertakings. After graduating from Atlanta University in 1894, he returned to Jacksonville, taught school, and became a school principal. While teaching he also studied law and became the first African-American to pass the Florida bar exam, although he did not practice law.

He and his brother, John Rosamond Johnson, dreamed of writing an operetta and presenting it on Broadway. In 1899 they left for New York City, where they teamed up with songwriter Bob Cole and wrote a number of successful songs, including *Under the Bamboo Tree*. He and his brother also wrote *Lift Every Voice and Sing*, which became known as the black national anthem.

But Johnson felt his work in New York City wasn't satisfying enough and he left for Washington, D.C., where he took an exam for the consular service. In 1906 he was appointed U.S. Consul to Venezuela and then to Nicaragua, leaving the service in 1912, the same year his first novel, *The Autobiography of an Ex-Colored Man*, was published, first anonymously and later under his own name.

Johnson joined the staff of the NAACP in 1916 and served as executive secretary from 1920 to 1930. Always an activist, he investigated charges of brutality to Haitians and pushed for passage of an anti-lynching bill in Congress. After retiring from the NAACP he became the first African-American poet to teach creative writing in a black university when he became a professor at Fisk University. Best known today for his poetry, his books of verse include *God's Trombone, Fifty Years and Other Poems,* and *Selected Poems.* He published his autobiography, *Along This Way,* in 1933 and died five years later.

WHO WAS THE FIRST AFRICAN-AMERICAN WOMAN TO WIN A GUGGENHEIM FELLOWSHIP?

Nella Larsen was the leading woman writer of the Harlem Renaissance, a period of creative expression by African-Americans during the late 1920s. After publishing short stories and two novels, Larsen became the first African-American woman to win a Guggenheim fellowship—a prestigious award made to scholars, writers, and artists. But Larsen never published again, and soon disappeared from the literary scene.

Larsen was born in Chicago in 1891 and professed to be the daughter of an African-American mother and Danish sailor father, although her claim was later disputed. She graduated from Lincoln Hospital's nursing school in New York City and pursued a nursing career until 1921, when she became a librarian at the Harlem branch of the New York Public Library.

Larsen's first writing appeared in *The Brownies' Book,* a magazine for African-American children. She published two short stories for adults and then, in 1928, a novel, *Quicksand,* the despairing story of an educated black woman unable to find her place in the world. Her next novel, *Passing,* published the following year, was equally tragic in its portrait of an African-American woman searching for her identity.

With the Guggenheim fellowship that she won in 1930, Larsen traveled to Europe to write another novel, but publishers rejected her work. Back in New York, she returned to nursing and by 1944 had become chief nurse at Gouverneur Hospital. She retired in 1963 and died a year later.

WHAT WAS THE FIRST MYSTERY NOVEL BY AN AFRICAN-AMERICAN?

The *Conjure Man Dies: A Mystery Tale of Dark Harlem,* published in 1932, was the first mystery novel written by an African-American. Its author was Rudolph Fisher, a physician who pursued medical studies at Washington's Howard University and at Columbia University in New York City, where he remained to practice medicine.

The Conjure Man Dies is the story of the murder of an African seer in Harlem, a case that is solved with the help of a young black doctor. The New York Times book reviewer at the time called it "a puzzling mystery yarn" and "a lively tale of Harlem." Fisher's first published work, a short story entitled *The City of Refuge,* appeared in the Atlantic Monthly in 1923.

His first novel, *The Walls of Jericho*, was published five years later. *The Conjure Man Dies* was adapted as a play by Arna Bontemps and Countee Cullen for New York's Federal Theatre Project. It opened there in 1936, two years after Fisher's death at the age of thirty-seven.

WHO WROTE THE FIRST NOVEL BY AN AFRICAN-AMERICAN TO BECOME A BOOK-OF-THE-MONTH CLUB SELECTION?

Richard Wright was born on a plantation in Roxie, Mississippi, and left school after the ninth grade, when he was sixteen years old. He first went to Memphis, Tennessee, and then on to Chicago. In 1932 he joined the Communist Party, which he quit twelve years later. His first writing was published in the Communist press, including *The Daily Worker* and *Left Front* magazine.

Wright's first book, *Uncle Tom's Children*, published in 1938, was a collection of four novellas about the South. His next book, *Native Son*, a novel about a young black man who commits a murder in a moment of panic, was published in 1940. It created a sensation, becoming a best seller, the first novel by a African-American writer selected by the Book-of-the-Month Club, and the first to enter the mainstream of American literature.

Wright lived in Mexico in the early 1940s, moving to Paris in 1946 and staying there until his death in 1960. In 1945 he published *Black Boy*, an autobiographical account of his childhood in the South. The second part of his autobiography, *American Hunger*, was not published until 1977. His other works include *The Outsider* and *The Long Dream*. *Eight Men*, a collection of stories about African-American men oppressed by their surroundings, was published a year after his death.

WHAT NOVEL WAS THE FIRST BY AN AFRICAN-AMERICAN WOMAN TO SELL OVER ONE MILLION COPIES?

The Street, by Ann Petry, published in 1946, is the story of a young woman struggling to raise her son in New York City's Harlem. Petry's first novel, it was also the first by an African-American woman to sell more than one million copies.

Petry was born in 1911 in Old Saybrook, Connecticut, where her father and grandfather ran a drugstore. As a child she loved to read, and at the age of fourteen she knew she wanted to be a writer. She wrote poetry and short plays in high school, but after graduation she followed the family tradition and studied pharmacy. She earned a degree from the Connecticut College of Pharmacy in 1931, worked in the family drugstore for a time, then married and moved to New York City in 1938.

Richard Wright

Her first job in New York was in the advertising department of the *Amsterdam News*, an African-American newspaper. She then became a reporter and editor for another weekly, *The People's Voice*. Petry's first published story, "On Saturday the Siren Sounds at Noon," appeared in *The Crisis* magazine in December, 1943. An editor at a major publishing company who read the story encouraged her to write a novel, which she completed in 1946 and titled *The Street*.

After the success of *The Street*, Petry continued to write, publishing short stories, children's books, and two other novels. Her 1953 book, *The Narrows*, examines the lives of African-Americans in a New England town, and a biography, *Harriet Tubman: Conductor on the Underground Railroad*, was published in 1955. *The Street*, with its realistic portrayal of life in Harlem in the 1940s, was reissued in 1992, when Petry was eighty-one years old.

WHO WROTE THE FIRST NOVEL BY AN AFRICAN-AMERICAN TO BE BOUGHT BY HOLLYWOOD?

Frank Yerby became a best-selling author with his very first book, *The Foxes of Harrow*, which was published in 1946. A historical melodrama, it is set in the South before the Civil War. Selling over one million copies, the novel was the first by an African-American writer to be purchased by a Hollywood studio; it was made into a 1947 film starring Rex Harrison and Maureen O'Hara.

Yerby was born in 1916 in Augusta, Georgia, and was educated at Paine College, Fisk University, and the University of Chicago. During World War II he worked in defense plants in Dearborn, Michigan, and Jamaica, New York. After the success of his first book, Yerby settled in Madrid, Spain, and went on to write more than thirty historical novels, most of which became best sellers. His books include *An Odor of Sanctity*, set in medieval Spain; *Goat Song*, set in ancient Greece; and *Judas, My Brother*, set in the time of Jesus. His 1971 novel, *The Dahomean*, was an exploration of his African ancestry, and he published a novel about slavery, *A Darkness at Ingraham's Court*, in 1979.

WHO WAS THE FIRST AFRICAN-AMERICAN WOMAN SCIENCE FICTION WRITER TO BE PUBLISHED?

Born in 1947 in Pasadena, California, Octavia Butler was a shy, awkward child who spent her happiest hours in the public library. She said that she began writing when she was about ten years old to escape loneliness and boredom. Outstanding in a genre dominated by white male writers, Butler has won the top two honors in science fiction, the Nebula and Hugo awards. A science fiction newsletter, *Locus*, called her books "some of the most powerfully disquieting science fiction of recent years."

Butler turned to science fiction because she enjoyed reading it, she told an interviewer, and submitted her first stories to science fiction magazines when she was only thirteen. She later supported herself with a succession of jobs while trying to become established as a writer. Her first story was published in *Clarion*, an anthology of work from the Clarion Science Fiction Writers' Workshop that she attended in 1970. Five years later, laid off from a job that she hated, she managed to write three books in one year; all were published. They were the first in a string of successful novels.

Butler's leading characters are usually independent African-American women, and her themes deal with genetic engineering, alien beings, and the use of power. Her first five novels are set in a universe she calls "Pat-ternist." In 1979 she broke away from that theme with her novel *Kindred*, which uses a time travel device to explore slavery in America. Among her other books are the *Xenogenesis* trilogy—*Dawn, Adulthood Rites*, and *Imago*. "I didn't realize that writing was supposed to be work," she was quoted as saying. "It was too much fun. It still is."

WHO WAS THE FIRST AFRICAN-AMERICAN TO WIN A PULITZER PRIZE?

In May 1950, Gwendolyn Brooks, a Chicago poet, was awarded a Pulitzer Prize for her collection of poems, *Annie Allen*. Brooks was born in 1917 in Topeka, Kansas, and her parents moved to Chicago when she was an infant. Even as children, she and her brother were encouraged to read the Harvard Classics and the poetry of Paul Lawrence Dunbar.

Brooks began writing when she was still a child, and by 1968 she had been named Poet Laureate of Illinois, succeeding Carl Sandburg. She gave much of her time to nurturing budding poets, including schoolchildren, prisoners, and homeless people. Her works include *A Street in Bronzeville*, *In the Mecca, Maud Martha*, and an autobiography, *Report From Part One*.

Asked in an interview if her poetry had a racial element, Brooks said, "Yes, it is organic, not imposed. It is my privilege to present Negroes not as curios but as people."

WHO WAS THE FIRST AFRICAN-AMERICAN WRITER TO WIN THE NATIONAL BOOK AWARD?

In 1953 Ralph Ellison's novel *Invisible Man* won the National Book Award for fiction, a yearly award for outstanding writing. Ellison's impressive reputation rests solely on this landmark first novel, a memorable account of the plight of the African-American in the United States.

Ellison was born in 1914 in Oklahoma City. His father died when he was three and his mother supported the family by doing domestic work. Ellison majored in music at Tuskegee Institute and went to New York City in 1936 to study music and sculpture. He became involved in the WPA Writers Project, developing friendships with the African-American writers

Langston Hughes and Richard Wright, and began publishing essays, reviews, and short stories in various publications.

After serving in the merchant marine during World War II, Ellison received a fellowship that allowed him to write *Invisible Man*. He spent the rest of his career teaching at several colleges and universities and published only one more book—a 1964 collection of essays called *Shadow and Act*.

WHO WAS THE FIRST AFRICAN-AMERICAN WOMAN TO WIN THE PULITZER PRIZE FOR FICTION?

A novelist, essayist, short story writer, and poet, Alice Walker had published several books before winning the Pulitzer Prize in 1983 for her novel, *The Color Purple*. Walker was born in 1944 in Eatontown, Georgia, where her parents were sharecroppers and dairy farmers. An accident when she was eight years old—she was blinded in one eye after being shot by her brother's BB gun—led her to develop a shy and solitary nature. Much of her school years were spent reading and writing poetry, and she was the valedictorian of her high school graduating class.

Walker won a scholarship to Spelman College in Atlanta, but in her sophomore year transferred to Sarah Lawrence College in Bronxville, New York. While still in college, she wrote a series of poems about suicide, love, and civil rights. The collection, entitled *Once*, was published in 1968.

After college Walker continued to write while becoming active in the civil rights movement. She lived for seven years in Mississippi with her husband, a white civil rights lawyer (they were divorced in 1977). While in the South, she was writer-in-residence at Jackson State and Tougaloo colleges. Her first novel, *The Third Life of Grange Copeland*, was published in 1970, and six years later she published her second novel, *Meridien*, about her experiences in the civil rights movement.

Her 1982 novel, *The Color Purple*, the story of an African-American woman's life, won not only the Pulitzer but also the American Book Award, and was made into a film in 1985. Her other books include *The Temple of My Familiar* and *Possessing the Secret of Joy*.

WHO WAS THE FIRST AFRICAN-AMERICAN POET LAUREATE OF NEW YORK STATE?

Audre Lorde was born in 1934 in New York City, where she attended Catholic schools. An avid reader of poetry, she eventually started writing her own; her first published poem appeared in *Seventeen* magazine when she was still in high school. She graduated from Hunter College, received a master's degree in library science from Columbia University, and worked as a librarian and teacher during the 1960s.

Audre Lorde

Nineteen sixty-eight was a banner year for Lorde: she was appointed poet-in-residence at Tougaloo College in Mississippi, she was a visiting professor at Atlanta University, and she published her first volume of poetry, *The First Cities*. An outspoken feminist and lesbian, during her life Lorde published seventeen volumes of poetry, essays, and autobiography, all reflecting her aversion to racial and sexual prejudice. She became an English professor at Hunter College and lectured throughout the United States, Africa, and Europe. In 1989 a collection of her essays, *A Burst of Light*, won an American Book Award.

In 1980 Lorde wrote *The Cancer Journals*, which described the beginning stages of the disease that finally took her life in 1992 at the age of fifty-eight. Before her death she was awarded honorary degrees from Hunter, Haverford, and Oberlin colleges, and received the Walt Whitman Citation of Merit in 1991, making her the Poet Laureate of New York State.

WHO WAS THE FIRST AFRICAN-AMERICAN TO READ HER OWN POEM AT A PRESIDENTIAL INAUGURATION?

Chosen by President Bill Clinton to create a poem for his January 1993 inauguration, Maya Angelou read her composition, *On the Pulse of Morn-*

ing, to a spellbound nation. Later that year, she published *Wouldn't Take Nothing for My Journey Now*, a collection of essays about such subjects as religion, death, racism, and motherhood.

Born Marguerite Johnson in 1928 in St. Louis, Missouri, and raised in Clinton's home state of Arkansas, Angelou moved to California when she was in ninth grade. At the age of fifteen, after hounding the Market Street Railway Company for weeks, her tenacity was rewarded and she was hired as the first African-American streetcar conductor in San Francisco.

Angelou's varied and colorful career included a role in the opera *Porgy and Bess* during its twenty-two nation tour in 1954 and a four-year stint on the staff of the University of Ghana beginning in 1963. Angelou's screenplay, *Georgia, Georgia*, was the first by an African-American woman to be made into a film, and she received an Emmy nomination for her performance in the television miniseries "Roots." By 1993, this actress, singer, dancer, playwright, author, lecturer, and civil rights activist had written twelve books of poetry and autobiography, including *I Know Why the Caged Bird Sings*, which was nominated for a National Book Award, and was a professor of American studies at Wake Forest University in North Carolina.

WHO WAS THE NATION'S FIRST AFRICAN-AMERICAN POET LAUREATE?

In May 1993, Rita Dove, a Pulitzer Prize-winning writer, was chosen to be the country's new Poet Laureate, the first African-American to hold that position and, at forty, the youngest to be named. The position of Poet Laureate of the United States, which each appointee holds for one year, was created in 1986; those who preceded Dove include Robert Penn Warren, Richard Wilbur, Joseph Brodsky, and Mona Van Duyn.

Dove was born in Akron, Ohio. Her father was the first African-American research chemist to be employed by a leading tire manufacturer and her mother was a homemaker: they both encouraged her love of reading. Dove earned degrees from Miami University in Oxford, Ohio, and the University of Iowa. At the time of her appointment as Poet Laureate, she was a professor of English at the University of Virginia.

In 1987 Dove won the Pulitzer Prize in poetry for *Thomas and Beulah*, a collection inspired by the lives of her grandparents. She was the second African-American to win the Pulitzer for poetry. Her other books of poetry include *The Yellow House on the Corner*, *Museum*, *Grace Notes*, and *Selected Poems*, which was published in 1993. Her collection of short stories, *Fifth Sunday*, appeared in 1985 and a novel, *Through the Ivory Gate*, in 1992. Her poems and stories have appeared in many antholo-

Rita Dove

gies. Dove uses the African-American experience to inform her writing, which often draws from history and autobiography.

WHO WAS THE FIRST AFRICAN-AMERICAN TO WIN THE NOBEL PRIZE FOR LITERATURE?

On October 7, 1993, writer Toni Morrison joined her friends in a jubilant celebration—she had just been awarded the Nobel Prize for Literature. In making the announcement, the Nobel Committee said that the novelist "gives life to an essential aspect of American reality."

Morrison was born Chloe Anthony Woford on February 18, 1931, in Lorain, Ohio, a steel town near Cleveland. Her parents taught her to read before she started first grade. She earned degrees in English from Howard and Cornell universities and then embarked on a teaching career, first at Texas Southern University and then at Howard. There she married a Jamaican architect named Harold Morrison; they were later divorced.

Morrison left Howard in 1965 to work as an editor for Random House. In 1970 she published her first novel, *The Bluest Eye*, about a young African-American girl who longs to have blue eyes. Her second novel, *Sula*, published in 1973, was nominated for a National Book Award. Her 1977 book, *Song of Solomon*, became a best-seller, winning several prizes, including the National Book Critics Circle Award. *Tar Baby*, published in 1981, was also a success.

In 1987 she became a professor at Princeton University, and that same year she published *Beloved*, the story of a runaway slave who is captured and cuts her daughter's throat rather than have the child grow up in slavery. It won great critical acclaim and was awarded a Pulitzer Prize. Morrison published two books in 1992—a novel, *Jazz*, and a collection of essays, *Playing in the Dark: Whiteness and the Literary Imagination*. Discussing the liberating aspects of being an African-American woman writer, Morrison once told the *New York Times*: "My world did not shrink because I was a black female writer. It just got bigger."

MILITARY

WHO WAS THE FIRST AFRICAN-AMERICAN WOUNDED IN THE CIVIL WAR?

In April 1861 Nicholas Biddle, an escaped slave, attached himself to the Union troops that left Harrisburg, Pennsylvania, for Washington, D.C. The troops were marching to a train station in Baltimore when they were attacked by a hostile mob. Biddle was struck in the head and seriously injured.

With the assistance of his fellow soldiers, Biddle managed to continue the trip to Washington. He was resting on the floor of the Capitol when President Lincoln stopped to talk with him. When he recovered, Biddle continued to serve bravely throughout the war. After his death, a marker was placed on his grave in his native Pottsville, Pennsylvania, memorializing him for "shedding the first blood in the late war for the Union."

WHO WAS THE FIRST AFRICAN-AMERICAN NAVAL HERO?

Robert Smalls was born in Beaufort County, South Carolina, in 1839, and learned about ships and sailing from his father, a sailmaker and rigger. In 1861, just after the outbreak of the Civil War, Smalls was made a pilot of a Confederate steamboat, the *Planter*, that was being used to transport guns and ammunition for the rebel army. On the night of May 12, 1862, when the ship was docked in the harbor at Charleston, South Carolina, the white officers went ashore. After alerting the seven other African-American seamen who were aboard, Smalls put on the captain's dress uniform, took control of the ship, and steered it out of Charleston harbor.

Heading for Beaufort harbor, which had been seized by Union forces, Smalls and his crew steered the *Planter* past the guns of Fort Sumter and surrendered the ship to the officers of the Union fleet. This amazing exploit earned great praise for Smalls, and he served for the rest of the war as a pilot in the Union Navy.

After the war Smalls entered politics and in 1868 was elected to the South Carolina State Legislature. In 1876 he became a United States Congressman, serving four terms. President Benjamin Harrison later appointed him customs collector of the port of Beaufort, where he died in 1915 at the age of seventy-six.

WHO WAS THE FIRST AFRICAN-AMERICAN TO WIN THE CONGRESSIONAL MEDAL OF HONOR?

Sergeant William H. Carney was a member of the Massachusetts Fifty-fourth Infantry, the first black regiment recruited in the North to fight in the Civil War. On July 18, 1863, the men of the 54th led an assault on the

*Robert Smalls, pilot of
the gunboat* Planter, *1862*

Confederate fort, Battery Wagner, that protected the approach to Charleston Harbor in South Carolina. The commander of the regiment, Robert Gould Shaw, and many other soldiers were killed in the battle.

As the fighting raged on, Sergeant Carney was running beside the color-bearer just as the man was hit by a shell. Carney picked up the flag and led the final charge on the fort. The valiant soldier managed to reach the parapet, but was shot twice and severely wounded by Confederate soldiers. As he fell he held the flag high and passed it to his comrades, saying, "Boys, it never touched the ground."

For his heroism, Carney became the first African-American soldier to be awarded the Congressional Medal of Honor. The highest military award for bravery, the Medal of Honor was established by Congress in 1862 to be awarded for gallantry at the risk of life above and beyond the call of duty. In all, more than 180,000 African-Americans fought in the Union Army during the Civil War, and sixteen were awarded the Medal of Honor.

Major Martin Delaney

WHO WAS THE FIRST AFRICAN-AMERICAN ARMY MAJOR?

Late in the Civil War, Martin Delany, an editor, doctor, lecturer, writer, and anti-slavery activist, was appointed a major in the Union Army, for which he recruited two regiments of former slaves. Before his military career began, Delany had studied medicine at Harvard, published a newspaper, and in 1852 written a book that urged African-Americans to emigrate to Latin America or Africa. It was titled *The Condition, Elevation, Emigration and Destiny of the Colored People of the United States Politically Considered.*

After the Civil War Delany was an important figure in South Carolina, where he assisted ex-slaves in making the transition to free citizens. After serving on the Freedmen's Bureau for three years, he became a customs house inspector and then a trial judge in Charleston, South Carolina. In 1861 he wrote the official *Report of the Niger Valley Exploring Party*, which he led in 1859. His 1879 book, *Principia of Ethnology: The Origin of Races and Color*, pointed out the major contributions African-Americans had made to world civilization, a view that had never before been expressed.

Delany, who died in 1885, always emphasized his pride in being an African-American. In fact, the distinguished statesman Frederick Douglass wrote: "I thank God for making me a man simply, but Delany always thanks Him for making him a black man."

WHAT WERE THE FIRST AFRICAN-AMERICAN UNITS COMMISSIONED IN THE REGULAR ARMY?

In 1866 Congress passed a law creating six regiments of African-American regular army soldiers. Four of these regiments were infantry (they were later combined into two) and two were cavalry. The Native Americans of the western United States, against whom the 9th and 10th cavalries often fought, called these men the Buffalo Soldiers, possibly because of their courage.

For twenty-five years the Buffalo Soldiers patrolled the West, guarding wagon trains, constructing roads, building towns, protecting payrolls, chasing off cattle rustlers, and serving in the thick of the Indian wars. They fought in New Mexico, Arizona, Texas, Oklahoma, Colorado, and the Dakotas, fending off bands of Apache, Sioux and Cheyenne. Thirteen Buffalo Soldiers were awarded the Congressional Medal of Honor during the western campaigns.

The Buffalo Soldiers were called back East to fight in the Spanish-American War, participating with Teddy Roosevelt's Rough Riders in the attack on San Juan Hill in Cuba. They went on to serve with distinction in the Philippines and Mexico, in World War I and II, and in Korea, until 1952 when the army was integrated and the all-black units were disbanded.

WHO WAS THE FIRST BUFFALO SOLDIER TO RECEIVE THE CONGRESSIONAL MEDAL OF HONOR?

Sergeant Emanuel Stance was a member of one of the all-black regiments—known as the Buffalo Soldiers—who patrolled the West for twenty-five years after the end of the Civil War. On May 20, 1870, Stance was ordered to lead a detachment of soldiers from the fort in Kickapoo Springs, Texas, on a routine patrol along an old Indian trail. On the way they were involved in a skirmish with a band of Kickapoo Indians.

Returning to the fort the next morning, the group saw a band of Kickapoos pursuing a herd of government-owned horses. Stance ordered a charge and led his men in a running battle with the Kickapoos, finally driving them away. When he returned to the fort, his captain commended him for his courage and devotion to duty and recommended him for a Medal of Honor, which Stance received on July 24, 1870. He was the first of eighteen African-American soldiers to win the Medal of Honor during the Indian Wars.

WHEN DID THE U.S. NAVAL ACADEMY ACCEPT ITS FIRST AFRICAN-AMERICAN?

John Conyers, a native of South Carolina, was appointed by his congressman to attend the U.S. Naval Academy at Annapolis, Maryland, and entered in September 1872, twenty-two years after the academy was established. His appointment created a storm of controversy. Since hazing was a popular practice at the academy, some faculty members feared he would be tormented by his fellow midshipmen.

Although Conyers was the object of several hazing incidents, he was said to have borne them stoically. But his teachers eventually decided that he was deficient in mathematics and French, and he left Annapolis after his first year.

WHO WAS THE FIRST AFRICAN-AMERICAN GRADUATE OF WEST POINT?

Although he was not the first African-American to enter the U.S. Military Academy at West Point, Henry Ossian Flipper was the first to graduate. In 1870, seven years before Flipper's graduation, a young man named James Webster Smith was admitted to the academy, but in his fourth year he was judged deficient in the study of philosophy and dismissed. While at West Point, Smith was forced to live in a room by himself, and the other cadets refused to sit with him in the dining hall.

Henry Ossian Flipper, who had come to West Point from Georgia, was also mistreated. Although ostracized by his fellow cadets, he was determined to get through the four years and he succeeded. After graduation Flipper was assigned to the all-black 10th Cavalry, a unit of the Buffalo Soldiers, where he served with distinction. But in 1882 he was accused of mishandling commissary funds. Although he proclaimed his innocence, he was court-martialed and dismissed from the army.

Flipper embarked on a long career as a mining engineer, becoming the first African-American to gain recognition in that profession. At one point, he was named an assistant to the secretary of the interior. He retired to Atlanta, where he died in 1940, still trying to clear his name. It was not until 1978 that the army finally reexamined all trial records and determined that the charges against Flipper were unfounded. He was given an honorable discharge and his body was reinterred with military honors.

WHO WERE THE FIRST FOUR AFRICAN-AMERICAN SOLDIERS TO WIN THE MEDAL OF HONOR IN THE SPANISH-AMERICAN WAR?

On June 30, 1898, two transport ships, the *Florida* and the *Funita*, were approaching the harbor in Tayabacoe, Cuba, to deliver food and ammunition to Cuban insurgents. Fifty African-American cavalrymen were among the white Americans and Cubans aboard the two ships. A small group of Cubans and white Americans rowed ashore to survey the area, but they were fired upon by the enemy and their small boats were destroyed. Cuban rescue parties left the *Florida* four times to try to reach the stranded men but were turned back.

Finally, four African-American cavalrymen offered to try; they were Privates Dennis Bell, Fitz Lee, William Thompkins, and George Wanton. Ducking Spanish bullets, the men rowed to shore, rescued their comrades, and carried them safely back to the ship. For their courage, each of the four cavalrymen was awarded the Congressional Medal of Honor.

WHO WAS THE FIRST AFRICAN-AMERICAN SOLDIER TO WIN A CROIX DE GUERRE?

During World War I, Henry Johnson, a former porter in the Albany, New York, train station, joined the army and was assigned to the 369th Infantry. In May 1918 when Johnson was still a private, his unit, attached to French troops, was guarding a line of trenches. One night while he was on sentry duty, at least twelve German soldiers suddenly attacked. Johnson shot one, wounded two others, and continued to fight until the Germans retreated. Then, ignoring his own injuries, he went to the aid of a wounded comrade. In recognition of his courage, the French government awarded Johnson its highest military decoration for bravery in action—the Croix de Guerre.

WHO WAS THE FIRST AFRICAN-AMERICAN GENERAL?

Benjamin O. Davis, Sr., enlisted in the infantry in 1898 when he was twenty-one years old, starting a military career that would last for fifty years. Davis saw action in the Spanish-American War, World War I, and World War II, amassing many honors, including the Bronze Star and the Distinguished Service Medal.

From the time that he enlisted, Davis rose through the ranks, becoming a lieutenant colonel in 1920 and being named the first African-American brigadier general in the Army in 1940. Before his retirement in 1948, Davis played a major role in the movement toward desegregation of the armed forces.

WHO WAS THE FIRST HERO OF WORLD WAR II?

When Japanese planes attacked Pearl Harbor on December 7, 1941, U.S. Navy mess attendant Dorie Miller was collecting laundry on the battleship *West Virginia*. As planes roared overhead Miller rushed on deck, manned a machine gun, and began firing at the attackers. Before receiving the order to abandon ship, Miller had downed four enemy planes.

Miller's exploit made him the first hero of the war and within six months he was personally awarded the Navy Cross for extraordinary courage by Admiral Chester W. Nimitz. But what made his feat really remarkable was the fact that he, like most African-American sailors, was serving as a noncombatant in a segregated navy that had given him no training in the operation of guns.

After receiving the Navy Cross, Miller was sent to black communities around the country to promote the sale of war bonds. When this tour of duty ended he was returned to the war in the Pacific—as a mess attendant. In 1943 his ship, the aircraft carrier *Liscombe Bay*, was torpedoed by a Japanese submarine and sank with all hands. Dorie Miller was twenty-four years old.

After the war legislation was twice introduced to award Miller the Congressional Medal of Honor. It was defeated both times.

WHO WERE THE FIRST AFRICAN-AMERICAN FIGHTER PILOTS?

On March 7, 1942, the first group of African-Americans ever to undergo training as combat fighter pilots graduated from flying school at Tuskegee Institute in Alabama. Known as the Tuskegee Airmen, they were organized into the 99th Pursuit Squadron. Led by Captain Benjamin O. Davis, Jr., who was to become the first African-American brigadier general in the air force, the pilots were ordered to North Africa.

On the 99th's first mission, Lt. Charles B. Hall of Indiana won the Distinguished Flying Cross for shooting down a German plane. A year later the 99th was transferred to the all-black 332nd Fighter Group, which won praise in its many engagements in the skies over Italy and Germany.

WHO WAS THE FIRST AFRICAN-AMERICAN TO COMMAND A U.S. MERCHANT SHIP?

Although the army and navy were segregated during World War II, the merchant marine had been integrated from the beginning; it was not part of the armed forces and its members belonged to a labor union that prohibited discrimination. Before the end of the war, fourteen Liberty ships (cargo ships built during World War II) had been named after well-known African-Americans, four after black colleges, and four after African-American seamen who had lost their lives in the service.

In September 1942, when the Liberty ship *Booker T. Washington* was launched, an African-American captain, Hugh Mulzac, was in command. Mulzac was the first of four African-Americans assigned to command Liberty ships. By May 1944, he had guided the *Booker T. Washington* through the dangerous, submarine-infested waters of the Atlantic Ocean seven times.

WHO WAS THE FIRST AFRICAN-AMERICAN NURSE TO SERVE IN THE NAVY NURSE CORPS IN WORLD WAR II?

Phyllis Daley, a graduate of Lincoln School for Nurses in New York City, was commissioned as an ensign in the U.S. Navy Nurse Corps in 1945. Daley was the first of four African-American nurses to serve in World War II, and her appointment was a milestone in the effort to integrate the U.S. Navy.

WHEN DID THE FIRST AFRICAN-AMERICAN GRADUATE FROM THE U.S. NAVAL ACADEMY?

From the time the U.S. Naval Academy opened in Annapolis, Maryland, in 1850, until Wesley Brown was appointed in 1945, only five African-Americans were admitted, the first in 1872. All resigned or were dismissed, allegedly because of poor grades or disciplinary problems. When two black midshipmen left in the 1930s, one within his first month at the academy, African-American organizations protested, charging discrimination.

In June 1945, Wesley A. Brown of Washington, D.C., was appointed to the naval academy by New York Congressman Adam Clayton Powell, Jr. As a student at Dunbar High School in Washington, Brown had excelled academically, was active in German, chess, and photography clubs, and

Lt. Commander Wesley A. Brown

participated in tennis and track. His teachers encouraged him to pursue a military career.

Brown's first year at the naval academy was an ordeal; he was harassed by classmates and reprimanded by teachers at any provocation. But he persevered, and in June 1949 became the first African-American to graduate from the academy. After a twenty-year career in the navy, Brown retired as a lieutenant commander and joined the faculty of Howard University. In 1989, when he celebrated the fortieth anniversary of his graduation from the naval academy, Brown received tributes from many other graduates, including former President Jimmy Carter.

WHO WAS THE FIRST AFRICAN-AMERICAN NAVY PILOT?

Ensign Jesse L. Brown of Hattiesburg, Mississippi, was the first African-American to be commissioned as a navy pilot. In December 1950, Brown was shot down near the Chosin Reservoir in North Korea. He had just taken off from the aircraft carrier *Leyte* when his plane crashed into a snow-covered mountain. Seeing that Brown was trapped in the wreckage, a white pilot from Massachusetts, Lieutenant Thomas J. Hudner, Jr., landed his plane on the icy slope and rushed to Brown's side, where he tried unsuccessfully to free the injured flyer. Hudner radioed for help but the rescue pilot arrived too late to save Brown's life.

After his death Brown was awarded the Distinguished Flying Cross and Air Medal for bravery. In March 1972 he was further honored when the destroyer escort *Jesse L. Brown* was launched from Avondale Shipyards in Louisiana. It was the first ship named for an African-American navy officer.

WHO WAS THE FIRST AFRICAN-AMERICAN TO EARN A MEDAL OF HONOR IN THE KOREAN WAR?

When William Thompson was just a youngster, a minister noticed him sleeping in a park and took him to the New York Home for Homeless Boys. Thompson remained a resident there until just after his eighteenth birthday in 1945, when he was drafted into the army. Thompson was honorably discharged a year and a half later and returned to New York, but he had trouble adjusting to civilian life and eventually reenlisted in the regular army.

Thompson was with the first American troops to arrive in South Korea in June 1950. Six weeks later, in the dark of night, his platoon came under a surprise attack by enemy forces. Private First Class Thompson set up his machine gun in the enemy's path and swept them with his fire, allowing the rest of the platoon to withdraw to a better position. Although the foe continued to charge toward him, tossing grenades and firing, Thompson, badly wounded, refused orders to retreat. Finally an enemy grenade exploded nearby, killing him. In June 1951 Thompson was posthumously awarded the Congressional Medal of Honor.

WHEN DID THE AIR FORCE APPOINT ITS FIRST AFRICAN-AMERICAN BRIGADIER GENERAL?

In October 1954, Benjamin O. Davis, Jr., made air force history by becoming the first black brigadier general in that branch of the service. The son of Benjamin O. Davis, Sr., the first African-American general in the army, the younger Davis graduated in 1936 from the U.S. Military Academy, the first black West Point graduate in the twentieth century.

Davis's treatment at the Academy was almost intolerable, he once told a group of students. "The greatest indignity was neglect," he said. "No cadet speaking to me the entire time I was at West Point except in the line of duty...I made up my mind that I wasn't going to let these people make me leave. I said to myself, 'I'm a better man than they are because I'm more human.'"

Soon after the start of World War II, when the military was still racially segregated, Davis was chosen to head the 99th Pursuit Squadron, consisting of African-American pilots trained at Tuskegee Institute. His outstanding performance earned him several military decorations, including the Distinguished Flying Cross and the Silver Star.

After the war, Davis became the first African-American to command an air base—Godman Field in Kentucky. He also commanded bases in Korea, Germany, the Philippines, and Taiwan, rising to the rank of three-star general before his retirement in 1970.

WHO WAS THE FIRST AFRICAN-AMERICAN TO BECOME A COLONEL IN THE U.S. ARMY NURSE CORPS?

Margaret Bailey, a native of Selma, Alabama, studied at the Fraternal Hospital School of Nursing in Montgomery and earned a degree from San Francisco State College. Bailey joined the army in June 1944 and filled assignments in hospitals throughout the United States and overseas, serving as a psychiatric, medical, and surgical nurse.

In 1964 Bailey become the first African-American army nurse to attain the rank of lieutenant colonel and in January 1970 she became the first to become a full colonel in the U.S. Army Nurse Corps.

WHO WAS THE FIRST AFRICAN-AMERICAN SOLDIER AWARDED THE CONGRESSIONAL MEDAL OF HONOR IN THE VIETNAM WAR?

Milton Lee Olive III, a native of Chicago, joined the army in 1964 when he was nineteen years old. A year later he was sent to Vietnam. On October 22, 1965, Olive and his platoon were creeping through the jungle when

Lt. Benjamin O. Davis, Jr. as commander of the 99th Pursuit Squadron

they stumbled into a Viet Cong ambush. A grenade landed near Olive and four other soldiers. He immediately threw his body on it as it exploded, sacrificing his own life to save the lives of his comrades.

Six months later, President Lyndon Johnson posthumously awarded the Congressional Medal of Honor to the courageous African-American soldier, presenting the award to Olive's father in a White House ceremony.

WHO WAS THE FIRST AFRICAN-AMERICAN ADMIRAL IN THE U.S. NAVY?

Samuel Gravely began his navy career in 1942 when he enlisted in the U.S. Naval Reserve. He was later commissioned as an ensign, and served in various assignments during World War II until he was released from active duty in 1946. Three years later he returned to the navy, where he was given increasingly responsible duties. In January 1962 he was made commander of the destroyer escort USS *Falgout*, becoming the first African-American to command a warship since the Civil War. He was later made captain of another warship, the USS *Taussig*.

Gravely made military history once again in 1971 when he became the first African-American to reach the rank of rear admiral. During his service in World War II, Korea, and Vietnam, Gravely won many decorations, including the Meritorious Service Medal and the National Defense Service medal with bronze star.

WHO WAS THE FIRST AFRICAN-AMERICAN TO COMMAND A U.S. ARMY DIVISION?

Before beginning his illustrious army career, Major General Frederic Davison earned a bachelor's degree from Howard University in 1938 and, after completing his ROTC training, was commissioned a second lieutenant in the infantry reserve. He later received master's degrees from both Howard and George Washington universities.

In March 1941, soon after the United States entered World War II, Davison was called to active duty in the army, leading an all-black company in North Africa and Italy. He left the army in 1946 and enrolled in Howard University medical school but a year later returned to the service. In 1968 he was appointed brigade commander of the 199th Light Infantry Brigade in Vietnam. Davison became the first African-American officer to lead a U.S. Army division when he took command of the Eighth Infantry Division in Germany in the spring of 1972.

WHO WAS THE FIRST AFRICAN-AMERICAN FOUR-STAR GENERAL?

Daniel James, Jr., who was nicknamed "Chappie," was born in Pensacola, Florida, in 1920. His mother, Lillie James, ran a school for African-American children in their home. James studied at Tuskegee Institute in Alabama

Rear Admiral Samuel L. Gravely, Jr.

and became a member of the Tuskegee Airmen, a group of African-American combat fighter pilots who served in the segregated army air force in World War II. An early civil rights activist, James, along with other Tuskegee Airmen, led sit-ins at white officers' clubs on several army bases.

James flew 101 combat missions as a fighter pilot during the Korean War and 78 more in Vietnam. In 1976 he became the first African-American four-star general in U.S. military history. A national spokesman for black self-esteem, James was being considered as a candidate for lieutenant governor of Florida, but he died of a heart attack in 1978, only a few weeks after his retirement.

WHEN WAS THE FIRST AFRICAN-AMERICAN WOMAN ADMITTED TO THE U.S. NAVAL ACADEMY?

Women were admitted to the U.S. Naval Academy in Annapolis, Maryland, for the first time in 1976. Of the eighty-one women who entered the academy that year, one was an African-American—Janie Mines, an eighteen-year-old from Aiken, South Carolina. A member of the Navy Junior ROTC at her high school, Mines majored in political science at the naval academy, where she was a squad leader, a midshipman drill instructor, and a regimental adjutant.

In 1980 Mines became the first African-American woman to graduate from the academy. After being trained as a supply officer, she was assigned to supervise three dining halls at the Naval Training Center in Orlando, Florida. Her sister, Gwen Mines, entered the naval academy a year after Janie and graduated in 1981.

WHO WAS THE FIRST AFRICAN-AMERICAN WOMAN GENERAL?

Five years after completing her nurse's training at Harlem Hospital in New York City, Hazel Johnson joined the army, and in May 1960 she was commissioned as a first lieutenant in the U.S. Army Nurse Corps. While in the service she earned a bachelor's degree from Villanova University, a master's from Columbia, and a Ph.D. from Catholic University. In 1979, at the age of fifty-two, she was promoted to brigadier general, the first African-American woman general in United States military history.

Johnson was chief of the army nurse corps from 1979 to 1983, when she retired. She then served as director of the government affairs division of the American Nursing Association, leaving after three years to become a nursing professor at George Mason University in Virginia.

WHO WAS THE FIRST AFRICAN-AMERICAN CHAIRMAN OF THE JOINT CHIEFS OF STAFF?

When General Colin L. Powell retired from the military in 1993, he ended a thirty-five-year career that culminated in serving as the nation's top uniformed military officer—the Chairman of the Joint Chiefs of Staff. Powell was born in New York City's Harlem in 1937 and grew up in the South

Bronx. He graduated from the City College of New York with a degree in geology and a commission as a second lieutenant in the Army ROTC.

Progressing in the army to command positions in the United States, Korea, Vietnam, and Germany, he was named national security adviser by President Ronald Reagan in 1987. Two years later President George Bush made Powell the Chairman of the Joint Chiefs; he was the first African-American and the youngest man ever to hold that office.

In his last speech as chairman on September 28, 1993, Powell said, "I've been a soldier all my life. I've never wanted to be anything else. I have loved every single minute of it, and I thank the nation for having given me the opportunity to serve in the proud armed forces of the United States."

President Clinton, who awarded Powell his second Presidential Medal of Freedom, said at the general's farewell ceremony that he symbolized a victory "for the principle that in our nation, people can rise as far as their talent, their capacity, their dreams, and their discipline will carry them."

WHO WAS THE FIRST AFRICAN-AMERICAN WOMAN GENERAL IN THE AIR FORCE?

Early in life, Brigadier General Marcelite J. Harris, a native of Houston, Texas, wanted to be an actress. Harris, born in 1943, enrolled in Atlanta's Spelman College to study speech and drama. During her senior year she joined a USO tour of military bases in France and Germany, and a year later, in need of a job and remembering the excitement of her travels abroad, she decided to join the U.S. Air Force.

Her first assignments were in California and Germany, and during the Vietnam War she was an aircraft maintenance supervisor at an air base in Thailand. She went on to fill military assignments in different parts of the country and in Japan—including a stint as White House social aide to President Jimmy Carter—and to win a number of decorations and awards.

Harris earned many "firsts"—such as becoming the first woman aircraft maintenance officer in the air force—and reached the pinnacle of her profession in September 1990 when she was promoted to brigadier general and became vice commander of the Oklahoma City Air Logistics Center at Tinker Air Force Base. In July 1993 Harris was assigned to Randolph Air Force Base in Texas as director of technical training, Air Education and Training Command. In this position, she assumed responsibility for the policy and management of the technical training of graduates in more than 245 different specialties.

Brig. General Marcelite Harris

MUSIC

WHO WAS THE FIRST AFRICAN-AMERICAN CONCERT ARTIST TO WIN RECOGNITION OUTSIDE THE UNITED STATES?

Elizabeth Taylor Greenfield was born in 1809 in Natchez, Mississippi, the daughter of an African father and a Seminole Indian mother. She was brought to Philadelphia when she was one year old and raised by a Quaker, Mrs. Greenfield. Her musical talent soon became evident and she was encouraged to pursue it. She was said to be awkward and unattractive and mostly self-taught, since white teachers refused her as a student. However, the quality and range—three and one-half octaves—of her voice made her increasingly popular.

When her patron died in 1844, Greenfield moved to Buffalo and began touring New York, the New England area, and the Midwest, performing ballads and arias from operas. In 1851 she sang to great acclaim before the Buffalo Musical Association, and a year later she performed in Albany for an audience that included the New York State governor and his family, members of both houses of the legislature, and other officials. In 1853 she made her New York City debut in Metropolitan Hall.

Despite Greenfield's success, controversy followed her everywhere. Riots were sometimes threatened when she performed and police often guarded her concerts. Although most of her performances were in the Northeast, African-Americans were either denied admission or forced to sit in the balcony. As a result, the black press attacked her for furthering segregation.

Famous nationwide and known as "The Black Swan," Greenfield sailed for England in 1854 to give a command performance for Queen Victoria at Buckingham Palace. Returning to America, she settled in Philadelphia, where she gave concerts, opened a studio, and taught voice. She died in 1876.

WHO WAS THE FIRST AFRICAN-AMERICAN TO GAIN RECOGNITION AS A CONCERT PIANIST?

Born into slavery in 1849 near Columbus, Georgia, Thomas Greene Bethune was blind from birth. When he was about four years old his owner, James Bethune, bought a piano, and legend has it that the child wandered into the living room at night and began to play tunes he had heard during the day. Amazed by his ability to imitate any piece by ear, the Bethune family encouraged him to use the piano whenever he wished, and played music for him so he could develop a repertoire.

By the time he was about five, Bethune was performing for private groups. He made his formal debut in 1857 at Temperance hall in Columbus. Known as "Blind Tom," he continued to give recitals during the Civil

War; even after the emancipation of slaves, the Bethune family continued their control over him. For almost thirty years he performed throughout the United States, Europe, and South America. It was said that he could play 7,000 pieces and that he composed more than 100.

WHAT WAS THE FIRST SINGING GROUP TO PERFORM SPIRITUALS THROUGHOUT THE WORLD?

Trying to save their struggling college, eleven student singers at Fisk University—six young women and five young men, all of whom had emerged from slavery—left their Nashville, Tennessee, campus in October of 1871 accompanied by two teachers. Stopping in Ohio, the group, which called itself the Fisk Jubilee Singers, gave its first concert of spirituals on a cold night in Cincinnati. They went on to Wilberforce University, an all-black school, where a bishop gave them his blessing.

As the singers traveled northward through the cold countryside, their skimpy clothing offered little protection from the icy weather. In many towns they were turned away from hotels and driven out of railroad station waiting rooms because of their race.

A concert they gave in Oberlin, Ohio, was praised in the press, and word of the talented singers began to spread across the country. They made their way eastward to New York State and stopped for a time in Brooklyn, where the theologian Henry Ward Beecher had arranged a concert. As their fame grew they performed before eminent citizens of New York City and were asked to sing for the President of the United States.

After returning to the Fisk campus three months after their departure to present $20,000 they had earned, the Fisk Jubilee Singers responded to invitations to perform across the country and overseas. They traveled and sang abroad for seven years, and managed to raise $150,000 to give to Fisk University. Part of the money was used to build the first brick building on the campus; it was named Jubilee Hall.

WHO WAS THE FIRST AFRICAN-AMERICAN VIOLINIST TO TOUR THE U.S.?

Joseph Douglass, born in 1871, was the grandson of the great abolitionist Frederick Douglass. Both Joseph's grandfather and father were violinists, so as a youngster he, too, was given lessons on the instrument. When he was not yet twenty his grandfather sent him to Boston to study at the New England Conservatory of Music.

Douglass returned to his native Washington, D.C., and began giving concerts. He first attracted a wide audience when he played at the Chicago World's Fair in 1893. Soon he embarked upon what was to be thirty years of touring throughout the United States. It was said that he played at every

African-American educational institution in the country and in most of the churches. At the same time, he taught at Howard University and occasionally conducted orchestras.

WHO IS SAID TO BE THE FIRST JAZZ MUSICIAN?

Charles "Buddy" Bolden, a barber and cornet player, became known throughout the Storyville section of New Orleans for the brass bands he led along the streets, wailing out blues and ragtime on his horn. Bolden and his bands played for dances, funerals, and Mardi Gras celebrations. At funerals, they would parade through the streets to the cemetery and back, marching to the tunes of old hymns they had set to jaunty rhythms.

It was said that Buddy Bolden was one of the loudest cornet players in the world. In fact, a story is told about the two amusement parks that existed in New Orleans at the time, one of which was preferred by Bolden. When he and his band arrived there he would blow a call on his cornet and all the people in the other park would rush over to hear him play.

Legend has it that Buddy Bolden first improvised in the style later called jazz in a New Orleans dance hall in 1894, and many think of him as the first musician to play jazz, at least the first in New Orleans. But Bolden was a heavy drinker; his health deteriorated and he began to show signs of insanity. In 1907 he was committed to a mental hospital and he died there twenty-four years later.

WHAT WAS THE FIRST RAG PUBLISHED BY AN AFRICAN-AMERICAN COMPOSER?

In 1897 Thomas Million Turpin, a pianist from St. Louis, Missouri, published "Harlem Rag," the first ragtime piece to be published by an African-American composer. Turpin, who was born about 1873, was a self-taught musician. When he was young he worked in his father's saloon, and in 1900 he and his brother opened their own place, the Rosebud Cafe. It became a gathering place for ragtime pianists.

Turpin was an impressive figure; he was over six feet tall and when he grew older he weighed about three hundred pounds. This ragtime pioneer wrote several appealing, tuneful pieces, including "Rag-Time Nightmare" and "St. Louis Rag," in honor of the St. Louis World's Fair. His last published rag, a more complex work, was the 1904 "Buffalo Rag."

WHO WAS THE FIRST COMPOSER OF GOSPEL HYMNS?

Charles A. Tindley was born in Maryland in 1859. For many years he was a traveling preacher, singing at religious camp meetings. After deciding to study for the ministry he settled in Philadelphia, and it was there in 1902 that he founded the East Calvary Methodist Episcopal Church.

Tindley was the composer of many gospel hymns, most of which were copyrighted between 1901 and 1906. Two of his most famous hymns are "We'll Understand It Better By and By" and "Stand By Me." When the famous composer Thomas A. Dorsey heard Tindley's spiritual "I Do, Don't You" at a National Baptist Convention in the mid-1920s, he was inspired to leave popular music and start writing gospel songs. Although Dorsey is sometimes referred to as the first gospel composer, he always gave Tindley credit for originating this form of music.

WHO WAS THE FIRST AFRICAN-AMERICAN TO GAIN FAME AS A COMPOSER OF CONCERT MUSIC?

When Harry Burleigh was just a child he was inspired to become a singer after hearing performers in his home town of Erie, Pennsylvania, where he was born in 1866. He was unable to afford lessons, but often sang in local churches. When he was twenty-six he went to New York where he was awarded a scholarship to study at the National Conservatory of Music. Two years later he became a baritone soloist at the eminent St. George's Protestant Episcopal Church, a position he held for more than fifty years. In 1900 he was hired as a soloist at another house of worship, Temple Emanu-El; he sang at services there for twenty-five years.

Burleigh attracted wide audiences on his concert tours, and even sang for members of the British royal family. He studied with the Czech composer Antonin Dvorak, introducing him to spirituals, which Dvorak incorporated into his *New World* Symphony. In 1898 Burleigh himself became a composer, producing more than 300 songs, including spirituals in the style of art songs. His works, which were favorites of concert artists, include the popular "Deep River." He died in 1949.

WHO WAS THE FIRST GREAT JAZZ COMPOSER?

Jelly Roll Morton, born Ferdinand Joseph La Menthe in New Orleans in 1885, got an early start on an amazing musical career. As a child, before settling on the piano as his instrument, he played harmonica, drums, trombone, violin, and guitar. He was part of a strolling quartet that sang spirituals and he hung around the famous New Orleans brass bands, hoping to be asked to fill in. By the time he was fourteen, his father had disappeared and his mother had died. He went to live with his grandmother, but she ordered him out of the house when she learned he was playing piano in a bordello.

That was the beginning of his lifelong career as a traveling musician. He worked in Biloxi, Houston, Chicago, San Francisco, New York, New

Orleans, Tijuana, Las Vegas, and many other cities. When piano work was slow he turned his hand to running hotels and night clubs. He was a pool shark, gambler, bandleader, and comedian. In his front tooth he wore a diamond that he plucked out and pawned when his funds got low. To top it all off, he claimed he invented jazz.

In 1902 at the age of seventeen he wrote his first blues, "New Orleans Blues," soon followed by "King Porter Stomp," "Jelly Roll Blues," and "Wolverine Blues." All big hits at the time, these tunes merged ragtime, blues, and brass band music into a new jazz style. These works alone could have earned him the title of the first great jazz composer, but he went on to write "Black Bottom Stomp," "Kansas City Stomp," "Winin' Boy Blues," and "Georgia Swing." In all, Morton claims to have written 1,400 compositions. If he alone didn't invent jazz, he was certainly among the few originators. He died in Los Angeles in 1941 at the age of fifty-six.

WHO FIRST SANG THE BLUES IN TRAVELING SHOWS?

The influential blues singer known as Ma Rainey was born Gertrude Pridgett in 1886 in Columbus, Georgia. She made her stage debut at the age of fourteen in a talent show at a local opera house. Four years later she fell in love with Will Rainey, a singer and comedian known as "Pa" who had stopped in Columbus with a traveling minstrel show. The two soon married and toured with the Rabbit Foot Minstrels and other traveling shows for many years. Billed as Ma and Pa Rainey, they performed a song-and-dance act, but it was Ma Rainey's blues singing that pulled in the audiences. She is believed to be the first vocalist to sing the blues in minstrel shows, and she became known as the "Mother of the Blues."

Resplendent in glamorous ensembles, Rainey performed for devoted fans throughout the South. In 1923 she started making records; two of her earliest recorded songs were "Bo Weevil Blues" and "Southern Blues." She was accompanied by Lovie Austin's Blue Serenaders, a group comprised of a clarinet, cornet, violin, and piano. When her recording career ended in 1929 she had cut almost 100 songs, performing with such outstanding musicians as Louis Armstrong, Kid Ory, and Fletcher Henderson.

Rainey's popularity had begun to diminish by 1930, and she retired three years later. She died of heart disease in 1939, at the age of fifty-three.

WHO WROTE THE FIRST AFRICAN-AMERICAN OPERETTAS?

The multi-talented Robert "Bob" Cole became involved in show business in New York City in the 1890s. He was a singer, dancer, actor, and writer— he could write complete musicals, including words and music. In about 1898 Cole teamed up with J. Rosamond Johnson, the older brother of the

Robert Cole and J. Rosamond Johnson

poet James Weldon Johnson. Rosamond Johnson was a classically trained musician; he had studied at the New England Conservatory of Music and in London.

Cole and Johnson were a successful match. Together they wrote songs, vaudeville acts, and full-length productions, and they became the first

African-American songwriters to sign a contract with a Broadway music publisher. In 1906 the two produced the first true African-American operetta, *The Shoo-Fly Regiment*, with lyrics by James Weldon Johnson. They both appeared in their second operetta, *The Red Moon*, which opened in 1908.

In 1910 Cole and Johnson returned to vaudeville, setting off on a lengthy tour. On the final night of the tour, at New York City's Fifth Avenue Theater, Cole collapsed. He was hospitalized for several months, and in August 1911, while in a private sanitarium in the Catskill Mountains, he drowned in a nearby lake.

After his partner's death Johnson turned to more serious music. He published collections of spirituals and folk songs, taught for several years at the Music Settlement School in New York, and composed a number of choral works, including *Walk Together, Children*. With his brother, James Weldon, he wrote "Lift Every Voice and Sing," which became known as the Negro National Anthem.

WHO WROTE THE FIRST RAGTIME OPERA?

Scott Joplin was born into a musical family in Texarkana, Texas, in 1868. His father, a former slave, was a violinist and his mother played banjo and sang. He learned the basics of classical music from local teachers, and left home to seek his fortune when he was not yet twenty years old.

After touring parts of the country as a traveling pianist, Joplin moved to Sedalia, Missouri, where he enrolled in college to study composition and soon began composing piano rags. In 1899 his first ragtime piece, "Original Rags," was published, followed later that year by his first big hit, "Maple Leaf Rag." Although his piano rags were very popular, Joplin's goal was to compose ragtime pieces that would receive as much respect as classical music. In 1902 he wrote a ballet, *The Ragtime Dance*, that was ignored by the public. A year later he composed a ragtime opera, *A Guest of Honor*, but couldn't get it published.

Joplin settled in New York City in 1909 and began writing another opera, *Treemonisha*, which he completed two years later. He spent most of his money in a futile attempt to get it produced. Increasingly depressed, he eventually became gravely ill with dementia and died in 1917 at the age of forty-nine.

Ragtime music experienced a revival in the early 1970s, when Joplin's collected works were published and a recording of his piano rags became a best-seller. In 1974 his music reached a mainstream audience when his composition, "The Entertainer," was used in the soundtrack of the Paul Newman movie, *The Sting*. And his dream finally came true, too late for him to appreciate it, when *Treemonisha* was given a premiere performance in 1972 in Atlanta, and was presented later that year at Wolf Trap Park in

Virginia. The opera was produced several times in subsequent years, including a 1975 Broadway performance by the Houston Grand Opera Company. In 1974 Joplin was honored with a bronze plaque on his grave in St. Michael's Cemetery in Astoria, New York.

WHO WAS THE FIRST TO ORGANIZE AFRICAN-AMERICAN MUSICIANS?

James Reese Europe, considered the most influential African-American musician in New York City in the early 1900s, was born in Mobile, Alabama, in 1881 and grew up in Washington, D.C. His mother played piano, and Europe and his brother and sister all became professional musicians. In 1904 Europe went to New York and managed to find work playing the piano in small clubs. He soon began directing musical comedy shows—*The Shoo-Fly Regiment* in 1906 and *Mr. Lode of Koal* three years later.

In 1910 Europe established the Clef Club, the first attempt to organize black musicians. Members of the Clef Club paid dues and were hired out in various combinations as dance bands. Europe's bands emphasized African-American rhythms and leaned heavily on banjos, mandolins, and pianos. In 1912, in a benefit concert at Carnegie Hall, he conducted a 125-piece orchestra that amazed the audience. The next year he resigned from the Clef Club and led several other musical groups, including the Negro Symphony Orchestra and the National Negro Orchestra. He always made a point of featuring the work of African-American composers.

In 1914 Europe began an association with the popular white ballroom dance team of Vernon and Irene Castle, for whom he composed music and invented some dances, including the fox-trot and the turkey trot. Vernon Castle was killed in a plane crash in 1917, the same year the United States entered World War I, and Europe became the bandmaster of an all-black army unit, the 369th Infantry. His band, called the "Hellfighters," caused a sensation wherever it played, and when the war ended its members left the army and embarked on a nationwide tour, making several successful records.

Europe's life came to a shocking finale when he was only thirty-eight years old. While his band was performing at Mechanics Hall in Boston a maddened ex-band member shot and killed the talented musician. The loss was felt by so many fans that New York City gave him a public funeral, the first ever for an African-American.

WHO WAS THE FIRST MAN TO WRITE A BLUES COMPOSITION?

Born in Florence, Alabama, in 1873, William Christopher Handy was the son and grandson of Methodist ministers. Learning to play the cornet by

James Reese Europe and his Clef Club band

ear, he led a quartet that played at the Chicago World's Fair in 1893. Known as W.C. Handy, he then toured with the Mahara Minstrels, organized another band, and finally ended up in Memphis. It was there that he founded a music publishing company with a lyricist and businessman named Harry Pace.

In 1905 Handy organized the Pythian Band and made African-American folk music its specialty. Handy was now composing his own songs, using the blues form and the rhythms and tunes he'd picked up listening to laborers and sharecroppers in the streets and saloons of the South. In 1909 he wrote a campaign song for a Memphis mayoral candidate named Edward H. Crump. The tune was published in 1912 as "Memphis Blues" and became an immediate hit. In 1914 he wrote the classic "St. Louis Blues," and four years later he and Pace moved their publishing company to New York.

Blues remained Handy's major interest for the rest of his life. He wrote several blues anthologies and, in 1941, published his autobiography, *Father of the Blues*. W.C. Handy died in 1958, the same year that Hollywood released *St. Louis Blues*, a fictionalized story of his life starring Nat King Cole.

WHO WAS THE FIRST AFRICAN-AMERICAN TO EARN A MASTER'S DEGREE IN MUSIC?

Nora Holt was born in Kansas in 1885 and started taking piano lessons when she was still a child. She earned a bachelor's degree from Western University in Kansas and in 1918 received a master's degree in music from Chicago Musical College. For her thesis she composed a symphonic rhapsody for string orchestra, basing it on the spiritual "You May Bury Me in the East."

After college Holt became an active participant in the world of music. She was a music critic for the *Chicago Defender* newspaper and published a magazine called *Music and Poetry*. She was president of the Chicago Music Association and helped organize the National Association of Negro Musicians. During the 1920s and '30s Holt traveled in the United States and abroad, working for a time as a nightclub entertainer.

After returning to the U.S. she taught in Los Angeles schools for a few years, then moved to New York City. In 1944 she became music critic of the *Amsterdam News* and produced a classical music program for radio. In 1945 she joined the Music Critics Circle of New York, becoming the first African-American member of this professional organization.

WHO WAS THE FIRST AFRICAN-AMERICAN WOMAN TO BECOME A CONCERT PIANIST?

Hazel Harrison, born in Indiana in 1883, was given piano lessons before she was five years old, and she was soon performing at local gatherings. After she finished high school she went to Europe to study and in 1904 was invited to play in Berlin, Germany. She stayed in Europe for several years, studying and performing. Returning to the United States after the outbreak of World War I, she made her debut in Chicago in 1919 and in New York City in 1922.

Harrison gave concerts throughout the United States, playing classical pieces and compositions by African-Americans. In 1931 she began teaching at Tuskegee Institute in Alabama, where she was appointed head of the piano department; she also taught at Howard University and Alabama State College. The leading African-American pianist of her day, she performed until she retired at the age of eighty.

WHO WAS THE FIRST SINGER TO RECORD THE BLUES?

When Mamie Smith cut the record of "Crazy Blues" in August 1920, it was because of the persistence of an ambitious songwriter named Perry Bradford. Bradford had been trying to convince record companies to let Smith record his songs, but the owners feared there would be no market for records by an African-American singer.

Finally, in February 1920, Okeh Studios recorded Smith singing "You Can't Keep a Good Man Down" and "That Thing Called Love." The disc was such a hit that Smith was called back in August to cut "Crazy Blues," the first blues record ever made. "Crazy Blues" was a phenomenal success, selling more than 800,000 copies.

Smith's recording career lasted until 1931. She toured the country with her own revue and band, the Jazz Hounds, and she starred in musicals and

Mamie Smith

film shorts. It was said that in her heyday she owned two apartment houses and performed in a $3,000 cape trimmed with ostrich feathers. But she reportedly died in poverty and obscurity.

WHO WAS THE FIRST WOMAN TO PLAY PIANO IN A JAZZ BAND?

Lil Hardin took her first piano lessons from Miss Violet White when she was about five years old and until she was in her teens she played only marches, hymns, and the classics. Born in Memphis, Tennessee, in 1898, she studied music at Fisk University. In 1917 she moved with her family to Chicago and began a career as a song demonstrator in a music store. The store owner helped her get a job playing piano with a New Orleans band and her career in jazz began to take off. She played in a band led by Freddie Keppard, led her own band for a time, and, in 1922, became the pianist for King Oliver's Creole Jazz Band.

Hardin's piano can be heard in a 1923 recording of Oliver's "Dipper-mouth Blues," in which Louis Armstrong plays second cornet. A year later, Hardin and Armstrong were married. She wrote a driving cornet solo for her new husband on one of her jazz compositions, "Struttin' With Some Barbecue."

After encouraging Armstrong to join Fletcher Henderson's band in New York City, Hardin went on to form a number of her own bands. In 1925 and '26, she led a group called Madame Lil Armstrong's Dreamland Syncopators, and in the '30s she led all-women groups and an all-male big band. She later performed as a soloist.

Although Hardin and Armstrong were divorced in 1938, she played at a 1971 memorial service held in his honor in Chicago. On stage, during her performance, Hardin collapsed and died.

WHO WAS THE FIRST PIANIST TO RECORD A JAZZ SOLO?

Known as the "father of the stride piano," James Price Johnson was born in New Brunswick, New Jersey, in 1891. From his mother he learned of the Southern black dances with African roots called "ring shouts," later to become the foundation of his stride piano style, in which the left hand plays a steady, driving beat. However, his early training was in classical piano, taught to him for four years by an Italian music teacher.

Johnson moved to New York while still in his teens and developed his piano style playing in small clubs and accompanying blues singers. He began composing his own tunes and had some of them published as early as 1917. That year he began making piano rolls and soon became the country's most popular piano roll musician. His earliest recording, "Harlem

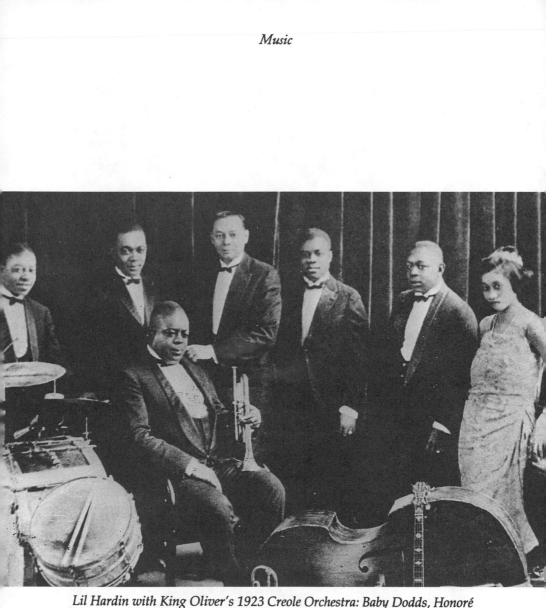

Lil Hardin with King Oliver's 1923 Creole Orchestra: Baby Dodds, Honoré Dutrey, Oliver (seated), Louis Armstrong, Johnny Dodds, Lil Hardin

Strut," was released on the Black Swan label in 1921, and was soon followed by "Carolina Shout," a favorite of jazz fans, on the Okeh record label.

A leading figure in the transition from ragtime to jazz, Johnson began writing scores for shows in the early 1920s. In all, he composed eleven

James P. Johnson

musicals, including *Keep Shufflin'* and *Runnin' Wild,* in which a new dance was introduced with Johnson's tune, "The Charleston." He also wrote such favorites as "If I Could Be With You" and "Old Fashioned Love."

Johnson wanted to prove himself a composer of concert music using jazz and African-American themes, but his works, including *Yamekraw: A*

196

Negro Rhapsody and *Harlem Symphony* received little attention. He presented his last revue, *Sugar Hill,* in 1949 and two years later suffered a paralyzing stroke. He died in 1955.

WHAT WAS THE FIRST JAZZ BAND TO CUT A RECORD?

The great jazz trombonist Edward "Kid" Ory was born in LaPlace, Louisiana, around 1886. He was still in his teens when he organized his first band. In 1913 he brought a band to New Orleans, where he led various combos and was the first to hire such illustrious musicians as Louis Armstrong, Joe "King" Oliver, and Johnny Dodds. In 1919 Ory moved on to Los Angeles, and it was there in 1922 that he made the first jazz record, leading Kid Ory's Sunshine Orchestra.

During the 1920s Ory made many other records, but always with other groups, including Armstrong's Hot Five and Hot Seven, and Jelly Roll Morton's Red Hot Peppers. After a lull during the Depression years of the 1930s, Ory was rediscovered in the '40s and became a major figure in the emerging popularity of traditional jazz. He died in Hawaii in his mid-eighties.

WHO WAS THE FIRST AFRICAN-AMERICAN TO SING WITH A MAJOR SYMPHONY ORCHESTRA?

Roland Hayes was born in rural Georgia in 1887; his parents were struggling tenant farmers. When he was twelve his father died and the family moved to Chattanooga, Tennessee, where the young Hayes found work wherever he could, as a laborer, farmhand, waiter, and messenger. He managed to earn enough money to enter Fisk University, and in 1911 toured with the Fisk Singers, who were then a quartet. When the group reached Boston, Hayes decided to settle there. He studied voice and began performing as a concert singer.

In 1920 he traveled abroad and for the next three years he sang in the major cities of Europe, becoming a celebrity in the music world. Accounts of his concert at Buckingham Palace before King George V attracted the attention of American impresarios, who were interested in representing him when he returned to the United States. His groundbreaking performance with the Boston Symphony Orchestra in November 1923 evoked acclaim from critics, as did his recitals in New York City, where admirers packed the concert halls.

Through the 1940s Hayes was considered the world's preeminent concert tenor. In 1950 he was appointed to the music faculty of Boston University, and in 1962, at his seventy-fifth birthday concert in New York's Carnegie Hall, every seat was filled. Hayes died in 1976 at the age of eighty-nine.

WHO WAS THE FIRST AFRICAN-AMERICAN WOMAN TO BE INTERNATIONALLY RECOGNIZED AS A CHORAL DIRECTOR?

Eva Jessye was born in Coffeyville, Kansas, in 1895. From early childhood she had an innate understanding of music, and by the time she was twelve she had organized a girls' singing group. She met the composer Will Marion Cook when he brought a musical production to her town; Cook was to become her mentor.

After studying at Kansas Wesleyan University, Jessye went to New York in 1922 to work with Cook. She organized the Eva Jessye Singers, a leading choral group that performed widely. In 1929 Jessye went to Hollywood to serve as choral director of the all-black film *Hallelujah!*, and in 1934 filled the same role for the Virgil Thomson opera *Four Saints in Three Acts*. A year later she trained the chorus for the first production of George Gershwin's folk opera *Porgy and Bess*, traveling with the company from Broadway to England, Germany, Russia, and Australia.

The first African-American woman to succeed as a professional choir director, Jessye, who died in 1992, directed the chorus for a number of operas and composed several choral works, including *Paradise Lost and Regained* and *The Chronicle of Job*.

WHAT AFRICAN-AMERICAN SINGER WAS THE FIRST TO PERFORM WITH A EUROPEAN OPERA COMPANY?

The famed singer Lillian Evanti was born Annie Lillian Evans in 1890 in Washington, D.C. Her mother, a music teacher, discovered that the child had a lovely voice; when she was only four she gave her first solo performance. But Lillian chose to study education in college, and after graduation became a kindergarten teacher. Soon, however, she enrolled in Howard University to pursue a music degree. In 1918 she married one of her professors, Roy W. Tibbs, and created a new professional name by combining her name with his.

Evanti gave concerts in Washington for several years and in 1925 traveled to France, where she was awarded a contract with the Paris Opera. She made her debut singing the title role in Delibes's *Lakmé*. When she came home for a visit, her successes abroad were praised by local newspapers but her race was not mentioned.

Evanti continued to perform in operas throughout Europe, not returning to the United States until the early 1930s. She sang at the White House in 1934 for President and Mrs. Roosevelt, and later gave concerts for presidents Eisenhower and Truman. During the 1940s and '50s Evanti toured Latin American countries as a goodwill ambassador for the United States. She died in 1967.

WHO WAS THE FIRST MUSICIAN TO
INTRODUCE SCAT SINGING?

The renowned jazz trumpeter Louis Armstrong introduced scat sing-ing—using the voice as an instrument by substituting nonsense sounds for words—on an Okeh recording of "Heebie Jeebies" with the Hot Five band in 1926. Armstrong was born in New Orleans; he claimed the date was July 4, 1900, although some think it was earlier. Growing up in poverty, he spent most of his childhood on the streets. When he was thirteen he was arrested for a prank and sent to the Colored Waifs Home. There he was given a cornet and taught to read music.

After young Armstrong's release from the home he supported himself at various jobs until in 1918, when he was befriended by Joe "King" Oliver, a cornetist who led a popular jazz band. Armstrong played cornet on Mis-sissippi riverboats and with the Kid Ory band for a time, and then traveled to Chicago in 1922 to join King Oliver's Creole Jazz Band. It wasn't until two years later, when he went to New York City to play with Fletcher Henderson, that Armstrong switched to trumpet and began vocalizing in his distinctive husky voice and demonstrating his scat singing style.

The outstanding recordings of Armstrong's Hot Five and Hot Seven groups in the mid-1920s were to make him an historic figure in jazz history. Known by his nickname "Satchmo," he grew to be an international star, attracting wide audiences around the world; he was referred to as Amer-ica's "Ambassador of Jazz." After Armstrong's death in 1971 a park in New Orleans was named after him and a statue of him by the African-American sculptor Elizabeth Catlett was erected there.

WHO WAS THE FIRST WOMAN TO
LEAD AN ALL-MALE JAZZ BAND?

Blanche Calloway was the older sister of the famous bandleader and scat singer, Cab Calloway. Born in 1902 in Baltimore, Blanche sang in the choir of the Presbyterian church where her mother was an organist, and studied music at Morgan State College. When she was nineteen years old, a song-and-dance show, *Oma Crosby and her Five Cubanolas*, passed through town. Calloway auditioned for a job and was hired. As her career developed, she appeared in the musicals *Shuffle Along* and *Plantation Days*, and headlined for a time as a vocalist in her brother's band.

In 1931 Calloway became the leader of her own all-male band, Blanche Calloway and her Joy Boys, delighting audiences with her combination of conducting, singing, and dancing. The group lasted for seven years, and in 1940 Calloway organized an all-female big band. She later moved to Washington, D.C., where she managed nightclubs and directed the career of singer Ruth Brown. In Miami, Florida, where she eventually settled,

Calloway embarked on a twenty-year radio career, becoming the first woman disc jockey in the United States.

WHO FOUNDED THE FIRST GOSPEL PUBLISHING COMPANY?

Thomas A. Dorsey, the foremost composer of gospel music, wrote his first successful gospel song, "If You See My Saviour," in 1926 and founded his publishing company, Dorsey House, six years later. Dorsey, born in 1899 near Atlanta, Georgia, was the son of a country preacher. It is said that he walked four miles a day four days a week to take piano lessons. He later studied at the Chicago College of Composition and Arranging, and one of his compositions, "Riverside Blues," was recorded by King Oliver's Creole Jazz Band.

As a young musician known as Georgia Tom, he played blues piano in saloons and bordellos in Chicago and Gary, Indiana, where he lived, and for a time was the accompanist for blues singer Ma Rainey. But Dorsey's life turned around when he attended the National Baptist Convention in Chicago and heard a chorus sing a spiritual called "I Do, Don't You?" He resolved to leave popular music and devote himself to composing spirituals.

Dorsey's compositions melded the blues with religious themes. He called them gospel songs to differentiate them from gospel hymns. His best-known gospel song, "Take My Hand Precious Lord," was made famous by Mahalia Jackson, who once toured with Dorsey, and has been translated into more than fifty languages. The song was inspired by a tragic loss Dorsey suffered when his wife died in childbirth and the baby passed away a day later.

In the 1930s Dorsey's music began spreading across the land, and by the time he died in 1993 at the age of ninety-four he had written more than 1,000 gospel songs.

WHO WAS THE FIRST AFRICAN-AMERICAN WOMAN TO BE RECOGNIZED AS A COMPOSER?

Florence Price was born in Little Rock, Arkansas, in 1888. When she was still a baby she moved to Chicago with her father, a dentist, and her mother, a soprano and pianist. She took her first piano lessons from her mother, and also learned to play organ and violin. After high school Price enrolled in the New England Conservatory of Music, where she studied composition and wrote a string trio and a symphony.

Back in Little Rock, Price taught music at a local college and gave private lessons, moving to Chicago in 1927 to further her studies. In 1932 a symphony she composed won an award in a music competition, and a year later it was performed by the Chicago Symphony Orchestra at the Chicago World's Fair.

Price wrote symphonies, concertos, art songs, chamber pieces, and arrangements of black spirituals; she was especially known for her adaptation of "My Soul's Been Anchored in the Lord." The first African-American woman to gain recognition as a composer, her works were performed by instrumentalists, orchestras, and singers throughout the country.

WHO WAS THE FIRST AFRICAN-AMERICAN SINGER TO APPEAR WITH A MAJOR OPERA COMPANY?

In July 1933, Caterina Jarboro, a soprano, sang the title role in Verdi's opera *Aida* with the Chicago Civic Opera at the Hippodrome Theater in New York City. Long before she became the first African-American prima donna of an opera company, Jarboro had sung in the chorus of two popular musicals of the early 1920s, *Shuffle Along* and *Running Wild*. She eventually traveled abroad to study voice and stayed for seven years, performing to acclaim throughout Europe.

Reports of Jarboro's great success reached the United States, and she finally returned to make her American operatic debut with the Chicago Civic Opera. When she appeared in *Aida*, the theater was filled with opera fans, both black and white, who showered her with applause and flowers as she knelt on stage after the final curtain. But Jarboro was unsuccessful in establishing a career in the United States; she returned to Europe where she continued to perform in leading opera houses.

WHAT WAS THE FIRST BROADWAY OPERA WITH AN AFRICAN-AMERICAN CAST?

A somewhat bizarre opera entitled *Four Saints in Three Acts* opened on Broadway in February 1934 with a cast that was made up completely of African-American singers. Composed by Virgil Thomson and written by Gertrude Stein, the opera was about two Spanish saints of the sixteenth century. It featured beautiful settings and costumes, colorful lyrics that made little sense, and performers who moved in a dramatic, stylized manner. The opera starred Edward Matthews as St. Ignatius, and the chorus was trained by the African-American choir director Eva Jessye.

Four Saints in Three Acts ran for forty-eight performances, making it the longest-running modern American opera to that date. Over the years it was revived several times.

WHO WAS THE FIRST AFRICAN-AMERICAN
TO HAVE A SYMPHONY PERFORMED
BY A MAJOR ORCHESTRA?

Born in Mississippi in 1895, William Grant Still studied violin as a child, but he enrolled in Ohio's Wilberforce University planning to major in science and become a doctor. Soon, however, he formed a string quartet, began writing his own compositions, and became director of the college band. He left Wilberforce to play in dance bands, and at the age of twenty-one enrolled at Oberlin College Conservatory of Music.

After serving in World War I, Still went to New York City, where he worked as musical director of the Black Swan Phonograph Company and played in W.C. Handy's dance band. In 1921 he was hired as an oboist for the show *Shuffle Along*. Studying at the New England Conservatory of Music and with the French composer Edgar Varese, Still began composing large-scale works in the mid-1920s. In 1931 his *Afro-American Symphony* was performed by the Rochester Philharmonic; it was the first time a major symphony orchestra had performed a work by an African-American composer. Four years later the symphony received its New York premiere when it was played by the New York Philharmonic in Carnegie Hall.

William Grant Still

As his career developed, Still continued to make history in the world of concert music. In 1935 he became the first African-American to conduct a major symphony orchestra, when he led the Los Angeles Philharmonic in a concert of his own works. At radio station WNBC he was the first African-American to direct a white radio orchestra. And his opera *Troubled Island* was the first by a black composer to be performed by a major opera company, the New York City Opera, in 1949.

In the 1940s Still went to Hollywood, where he wrote the score for *Pennies From Heaven* and many other films. He later composed music for television series such as "The Perry Mason Show" and "Gunsmoke." In all, Still composed five symphonies, six operas, four ballets, and many other works.

WHO WAS THE FIRST AFRICAN-AMERICAN VOCALIST TO SING WITH A WHITE ORCHESTRA?

Lena Horne was only sixteen when she was hired for the chorus line at Harlem's Cotton Club. Dancing with twelve other young women, she made $25 a week that went to support her family. Born in Brooklyn in 1917, she had left high school to work at the famous night club, where her mother provided protection by sitting in her dressing room every night.

Horne stayed at the Cotton Club for two years and in 1936 appeared at the Apollo Theater as a vocalist with Noble Sissle's orchestra. After a road tour with Sissle she joined Charlie Barnet's popular band, becoming the first African-American to sing with a white orchestra.

In 1941 Horne went to Hollywood. Singing at the opening of a new nightclub, she was noticed by a scout from the MGM movie studio, which soon offered her a contract. She appeared in the all-black movies *Cabin in the Sky* and *Stormy Weather*, and later was given singing parts in white movies. By design, her scenes had nothing to do with the story and could be cut from the film when it was shown in the South. Finally, in 1969, she landed a dramatic role with the white actor Richard Widmark in the film *Death of a Gunfighter*.

Horne's Hollywood career gradually faded, and in 1957 she was beckoned to Broadway, where she was featured in the musical *Jamaica*. She continued to perform and make records, and in 1981 won a Tony award for her Broadway show *Lena Horne—The Lady and Her Music*.

WHO WAS THE FIRST FULL-TIME AFRICAN-AMERICAN CONDUCTOR OF SYMPHONIC MUSIC?

Born in New York's Harlem in 1915 to West Indian parents, Dean Dixon was introduced to classical music as a child when his mother took him to concerts at Carnegie Hall. He began violin lessons at an early age, and organized his own amateur musical groups, the Dean Dixon Symphony Orchestra and the Dean Dixon Choral Society, while he was still a student at DeWitt Clinton High School.

Dixon earned a bachelor's degree from the Juilliard School of Music and a master's from Columbia Teacher's College. In 1941 he made his first appearance as a conductor of a major orchestra when he led the NBC Summer Symphony in two concerts. He later conducted the New York Philharmonic, the Philadelphia Orchestra, and the Boston Symphony. But by the late 1940s conducting opportunities in the United States had all but disappeared, and Dixon traveled abroad to lead concerts in Paris. He settled in Europe, where he developed a distinguished career, serving as musical director of orchestras in Sweden, Germany, and Australia. In 1970 Dixon returned to his native country to conduct the New York Philharmonic in Central Park, attracting an audience of 75,000 music lovers. He died six years later in Switzerland.

WHO WAS THE FIRST AFRICAN-AMERICAN SINGER TO WIN THE NAUMBERG AWARD?

In 1944 the contralto Carol Brice became the first African-American musician to receive the prestigious Walter Naumberg award, which is presented to young performers with outstanding talent. A year later she made her Town Hall debut in New York City, garnering praise from critics.

Brice was born in 1918 in Sedalia, North Carolina, to a musical family; her parents were singers and her two brothers became professional musicians. She studied at Talledega College and the Juilliard School of Music. After winning the Naumberg award she toured extensively as a soloist. She also appeared in musicals, including *Finian's Rainbow* in 1960 and *Show Boat* a year later.

Brice reached a turning point in her lengthy performing career in 1974 when she and her husband, baritone Thomas Carey, became professors at the University of Oklahoma, where they founded a regional opera company. Brice died in 1985 in Norman, Oklahoma.

WHO WAS THE FIRST AFRICAN-AMERICAN MAN TO SING A LEADING ROLE WITH A MAJOR OPERA COMPANY?

In 1945 the baritone Todd Duncan made his debut with the New York City Opera singing the role of Tonio in *Il Pagliacci*, thus becoming the first African-American man to sing with a major opera company. Duncan had begun his professional career singing in films and Broadway musicals, and in 1935 he was chosen to play the role of Porgy in the first production of George Gershwin's folk opera, *Porgy and Bess*.

Duncan made his concert debut in 1944 at New York's Town Hall, and after his 1945 performance in *Il Pagliacci* he sang a leading role at the New York City Opera in Bizet's *Carmen*. He went on to give concerts throughout the world while maintaining a teaching career at Howard University.

WHO WAS THE FIRST GOSPEL SINGER TO GAIN INTERNATIONAL FAME?

Before she was five years old, Mahalia Jackson was singing in the choir of her Baptist church in New Orleans, Louisiana, where she was born in 1911. Her father, a devout minister, allowed only religious music to be played in his home, but young Mahalia heard the sound of the blues drifting through the windows of houses in the neighborhood. When her mother died the child went to live with an equally religious aunt, and she was strongly affected by the powerful, rhythmic singing of the Sanctified Church congregation next door.

When she was sixteen Jackson moved to Chicago with her aunt. Working as a laundress to support herself, she became an active member of the Greater Salem Baptist Church and joined a gospel group. She soon began performing alone, singing in African-American churches around the country. She met the great gospel composer Thomas Dorsey, and the two sometimes performed together.

In 1934 Jackson made her first record, "God Gonna Separate the Wheat from the Tares," but it received little attention. She opened a beauty salon and a flower business and didn't record again until 1946, when she cut "Move on Up a Little Higher." The record was a hit, selling nearly two million copies, and it made her famous. She sang in concerts, appeared on the Ed Sullivan television show, and in 1950 made her debut in New York's Carnegie Hall. She toured Europe and had her own radio and television programs in Chicago.

After singing at a rally in Montgomery, Alabama, Jackson allied herself with Dr. Martin Luther King, Jr., and became a fervent participant in the civil rights movement. During the 1963 March on Washington she sang on the steps of the Lincoln Memorial. Jackson, who some called the "Queen of Gospel Song," died in 1972 at the age of sixty-one.

WHAT AFRICAN-AMERICAN SINGER WAS THE FIRST TO PERFORM WITH THE METROPOLITAN OPERA?

As a child, Marian Anderson sang in the choir of the Union Baptist Church in Philadelphia, where she was born in 1897. In her teens she became the student of a distinguished voice teacher; members of her church

Mahalia Jackson

collected money to pay for her lessons. After giving recitals in Philadelphia and New York, Anderson traveled to Europe, where she studied and gave concerts in several countries. A spellbinding performance in Salzburg in 1935 moved the conductor Toscanini to remark, "A voice like yours comes once in a century."

Marian Anderson

Six months later Anderson returned to the United States for a highly acclaimed concert at New York's Town Hall. Critics hailed her as one of the "greatest singers of our time," and she was invited to sing at the White House for President and Mrs. Roosevelt. Despite Anderson's many triumphs, in 1939, because of her race, she was barred from singing in Washington, D.C.'s Constitution Hall by the Daughters of the American Revolution. Outraged by this insult to the great singer, Eleanor Roosevelt resigned from the D.A.R. in protest and sponsored an Easter Sunday concert on the grounds of the Lincoln Memorial, where Anderson received a tremendous outpouring of support from an audience of 75,000 people.

Although she performed hundreds of recitals around the country, America's opera houses were closed to her until January 7, 1955, when she sang the part of Ulrica in Verdi's *Un Ballo in Maschera* at the Metropolitan Opera House in New York City. She was the first African-American to sing on the stage of the Met. Another honor soon followed. In 1958, President Eisenhower appointed her delegate to the 13th General Assembly of the United Nations. Further recognition came in 1963 when Anderson became the first black woman to receive the Presidental Medal of Freedom, presented to her by President Lyndon Johnson. Anderson gave her farewell Carnegie Hall concert on Easter 1965. Her autobiography, *My Lord, What a Morning,* was published in 1956. Anderson died in April 1993 at the age of ninety-six at the home of her nephew, the conductor James DePriest, in Portland, Oregon.

WHO WAS THE FIRST AFRICAN-AMERICAN MALE SINGER TO BE FEATURED AT THE MET?

Just three weeks after Marian Anderson made her Metropolitan Opera debut on January 7, 1955, Robert McFerrin appeared on the stage of the Met singing the role of Amonasro in Verdi's *Aida.* McFerrin, born in 1921 in Marianna, Arkansas, grew up in St. Louis and studied music in Chicago and New York. A baritone, he began singing professionally in the 1940s.

McFerrin sang in Broadway musicals and with opera companies. In 1949 he appeared in the New York City Opera Company's production of *Troubled Island,* an opera by the African-American composer William Grant Still. After his Met debut in January 1955, he became the first African-American to accept a permanent position with the Metropolitan Opera. His son, Bobby McFerrin, gained popularity as a jazz vocalist in the late 1980s.

WHO LED THE FIRST JAZZ BAND SENT ABROAD BY THE STATE DEPARTMENT?

John Birks "Dizzy" Gillespie was born in Cheraw, South Carolina, in 1917. His father, who was a bricklayer, led a local band. Gillespie was just a youngster when he began learning to play the trumpet, and he was playing professionally while still in his teens. It is said that bandleader Teddy Hill gave Gillespie his nickname because of his eccentric clothing style and his love of practical jokes.

Robert McFerrin

After joining Cab Calloway's band in 1939, he met saxophonist Charlie Parker in Kansas City and they began work on the style that would soon be called bebop. Referring to Parker as "the other side of my heartbeat," Gillespie joined him in a quartet in 1945 that produced bop's most famous

John Birks "Dizzy" Gillespie

records. It is generally acknowledged that Gillespie, Parker, and Thelonius Monk founded the bebop movement.

Also in 1945, Gillespie formed the first of his big bands. He gradually became interested in Cuban rhythms and is considered the creator of Afro-Cuban jazz. In 1953 someone fell on his trumpet, bending it upward. Gillespie discovered he could hear its sound better that way. His tilted horn and ballooning cheeks became his trademarks.

In 1956 he put together a new big band and, at the request of the U.S. State Department, made a tour of the Middle East and South America. His was the first jazz band to be sent abroad by the U.S. government. His autobiography, *To Bop or Not to Bop*, came out in 1979 and he won Grammy awards in 1975 and 1980. He died of cancer in 1993. His wife, Lorraine, said one of his songs, "Dizzy's Dime," was playing on his tape recorder when he passed away in his sleep.

WHO WAS THE FIRST JAZZ PIANIST TO GIVE A CONCERT IN CARNEGIE HALL?

Although Erroll Garner had no formal training and never learned to read music, he became one of the world's most popular jazz pianists. Born in Pittsburgh, Pennsylvania, in 1921, he was the youngest of five children. When he was not yet three years old he started playing the piano; he could repeat the tunes he heard on his mother's records and those that the music teacher played for his older brother and sisters. He could play anything he heard. As a youngster he performed on a local radio station and played in clubs and on riverboats, learning new tunes and styles by listening to professional pianists.

In 1944 Garner went to New York where his lilting piano style soon won him a legion of fans. The first jazz musician to be represented by the leading impresario Sol Hurok, Garner toured widely in the United States and Europe. In 1950 he made his concert debut in the Cleveland Music Hall, and in 1958 he became the first jazz pianist to appear in concert at New York's Carnegie Hall.

Garner died in Los Angeles in 1977 at the age of fifty-six. He is especially remembered for his composition, "Misty." He said that he was inspired to write the song when he saw a rainbow through an airplane window.

WHO WAS THE FIRST AFRICAN-AMERICAN SINGER TO PERFORM A LEADING ROLE AT THE MET ON OPENING NIGHT?

Known as the first African-American diva, Leontine Price sang major roles at opera houses throughout the world. Born in 1927 in Laurel, Mississippi, Price's career path was decided when, at the age of nine, her mother took her to see a performance by the great singer Marian Anderson. Endowed with a glorious voice, Price graduated from Central State College in Wilberforce, Ohio, and won a scholarship to study at the Juilliard School of Music in New York City. When he heard her sing in a student production, the composer Virgil Thomson chose her for a role in his all-black opera, *Four Saints in Three Acts*.

Erroll Garner

Price made her Paris debut in 1952, her New York debut at Town Hall in 1954, and performed at leading opera houses in San Francisco, Vienna, and Milan. In January 1961 Price finally reached the stage of New York's famed Metropolitan Opera as Leonora in *Il Trovatore*, receiving a forty-two minute ovation from an ecstatic audience. And on the Met's opening night that fall she sang the leading role in the Puccini opera, *The Girl of the Golden West*. She was the first African-American singer to perform a leading role on an opening night at the Met. Price won many honors during her career, including the Presidential Medal of Freedom.

WHO WAS THE FIRST AFRICAN-AMERICAN TO SING "VENUS"?

Prompting a storm of protest, the grandson of composer Richard Wagner chose the mezzo-soprano Grace Bumbry to sing the role of the traditionally blond Venus in the opera *Tannhauser* at the famed Wagner Festival in Bayreuth, Germany, in 1961. Bumbry's performance was a huge success, and she made headlines throughout the world.

Born in Missouri in 1937, Bumbry sang in school and church choirs, and after graduating from high school she won first prize on the "Arthur Godfrey's Talent Scouts" television show, singing a Verdi aria. She studied voice at Boston and Northwestern universities, and made her operatic debut in 1962 with the Paris Opera Company in Verdi's *Aida*. She toured Europe and sang with several leading opera companies before appearing at Bayreuth. In February 1962, Bumbry was asked to sing at the White House by First Lady Jacqueline Kennedy, and that November she made her New York City debut at Town Hall.

WHO WAS THE FIRST AFRICAN-AMERICAN COUNTRY MUSIC STAR?

When he was a child in the cotton-growing region of Sledge, Mississippi, where he was born in 1938, Charley Pride listened to country music every Saturday night on the radio show "Grand Ole Opry." But Pride's first interest was baseball, and he played for several seasons with the Memphis Red Sox of the Negro American League.

Pride began making the switch to a country music career around 1960, when he sang between innings at baseball games. He signed a recording contract with RCA and cut his first record, "The Snakes Crawl at Night," in 1965. Two years later he became the first African-American singer to appear on the favorite show of his childhood, Nashville's "Grand Ole Opry." In 1969 he first hit the number one spot on the singles charts with "All I Have to Offer You (is Me)."

Pride went on to produce many more number one tunes, including "Kiss an Angel Good Morning" and "Mountain of Love," and became one of the country's top sellers of records. As that rarity—an African-American country music singer—Pride says he developed his style from listening to

Charley Pride

such country stars as George Jones and Hank Williams, as well as black blues singers B.B King and Sam Cooke.

WHO WAS THE FIRST AFRICAN-AMERICAN DIRECTOR OF A MAJOR ORCHESTRA?

Henry Lewis was born in Los Angeles in 1932 and, like many professional musicians, started piano lessons at an early age. He expanded his musical education, and by the time he reached sixteen he had become such an accomplished double bass player that he was hired to play with the Los Angeles Philharmonic Orchestra. Lewis served in the army in 1955 and '56, playing the bass in an army orchestra and conducting.

In 1961 Lewis made his professional debut as a conductor when he led the Los Angeles Philharmonic in two concerts. He was named musical director of the Los Angeles Opera Company in 1965, and three years later he left to become musical director of the New Jersey Symphony Orchestra, making him the first African-American director of a major orchestra in the United States. In 1972 Lewis made his debut with the Metropolitan Opera, conducting Puccini's *La Boheme.* He was the first African-American to lead an orchestra at the Met.

WHO WAS THE FIRST WOMAN INDUCTED INTO THE ROCK AND ROLL HALL OF FAME?

The Rock and Roll Hall of Fame, with headquarters in Cleveland, Ohio, began inducting members in 1986, and a year later installed its first woman—the famed singer Aretha Franklin. Notoriously shy and afraid of flying, Franklin did not attend the January 1987 induction ceremony; her award was accepted by her brother, the Rev. Cecil Franklin. When musician Keith Richards announced that "Lady Soul" would be the first woman in the Hall of Fame, the crowd that had gathered to attend the ceremony roared its approval.

Aretha Louise Franklin was born in 1942 in Memphis, Tennessee, and grew up in Detroit, where her father, the Rev. C.L. Franklin, was pastor of the New Bethel Baptist Church. Young Aretha, who played piano for the church choir and sang in a gospel quartet, performed her first church solo at the age of twelve and recorded her first single at about the same time for Chess Records.

In 1960 Franklin decided to move to New York City and try to make it as a singer. She was soon signed by Columbia Records, which issued her 1961 album, *Aretha.* She recorded a total of nine albums in a range of styles for Columbia before her contract ran out in 1966 and she was signed by Atlantic Records, where she began to focus on rhythm and blues. At Atlantic, where she was encouraged to freely express her gospel piano style, Franklin came into her own as a great soul singer. Her recordings of "I Never Loved a Man" and "Respect" hit the top of the charts. Her albums for Atlantic, *I Never Loved a Man* and *Lady Soul,* are considered soul masterpieces. Her career had its ups and downs during the '70s and '80s, and in 1992 many of her best numbers were collected in a four-CD set produced by Rhino/Atlantic, *Queen of Soul.*

WHO WAS THE FIRST AFRICAN-AMERICAN MUSICIAN TO WIN THE NAUMBERG PIANO COMPETITION?

In May 1992, twenty-six-year-old Awadagin Pratt won first prize in the Naumberg International Piano Competition, held at New York City's Lincoln Center. The award created a wave of interest sparked not only by Pratt's outstanding talent, but also by his long dreadlocks, the jeans and casual shirts he wore when performing, and the small lamp table he sat on instead of a piano bench. Pratt had already distinguished himself as the

Awadagin Pratt

first student in the history of Baltimore's Peabody Conservatory to earn diplomas in three areas—piano, violin, and conducting.

Pratt's parents, both professors, introduced him to classical music; his father, a native of Sierra Leone, was an organist in his youth. At the age of six Pratt asked his parents for conducting lessons; they gave him piano lessons instead. After high school he entered the University of Illinois but decided to transfer to the Peabody Conservatory, where he studied for six years.

As the winner of the Naumberg competition, Pratt was granted a two-year tour of the United States as guest soloist with several top orchestras, and a debut recording. When asked in a radio interview if he regarded himself as a role model, Pratt said that as an African-American in a white male profession, he would "try to do what I believe in and not be swayed."

RELIGION

WHO WAS THE FOUNDER AND FIRST BISHOP OF THE AFRICAN METHODIST EPISCOPAL CHURCH?

Born in 1760 to parents who were slaves, Richard Allen grew up in Delaware, where he developed a Christian faith so strong that he was able to convert his owner, who had allowed him to study religion. Allen purchased his freedom and eventually settled in Philadelphia where he preached at St. George's Methodist Episcopal Church, which had a white congregation that Allen encouraged African-Americans to join.

Most white churches of the time forced black communicants to sit in certain pews at the back of the church or in the gallery. One Sunday morning in 1787, when Allen and his colleague, Absalom Jones, were kneeling in prayer, a church trustee insisted that they move to the rear of the building. The two African-American leaders walked out of St. George's and never returned. Jones split from Allen and organized the St. Thomas Protestant Episcopal Church. Allen gathered a congregation and formed the Bethel African Methodist Episcopal Church, which opened its doors in 1787 as the first church in the country controlled and supported by African-Americans.

The church is said to be the oldest piece of property in the United States continually owned by black Americans. African Methodist Episcopal churches sprang up around Pennsylvania, Maryland, Delaware, and New Jersey, eventually uniting in 1816 to form a separate branch of Methodism with Richard Allen as its first bishop.

WHO WAS THE FIRST AFRICAN-AMERICAN EPISCOPAL PRIEST IN THE UNITED STATES?

Absalom Jones, a deeply religious former slave from Delaware, bought his freedom and settled in Philadelphia, where he and his colleague, Richard Allen, formed the Free African Society, a mutual aid society for African-Americans. Both men worshipped at St. George's Methodist Episcopal Church, but after being told they could not sit in the front pews they left the congregation and decided to start an African-American church. Jones, however, preferred the Anglican religious tradition while Allen was a Methodist.

Although they remained friends, the two took separate paths. Jones organized the St. Thomas Protestant Episcopal Church in 1794 and became its first minister. He was the first African-American in the nation to be ordained as an Episcopal priest.

Richard Allen

WHAT WAS NEW YORK CITY'S FIRST
AFRICAN-AMERICAN CONGREGATION?

In 1796, the Mother African Methodist Episcopal Zion Church was founded as the first black congregation in New York City. One of its founders, Peter Williams, was a former slave who had been bought by the trustees of the John Street Methodist Church in 1783. Williams worked as a sexton, purchased his freedom in 1785, and became a successful undertaker and tobacconist.

At that time, African-Americans who belonged to New York's white churches were forced to sit in the back pews or in the balcony, and could not bury their dead in church grounds. Williams and other black members of the John Street church decided in 1796 to form their own Methodist congregation.Because he had donated the land and much of the money to build the church, Williams laid the cornerstone of the Mother African Methodist Episcopal Zion Church on July 30, 1800, on a site at the corner of Church and Leonard streets. In 1821 the African Methodist Episcopal Zion group became an independent body, and a year later elected its first bishop, James Varick.

Mother A.M.E. Zion served as a station on the Underground Railroad—a system of helping slaves escape from the south—and Sojourner Truth, the abolitionist and suffragist, was among its members. The church is now located at 137th Street in New York City's Harlem.

WHAT WAS THE FIRST AFRICAN-AMERICAN ORDER OF CATHOLIC NUNS?

In July 1829 in Baltimore, four African-American women—two from Haiti, one from Baltimore, and one from Cuba—took their vows as nuns. Their order, the Oblate Sisters of Providence, was the first religious sisterhood for African-Americans in the history of the Catholic Church. Sister Mary Lange, who was from Cuba, became the superior.

The Oblate sisters established a school and orphanage for boys, and were praised for their service to the poor during a cholera epidemic in 1832. Using money that she had inherited, Sister Mary had a chapel constructed. Completed in 1837, St. Frances Chapel of the Oblate became the first church in the United States built for African-American Catholics.

WHO WAS THE FIRST AFRICAN-AMERICAN TO EARN A DOCTOR OF DIVINITY DEGREE?

James W.C. Pennington, born into slavery in about 1810, escaped from Maryland to Pennsylvania, where Quakers helped him travel to New York. There he learned to read and write, eventually becoming accomplished in German, Latin, and Greek. Records state that in 1841 he published the first history of African-Americans in the United States.

Pennington received a doctor of divinity degree in Heidelberg, Germany, in the 1840s—the first African-American to earn this degree. He became a Presbyterian minister and a fervent abolitionist. His autobiography was published in London in 1849; its full title was *The Fugitive Black-smith, or Events in the History of James W.C. Pennington, Pastor of a Presbyterian Church, New York, Formerly a Slave in the State of Maryland, United States.*

WHO WAS THE FIRST AFRICAN-AMERICAN CATHOLIC PRIEST AND BISHOP?

James Augustine Healy was born on a Georgia plantation in 1830. His father, an Irish immigrant, had challenged the state's laws by marrying Healy's mother, a slave. The family moved to Long Island and young Healy studied at a Quaker school and later earned bachelor's and master's degrees from a Jesuit college in Massachusetts. Deciding to become a Catholic priest, Healy was ordained at the Cathedral of Notre Dame in Paris in 1854.

When Healy returned to the United States, it was as the first black Catholic priest in the country. He was assigned to parishes in Boston, where he became known as "the children's bishop" because of his work with needy youngsters. His generous efforts on behalf of destitute and troubled people brought him to the attention of Pope Pius IX, who in 1875 appointed Healy the first African-American bishop in the United States, with jurisdiction over the states of Maine and New Hampshire.

Healy's brother, Patrick Francis, also had a distinguished career. He was the first African-American to earn a Ph.D. and in 1874 became president of Georgetown University.

WHO WAS THE FIRST AFRICAN-AMERICAN CHAPLAIN COMMISSIONED IN THE ARMY?

Bishop Henry McNeal Turner was born free in South Carolina in 1833. He studied for the ministry and joined the Methodist Church, later transferring to the African Methodist Episcopal Church. Starting as an itinerant preacher, Turner soon became a prominent minister. In 1963 President Lincoln appointed him the first African-American chaplain in the U.S. Army.

Turner was not only an outstanding clergyman, he also rose to prominence in politics. In 1867 the National Republican Committee assigned him to supervise the political organization of African-Americans in Georgia, and that same year he was elected to the State Constitutional Convention. The following year voters elected him to the state legislature, but after he was reelected in 1870 he was ousted because of his race. President Grant then appointed him postmaster of Macon, Georgia, but once again he was persecuted and forced to resign.

After serving in two other government positions, Turner left politics to devote himself wholly to his church. He died in 1915 in Windsor, Canada, at the age of eighty-two.

Bishop Henry McNeal Turner

WHO WAS THE FIRST AFRICAN-AMERICAN MINISTER TO PREACH BEFORE THE HOUSE OF REPRESENTATIVES?

Although Henry Highland Garnet was only twenty-eight years old when he went to Troy, New York, to serve as a minister, his life had been marked by many dramatic events. Garnet was born in 1815 in Maryland, where his family was enslaved. When he was a child his father, pretending to be traveling to a funeral, got passes for his family to leave the plantation. The Garnets escaped into Delaware, and with help from an antislavery advocate they were able to reach New York City.

There, young Henry studied at the African Free School and then accepted an invitation to attend Noyes Academy in Canaan, New Hampshire. Soon after Garnet and two friends arrived at the school, local farmers destroyed the building. Garnet ended up at the Oneida Institute in Whitesboro, New York, where he gained a reputation as a brilliant student.

When Garnet went to Troy in 1843 it was to serve as the pastor of the Negro Presbyterian Church and to start a school for black children. A passionate spokesman for African-American freedom, Garnet was invited to speak at the National Negro Convention in Buffalo, New York, at which African-Americans gathered from throughout the country to find ways to end slavery. Garnet made an eloquent plea for black people to resist slavery, by armed rebellion if necessary.

When slavery was legally abolished in 1865, President Lincoln arranged for Garnet to deliver a sermon before the House of Representatives. He became the first African-American to preach before this legislative body.

WHAT WAS THE FIRST SEMINARY FOR TRAINING AFRICAN-AMERICAN PRIESTS?

At the turn of the century, a Catholic priest, Father Aloysius Heick, left Illinois and traveled to Mississippi, intending to open a mission chapel and an industrial arts school for African-Americans in the town of Merigold. But opposition to his plan was so intense that he was forced to leave, and the project was abandoned.

Heick moved to Vicksburg, Mississippi, and in 1905 his order, the Society of the Divine Word, asked Rome for permission to start a seminary to train African-American priests and brothers. Permission finally was granted in 1920. The first seminary, called Sacred Heart College, was opened in Greenville, Mississippi, with fourteen students.

In 1923 the seminary moved to Bay St. Louis, Mississippi, and was renamed St. Augustine's Mission House. The first African-American priests were ordained in 1934 and that same year the first black candidates for brothers enrolled at the seminary. Although some black priests had been trained in integrated seminaries before St. Augustine's was established, it was the first set up exclusively to train African-American Catholic clergy.

WHEN DID THE EPISCOPAL CHURCH ORDAIN ITS FIRST AFRICAN-AMERICAN WOMAN PRIEST?

P auli Murray was born Anna Pauline Murray in Baltimore in 1910. When she was only three, her mother died, and she went to live with an aunt in North Carolina. She studied at Hunter College in New York City and earned a law degree from Howard University Law School, where she graduated first in her class. She also earned degrees from the University of California at Berkeley and Yale Law School. She practiced and taught law, and was a poet, writer, and advocate of the rights of women and minorities.

After deciding to enter the ministry, Murray earned a divinity degree and in 1977 became the first African-American woman to be ordained a priest in the Episcopal Church. Murray died in 1985. Her books include *Songs in a Weary Throat, Dark Testament and Other Poems*, and *Proud Shoes: The Story of an American Family.*

WHO WAS THE FIRST AFRICAN-AMERICAN WOMAN BISHOP OF A MAJOR RELIGIOUS ORGANIZATION?

L eontine Kelly was born in 1920 in Washington, D.C., where her father was a Methodist minister. Before she was ten years old the family moved to Cincinnati, and her mother co-founded the local Urban League. Kelly graduated from Virginia Union University and later earned a divinity degree from Union Theological Seminary in Richmond, Virginia. A schoolteacher at first, Kelly entered the ministry after the death of her husband, who had been minister of a Methodist church in Virginia.

In 1984 she was elected a bishop of the United Methodist Church, the first African-American woman to hold this position in a major denomination. She was consecrated in a multicultural ceremony in Boise, Idaho, attended by one thousand African-Americans, Latinos, Native Americans, and whites. She served as resident bishop of the United Methodist Church for the San Francisco Bay area until her retirement in 1988, when she became a visiting professor at the Pacific School of Religion in Berkeley.

WHEN DID THE EPISCOPAL CHURCH ORDAIN ITS FIRST WOMAN BISHOP?

I n February 1989, the Rev. Barbara Clementine Harris was consecrated a suffragan bishop of the Episcopal Diocese of Massachusetts, making her

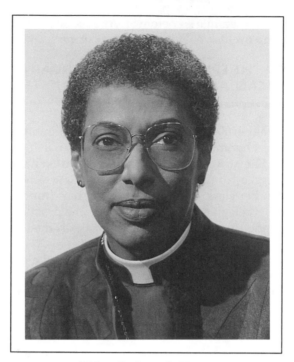

Bishop Barbara C. Harris

the first woman bishop in the Anglican Communion—a worldwide organization of churches derived from the Church of England.

Harris, who grew up in Philadelphia, was an early participant in the activities of her local church, starting a youth group there when she was still a teenager. After high school she attended a school of advertising and journalism and then took a job with a national public relations firm. In 1968 she joined the Sun Company as a community relations consultant and later headed Sun's public relations department. Eventually Harris made a decision to enter the ministry. She studied at Villanova University and in England, and was ordained an Episcopal priest in 1980.

A member of the Union of Black Episcopalians, Harris became active in many organizations, including the Prisoner Visitation and Support Committee and the National Episcopal AIDS Coalition. As a priest, Harris was an eloquent spokesperson for the rights of women, poor people, and African-Americans and other minorities. But because she was a woman, she had to overcome strong opposition from some conservative church members when she was named an Episcopal bishop.

WHO WAS THE FIRST AFRICAN-AMERICAN CHAPLAIN AT YALE UNIVERSITY?

In October 1992 the Rev. Frederick Jerome Streets was installed as the first African-American and the first Baptist to hold the position of University Chaplain at Yale. As chaplain, Streets assumed responsibility for a range of duties, including officiating at university functions; fostering religious life and ethical concerns; and counseling students, faculty, and staff on personal and spiritual matters.

Streets was born on the south side of Chicago in 1950. He lived with his grandparents for several years, and on Sundays his grandmother took him to churches where she played the piano. When he was eleven his family joined the Antioch Baptist Church and two years later the young Streets informed the pastor that he wanted to preach. After studying with the pastor for three years he preached his first sermon.

Streets went on to earn a bachelor's degree from Ottawa University in Kansas, a master's in divinity from Yale Divinity School, and a master's in social work from Yeshiva University. While studying at Yale he served on the New Haven Board of Aldermen.

Rev. Frederick Jerome Streets

In 1975, when he was twenty-five years old, Streets was named pastor of Mount Aery Baptist Church in Bridgeport, Connecticut, one of the city's oldest African-American Baptist churches. During that time he taught at Yale Divinity School and Hartford Seminary. Over the seventeen years that Streets served as pastor of Mount Aery, the church developed a housing program and a day care center and founded the first AIDS outreach service in the county.

SCIENCE & MEDICINE

WHO MADE THE FIRST CLOCK AND WAS THE FIRST AFRICAN-AMERICAN TO PUBLISH AN ALMANAC?

Born on a small tobacco farm near Baltimore, Maryland, in 1731, Benjamin Banneker received an eighth grade education as the only African-American child enrolled in a Quaker school near his home. At the age of twenty-three, assisted only by a picture of a clock, an English journal, and a geometry book, he designed and built the first clock in the colonies. Completed in 1754, the clock was entirely hand-carved of wood and struck the hours. It is said to have run for over forty years.

At the age of fifty Banneker began to pursue the study of astronomy, spending many nights outside, wrapped in blankets, observing the stars. Scientists, including Thomas Jefferson, took notice of him when he accurately predicted the solar eclipse of 1789. Three years later he published an almanac for farmers containing helpful seasonal information as well as weather predictions and the tide tables.

About this time President George Washington hired a Frenchman, Pierre l'Enfant, to provide a grand plan for the nation's new capital, and Banneker was chosen as surveyor. He and his Quaker friend, George Ellicott, chose the site for the Capitol and the White House, and laid out malls, avenues, circles, and parks. In 1972 l'Enfant suddenly left for France, taking the plans with him. Banneker and Ellicott put their heads together and, working only from memory, reconstructed the entire grand design.

In 1976, a stone marking the original southwestern boundary of Washington was made a memorial to Banneker and designated a National Historic Landmark, and in 1980 the U.S. Postal Service issued a commemorative stamp in his honor.

WHO WAS THE FIRST AFRICAN-AMERICAN PHYSICIAN IN THE UNITED STATES?

Born a slave in 1762, James Derham became a prominent doctor, one of the country's leading specialists in throat disorders. Derham learned his medical skills from three doctors, each of whom was his master. Encouraged by his third owner, Dr. Robert Love, Derham saved enough money as a medical assistant and apothecary to buy his freedom in 1783 and open a medical practice in New Orleans.

On a visit to Philadephia, Derham met Dr. Benjamin Rush, one of the country's most outstanding physicians. Rush took an interest in Derham's career and convinced him to move his practice to Philadelphia, where he gained great respect from his medical colleagues. As his practice expanded, Derham became known throughout the nation as an expert on the relationship between disease and climate.

WHO WAS THE FIRST AFRICAN-AMERICAN INVENTOR TO BE GRANTED A U.S. PATENT?

Thomas L. Jennings became the first African-American known to have patented an invention when, in 1821, he was issued a patent for a dry-cleaning process known as "dry scouring." Jennings, who owned a dry cleaning and tailoring business in New York City, was said to have used much of his profits to support the abolitionist cause. An activist for the rights of his people, Jennings served as assistant secretary of the First Annual Convention of the People of Color in June 1831 in Philadelphia.

WHO WAS THE FIRST AFRICAN-AMERICAN TO EARN A MEDICAL DEGREE?

In 1837 James McCune Smith, the son of a wealthy merchant, earned a medical degree from the University of Glasgow in Scotland and returned to New York City, where he opened a practice. An eloquent speaker and writer, Smith played an active role in the abolitionist movement.

Another African-American doctor, David J. Peck, was the first to earn a medical degree in the United States, graduating from Rush Medical College in Chicago in 1847. Peck opened a practice in Philadelphia.

WHO WAS THE FIRST TO PATENT A VACUUM SYSTEM FOR REFINING SUGAR?

In August 1843, the U.S. Patent Office issued Norbert Rillieux his first patent for a revolutionary system of refining sugar, an invention that completely changed the sugar industry. Rillieux, born in New Orleans in 1806, was the son of a slave and a plantation owner. He was sent to Paris to be educated and remained there as a teacher of applied mechanics.

Rillieux eventually returned to New Orleans and became an engineer in the sugar refining business. Before his 1843 invention, refining the juice of sugar cane into granular sugar was a laborious operation. His vacuum system was simpler and less expensive, and produced a higher quality sugar. The system was soon adopted by refineries throughout the country.

Although Rillieux's invention made him wealthy, his life was severely limited after the passage of the Fugitive Slave Act in 1850. Even though he was free, it was difficult to distinguish between free people of color and those who were slaves or fugitives. In 1854, when he was forced to carry a pass to travel around New Orleans, he left the country and returned to France, where he spent the next ten years deciphering Egyptian hieroglyphics. The European sugar industry eventually adapted his process to the refining of the sugar beet, which increased its production and added to Rillieux's wealth.

G. A. MORGAN.

BREATHING DEVICE.

APPLICATION FILED AUG. 19, 1912.

1,113,675.

Patented Oct. 13, 1914.

2 SHEETS—SHEET 1.

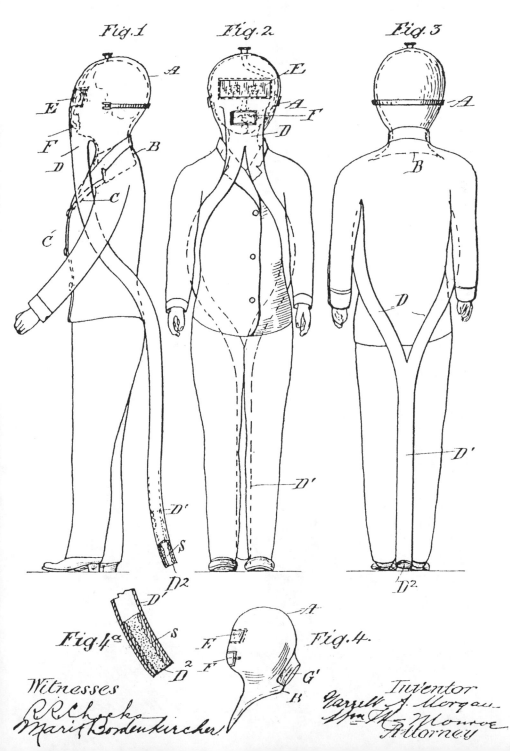

Fig. 1

Fig. 2

Fig. 3

Fig. 4ª

Fig. 4.

Witnesses

R R Cheeks

Marie Bordenkircher

Inventor

Garrett A. Morgan

Wm M Monroe

Attorney

1,475,024

G. A. MORGAN

TRAFFIC SIGNAL

Nov. 20, 1923.

Filed Feb. 27. 1922

2 Sheets-Sheet 1

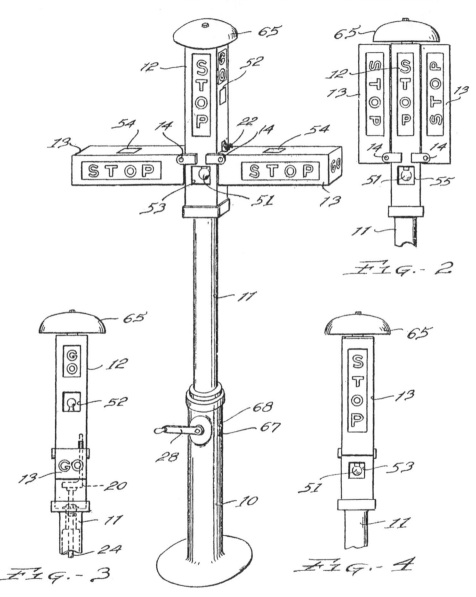

FIG.-2

FIG.-3

FIG.-4

FIG.-1

INVENTOR
Garrett A. Morgan,
By Baka & Macklin,
ATTORNEYS

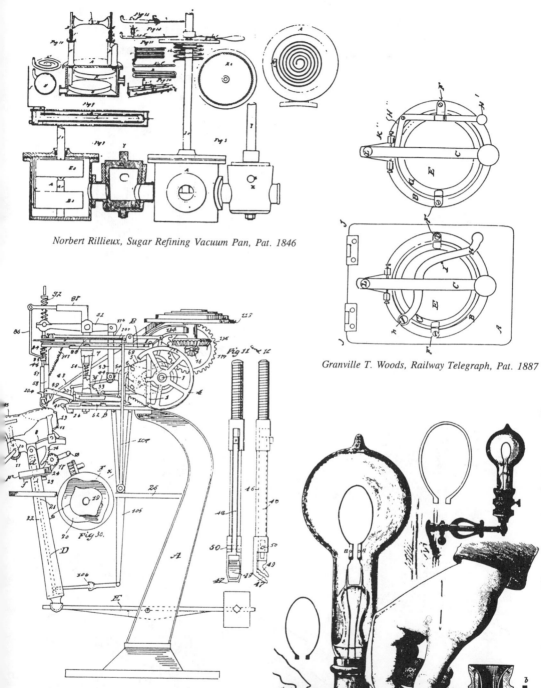

Norbert Rillieux, Sugar Refining Vacuum Pan, Pat. 1846

Granville T. Woods, Railway Telegraph, Pat. 1887

Jan Matzeliger's Lasting Machine, Pat. 1891

Lewis H. Latimer's Electric Lamp, Pat. 1881

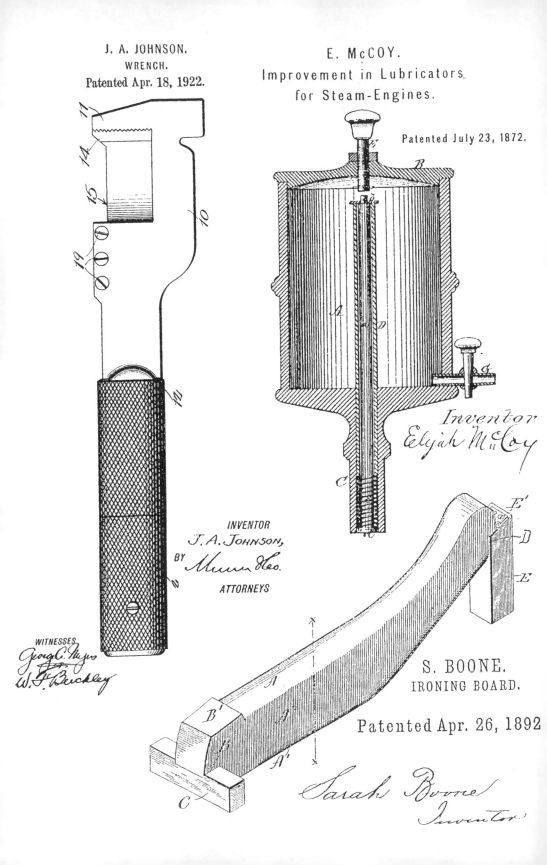

J. A. JOHNSON.
WRENCH.
Patented Apr. 18, 1922.

E. McCOY.
Improvement in Lubricators
for Steam-Engines.

Patented July 23, 1872.

Inventor
Elijah McCoy

INVENTOR
J. A. JOHNSON,
BY *Munn & Co.*
ATTORNEYS

WITNESSES
Geo. C. Myers
W. F. Beckley

S. BOONE.
IRONING BOARD.

Patented Apr. 26, 1892

Sarah Boone
Inventor

WHO INVENTED THE FIRST TOGGLE HARPOON FOR WHALING?

Lewis Temple was born in 1800 in Richmond, Virginia, and eventually settled in New Bedford, Massachusetts, where he worked as a blacksmith. The whaling industry was prominent in New Bedford at the time, and in his blacksmith shop Temple forged many of the harpoons used by whalers.

Told that the whales often were able to detach themselves and escape, Temple set to work to solve the problem. In 1848 he invented a toggle harpoon that made it more difficult for the whales to get away. The toggle harpoon was said to be the most important invention in the history of the whaling industry. But Temple neglected to patent his invention and never benefited from its profits.

WHO WAS THE FIRST AFRICAN-AMERICAN WOMAN TO EARN A MEDICAL DEGREE?

Rebecca Lee Crumpler was born in Richmond, Virginia, in 1833 and raised in Pennsylvania by her aunt, who acted as a doctor to others in her community. Inspired by her aunt, Crumpler became a nurse in Massachusetts in 1852. After her supervisors encouraged her to further her medical education, she entered New England Female Medical College in Boston, receiving a Doctress of Medicine degree in 1864. She was the first African-American woman to earn a medical degree in the United States.

Dr. Crumpler practiced medicine in Boston until after the Civil War, when she moved her practice to Richmond, where she worked with newly freed slaves. She eventually returned to Boston, and in 1883 she published a book on the subject to which she had devoted her life—medical care for women and children.

WHO DESIGNED THE FIRST AUTOMATIC LUBRICATOR AND INSPIRED THE TERM "THE REAL MCCOY"?

The child of escaped slaves, Elijah McCoy was born in 1844 in Canada and attended school in Michigan, where his parents eventually settled. He went to Edinburgh, Scotland, to serve an apprenticeship in mechanical engineering, but back in the United States he was unable to find a job in his field. He finally became a fireman on the railroad where one of his jobs was to oil the engine, which had to be done by hand while the train was stopped.

McCoy began experimenting with less tedious methods to oil machinery. In 1872 he patented his first invention, an automatic lubricator that supplied oil to moving parts while a machine was operating. He patented improvements over the years, and his lubricating device was soon used by manufacturers everywhere. Eventually customers inspecting pieces of machinery would routinely ask if it were "the real McCoy." The phrase is still used today to indicate authenticity.

McCoy acquired more than fifty patents in his lifetime; along with various lubricating devices, he invented an ironing table and a lawn sprinkler. He founded the Elijah McCoy Manufacturing Company in Detroit, and continued working on inventions until his death in 1929.

WHO WAS THE FIRST AFRICAN-AMERICAN NURSING SCHOOL GRADUATE?

Diminutive and energetic, Mary Elizabeth Mahoney developed an acquaintance with medicine early in life. Born in 1845, she was the eldest daughter in a large family, and assisted at the births of several of her younger brothers and sisters. She was in her early thirties when she entered the New England Hospital for Women and Children in Boston, the first nursing school in America.

All student nurses were required to do cleaning and laundry while pursuing their studies, and the regimen was so exhausting that only three out of a class of forty graduated in 1879; Mahoney was among them. She was an active suffragist, and after the passage of the nineteenth Constitutional amendment giving women the right to vote, she was thought to be the first African-American woman in Boston to register. Her nursing career continued for forty years, and in 1936 the National Association of Colored Graduate Nurses established the Mary Mahoney award for African-American nurses who made outstanding contributions to their profession.

WHO INVENTED THE FIRST ELECTRIC LIGHT WITH A CARBON FILAMENT?

The only African-American member of the famed "Edison Pioneers," Lewis Latimer was a man of many talents and accomplishments. Latimer, born in Chelsea, Massachusetts, in 1848, had a rough childhood. His father disappeared when he was ten years old and he sold copies of the abolitionist newspaper *The Liberator* to help support his family. When he and his brother were teenagers they were sent to a farm school for boys. They escaped, and Lewis joined the Union navy.

After the Civil War, he got a job as an office boy in a firm of patent lawyers. He eventually became the company's chief draftsman, and prepared the drawings for Alexander Graham Bell's application for his telephone patent, which was issued in 1876. Latimer soon began to work on his own inventions. In 1880 he took a job with an electric lighting company in Connecticut and created improvements in the incandescent light that Thomas Edison had invented one year earlier.

Latimer's most important invention, in 1882, was a long-lasting carbon filament for electric lamps. He was asked to install his lighting system in New York City, Philadelphia, and Canada. In 1884 Latimer joined the Edison Electric Light Company in New York, where he became chief draftsman and an expert witness in defending patents in court, and was one of the "Edison Pioneers," a group of inventors who worked for Edison.

In 1890 Latimer wrote a standard textbook, *Incandescent Electric Lighting, A Practical Description of the Edison System*. His interests were broad; he was a talented poet, artist, and musician. He spent his later years immersed in the study of literature, and before his death in 1928 he published a volume of his poetry.

WHO CREATED THE FIRST MACHINE TO MAKE A COMPLETE SHOE?

Jan Matzeliger emigrated to the United States from Dutch Guiana and in 1876, at the age of twenty-four, settled in Lynn, Massachusetts, which was the country's largest shoe manufacturing center. Since he had worked in machine shops in his native country, he was able to find a job in a shoe factory. He soon realized that there was no machine that could automatically "last" a shoe, that is, connect the upper part to the sole.

For years Matzeliger experimented with machines that would hold the shoe in place, stretch the leather down, and automatically tack it in place on the sole. Finally he achieved success, and in 1883 received a patent for the first lasting machine that would turn out a complete shoe. His invention revolutionized the shoe industry; the shoe-lasting machine was in demand throughout the world.

But Matzeliger remained a lonely man. He had devoted all his free time to his invention and the four improvements that followed, and he never married. He developed tuberculosis and died in 1889 before he could benefit from the great profits earned by his invention.

WHAT WAS THE FIRST PATENT AWARDED TO AN AFRICAN-AMERICAN WOMAN?

In July 1885 a patent was awarded to Sarah Goode, the owner of a Chicago furniture store, for a "folding cabinet bed," which was similar to today's convertible couch.

WHO INVENTED THE FIRST RAILROAD TELEGRAPH SYSTEM?

Granville T. Woods was born in Columbus, Ohio, in 1856. Forced to leave school when he was just ten years old, he went to work in a machine shop.

After moving to Missouri at the age of sixteen, Woods worked on the railroad and in a steel rolling mill. Developing an interest in electricity, he studied the subject in books and in college courses. For a time he drove a steam locomotive for the Danville and Southern Railroad, and in the early 1880s he opened his own company in Cincinnati, Ohio, and launched his career as an inventor.

In 1887 Woods patented a rail telegraph system that was designed to avert accidents by allowing messages to be sent between moving trains and between trains and railroad stations. The next year he invented a system for electric trains that utilized a pole extending to an overhead power line; the system was soon adopted for use with electric trolleys. Woods, who became known as the "black Edison," had secured more than sixty patents when he died in 1902. His inventions include the "third rail" that is now used on subways and a series of devices that led to the automatic air brake.

WHO WAS THE FIRST AFRICAN-AMERICAN WOMAN DENTIST?

Ida Gray was born in Tennessee in 1867. After attending high school in Cincinnati, where her family then lived, Grey earned a bachelor's degree from Ann Arbor College in Michigan. In 1890, when she graduated from the University of Michigan Dental School, she became the first African-American woman in the country to receive a Doctor of Dental Surgery degree. Gray then returned to Cincinnati, where she established a dental practice.

WHO INVENTED THE FIRST IRONING BOARD?

In 1892, an African-American woman, Sarah Boone, received a patent for an ironing board. She had devised a narrow wooden board with a padded covering supported by legs that could be collapsed. Before Boone's invention, ironing was done on tables or on boards laid across chairs.

WHO PERFORMED THE FIRST OPEN-HEART SURGERY?

Back in 1893, an African-American doctor named Daniel Hale Williams made history when he opened the chest of a young black man who had been stabbed in a fight, repaired the hole in the membrane surrounding his heart, and saved the man's life.

Williams, born in Pennsylvania in 1856, was left on his own at the age of eleven after his father's death. Supporting himself with various jobs, he learned the barbering trade and joined his sister in Wisconsin, where he worked as a barber and attended high school. He was hired as an assistant to a local doctor, who, impressed by his competence, sponsored his admission to Chicago Medical School. Williams graduated in 1883 and opened an office in Chicago, where his practice quickly grew.

Williams gained a reputation as a skilled surgeon, but because he was black he was not given a hospital appointment, and much of his surgery was performed in the homes of his patients. He became determined to open a hospital where African-American doctors and nurses could be trained and black patients would receive the best of care. In 1891 Williams founded Provident Hospital in Chicago, the first in the country with an interracial staff.

When James Cornish was stabbed in a bar brawl in 1893 and sent to Provident Hospital, Williams used an innovative technique to save his life. Without X-rays, antibiotics, or blood transfusions, the gifted surgeon made an incision in Cornish's chest and stitched up the wound. The patient recovered completely and the amazing operation made Williams famous throughout the country.

WHAT IS THE FIRST NATIONAL MONUMENT DEDICATED TO AN AFRICAN-AMERICAN?

In July 1953, the George Washington Carver National Monument, on a site near Diamond, Missouri, at the birthplace of this eminent scientist, became the first federal monument dedicated to a black American. Five years earlier, in January 1948, the U.S. Postal Service issued a commemorative stamp of Carver, who died of anemia in 1943.

George Washington Carver, born to parents who were slaves, became the first African-American graduate of Iowa State College in 1894. Hired to develop the agricultural department at Tuskegee Institute in Alabama, Carver was a pioneer in agricultural research and plant chemistry. He discovered a new method of organic fertilization, originated crop rotation as a means of restoring soil, and developed the peanut and the sweet potato as staples of farming in the South.

Carver was a pioneer in the field of chemurgy—finding new uses for agricultural products. He created 118 products from the sweet potato and more than 300 from the peanut, including soap, shampoo, vinegar, and wood stains.

WHO WAS COLORADO'S FIRST AFRICAN-AMERICAN WOMAN DOCTOR?

Dr. Justina Ford arrived in Denver, Colorado, in 1902, having just graduated from Hering Medical College in Chicago. When she applied for her Colorado medical license the examiner said he felt guilty taking her fee.

Dr. Justina Ford

"You've got two strikes against you to begin with," he said. "First of all, you're a lady, and second, you're colored."

Despite these seeming disadvantages, Dr. Ford established a long and successful practice, specializing in gynecology, obstetrics, and pediatrics. For several years she was denied hospital privileges and had to practice

244

home delivery. Known as the "Lady Doctor," Ford delivered more than 7,000 babies for people of many different backgrounds.

Dr. Justina Ford died in 1952 at the age of eighty-one. The Victorian house that was her home and office was placed on the National Register of Historic Landmarks, and was used to house the Black American West Museum and Heritage Center.

WHO WAS THE FIRST RECIPIENT OF THE NAACP'S SPINGARN MEDAL?

The Spingarn Medal was instituted in 1914 by J.E. Spingarn, who was then chairman of the board of the NAACP. It was designed to be presented annually for the highest achievement by an African-American in any field of endeavor. The first recipient of the Spingarn Medal, in 1915, was Ernest E. Just, then head of the department of physiology at Howard Medical School, for his biological research.

Ernest Just was born in 1883 in Charleston, South Carolina, where he attended an elementary school for African-American children. When he was seventeen years old his mother decided he should go North to further his education; he made his way to New York City by working on a ship. He soon earned enough money to enter Kimball Academy in Meriden, New Hampshire. His academic accomplishments there were outstanding and he graduated with honors in only three years.

In 1903 Just entered Dartmouth College, where he became intrigued by the study of biology, especially the development of the egg cell. After graduating magna cum laude he joined the teaching staff of Howard University and spent his summers conducting research on marine eggs at the Marine Biological Laboratories in Woods Hole, Massachusetts.

During his career Just published more than sixty papers on fertilization and parthenogenesis in marine eggs. His findings gave scientists new insight into the development of the cell. Just's 1939 book, *The Biology of Cell Life,* summarized his life's work.

WHO INVENTED THE FIRST TRAFFIC LIGHT AND GAS MASK?

In the early days of the automobile, traffic was controlled by a policeman sitting in a little tower at intersections, manually operating stop-and-go signals. This all changed when Garrett A. Morgan, after seeing an accident between an automobile and a horse-drawn carriage on a busy street, invented and patented the first automatic traffic light in November 1923.

Born in Paris, Kentucky, in 1877, Morgan received an elementary school education before leaving home and going to Cleveland, where he settled. He worked repairing sewing machines and then opened a tailoring shop.

It was there, while trying to make a lubricant for sewing machine needles, that he accidentally discovered a hair-straightening solution, which he sold as the G.A. Morgan Hair Refining Cream.

In 1916 Morgan came to public attention in a big way when, using a breathing device he had invented two years earlier, he took part in a dramatic rescue. A disastrous explosion had occurred in a tunnel below Lake Erie, trapping nearly thirty workers. Morgan and his brother, wearing his newly invented device, which he called a "Safety Hood," went into the smoke-filled shaft and pulled the workers to safety.

When they heard about the rescue, fire officials around the country placed orders for the Safety Hood, but many cancelled them when they learned that Morgan was an African-American. At this point the army saw the value of Morgan's invention, made some improvements on it, and the Safety Hood became the gas mask that saved thousands of lives in World War I.

WHO WAS NEW YORK'S FIRST POLICE SURGEON?

It was almost preordained that Louis Tompkins Wright should study medicine. His father, who died when Wright was four, was a graduate of Meharry Medical College. And his stepfather, Dr. William Fletcher Penn, was the first African-American to graduate from Yale Medical School. Encouraged by his stepfather to study medicine, Wright attended Harvard Medical School, graduating with honors in 1915. After his internship he practiced for a year in Atlanta, leaving to join the army medical corps in 1917.

When he was discharged from the service in 1919, Wright became the first African-American doctor on the staff of New York's Harlem Hospital, which was then in a white community. His appointment caused such furor that four white doctors resigned in protest, but twenty-three years later Wright became director of surgery of that same hospital.

In 1928 Wright was made the first African-American police surgeon in the history of the New York City Police Department. A specialist in head and neck injuries, he invented a brace for patients with neck fractures that is still used today. After developing an interest in cancer research, he founded the Harlem Hospital Cancer Research Foundation in 1948. His daughter, Dr. Jane Wright, a graduate of New York Medical College, where she became an associate dean, took over the foundation after her father's death in 1952.

WHO SET UP THE COUNTRY'S FIRST BLOOD PLASMA BANK?

Dr. Charles R. Drew, famous for his work in the preservation of blood, was a native of Washington, D.C., who first gained recognition as an outstanding athlete. At Amherst College, where he was a star in track and football, Drew won the Mossman Trophy as the athlete who had contributed the most to the school. Drew dreamed of becoming a doctor but could not afford medical school, so he took a job teaching biology and directing athletics at Morgan State College. Two years later he entered McGill University Medical School in Montreal, concentrating on research in blood transfusion.

After graduating from McGill, Drew became a teacher at Howard University Medical School, where he set up a program of residency training in surgery. A turning point in Drew's life came in 1938 when he won a research fellowship and went to New York City to do graduate work at Columbia University. While there, he developed techniques for separating and preserving blood, and determined that plasma could be stored much longer than whole blood. In 1939, Drew was instrumental in setting up a blood plasma bank at New York's Presbyterian Hospital, the first of its kind in the country.

When he finished his studies at Columbia University in 1940, Drew became the first African-American in the nation to receive a Doctor of Science degree in medicine. He returned to Howard Medical School to teach, but was soon asked to head a program to collect and process blood plasma for Britain, where German bombings were creating a critical need for blood. A year later, in 1941, Drew became head of an American Red Cross effort to collect blood for use by the American armed forces. But the military, in a shocking response, announced that blood from African-Americans would not be acceptable. After protests from around the country, the policy was revised: African-American blood would be accepted but kept separate!

Drew returned to Howard Medical School where he became head of the department of surgery and, in 1944, chief of staff of its teaching hospital. Drew received many honors and awards before his life came to an untimely end in 1950 when, on his way to a medical clinic in Alabama, his car went off the road and he was killed. But Drew's accomplishments live on. Schools all over the country have been named after him, and a medical center in California bears his name.

WHO WAS THE FIRST AFRICAN-AMERICAN AERONAUTICAL ENGINEER?

Douglas C. Watson fell in love with aircraft when he was still in grammar school. He set up a workshop in his basement to build model planes and read every issue of *Model Airplane News*. By the time he was in high school his models were winning competitions among New York City boys clubs.

When Watson entered New York University in 1937, he chose the engineering school, where he earned bachelor's and master's degrees. Watson graduated third in his class and was awarded the Chance-Vought Memorial Prize for his airplane design. But despite his outstanding record and the enthusiastic praise of his professors, Watson was the only member of his class not hired by an aeronautical company. Finally, with the help of his teachers, he was offered a job by an aircraft company in Pennsylvania, where he helped design a plane that won the firm a large army contract.

Watson spent most of his career with the Fairchild Republic Aviation Corporation in Farmingdale, New York. During his career he helped to develop the F-105 and F-84 jet fighters and played a major role in the design of the long-range P-47N, a bomber escort. After his retirement from Fairchild in 1978, he served as president of the Sabre Research Corporation, consulting engineers. He died in June 1993 at the age of seventy-three.

Watson was one of a family of achievers. His father, James S. Watson, was the first African-American judge in New York State; his sister, Barbara Watson, was the first African-American assistant secretary of state; and his younger brother, James L., was the second African-American state senator in New York.

WHO WAS THE FIRST AFRICAN-AMERICAN EMPLOYED BY AT&T'S BELL LABORATORIES?

W. Lincoln Hawkins's life was notable for hard work, solid achievement, and the deserved recognition of his peers and country. Born in Washington, D.C., in 1911, he graduated from Howard University and earned a master's degree from Rensselear Polytechnic Institute and a doctorate in chemistry from McGill University in Montreal.

Hired by Bell Laboratories, the prestigious research arm of AT&T, in 1942, Hawkins's most important inventions were additives that prolonged the life of plastic. He and a co-inventor found anti-oxidizing agents that gave plastic a useful life of seventy years. This was vital to AT&T because plastic shielding could now replace lead in protecting telephone cables.

In all, Hawkins was granted eighteen patents from the United States and 129 from foreign countries. He won honors from many professional societies and published fifty-five scientific papers and three books. He was a leader in efforts to promote scientific careers for other African-Americans, and helped to expand the science programs of predominantly black colleges.

In 1992, two months before he died, Hawkins received the National Medal of Technology from President Bush for his efforts on behalf of minority-group students.

WHO WAS THE FIRST AFRICAN-AMERICAN PROFESSOR AT HARVARD MEDICAL SCHOOL?

Dr. William Augustus Hinton, born in Chicago in 1883, earned a medical degree with honors in 1912 from Harvard Medical School, where he returned in 1949 as a professor of preventive medicine and hygiene. Hinton became famous throughout the world for his work in developing the Hinton test for the detection of syphilis and, with a Dr. Davies, the Davies-Hinton tests of blood and spinal fluid.

Although the NAACP wanted to present Hinton with its coveted Spingarn Medal in 1938, the doctor refused to take it, fearing that allowing the world to know he was African-American would be detrimental to the acceptance of his work.

WHO WAS THE FIRST AFRICAN-AMERICAN WOMAN TO BECOME A FELLOW OF THE AMERICAN COLLEGE OF SURGEONS?

Dorothy Brown's life did not have a promising start. Five months after her birth in 1919 in Troy, New York, her mother left her in an orphanage, where she remained for twelve years. Her future became more hopeful by the time she became a student at Troy High School; she had been taken in by loving, supportive foster parents.

Winning a four-year scholarship, Brown went on to study at Bennett College in Greensboro, North Carolina, graduating second in her class, and in 1948 she earned an M.D. from Meharry Medical College in Nashville, Tennessee. Brown was determined to become a surgeon, and in 1957 was appointed chief of surgery at Riverside Hospital in Nashville, a position she held until 1983. She was the first African-American woman surgeon in the South.

Her membership in the American College of Surgeons was not Brown's only first. She was the first single woman to adopt a child in the state of Tennessee and in 1966 she became the first African-American woman to serve in the Tennessee State Legislature.

WHO WAS THE FIRST AFRICAN-AMERICAN WOMAN TO HEAD A MAJOR TEACHING HOSPITAL?

From the time she graduated from high school at the age of fifteen, Florence Small Gaynor had to fight against racial obstacles to become a nurse. She first applied to Jersey City Medical Center, in the city of her birth, but was turned down because it did not admit African-Americans. To help support her family, she worked for a time at an electric plant and a doll factory. She was finally admitted to the nursing school at Lincoln Hospital in the Bronx, graduating as a registered nurse in 1946.

Gaynor held several nursing jobs while earning a bachelor's degree in nursing and a master's in public health; she was a public health nurse in New York City's East Harlem, a head nurse at a hospital in Manhattan, and a school nurse in Newark, New Jersey. She spent a summer at the University of Oslo in Norway studying the Scandinavian health system, and when she returned she pursued a career in hospital administration.

Rising through the ranks of hospital administration at a time when there were few women or African-Americans in such positions, Gaynor was chosen over nineteen male candidates in 1971 to be executive director of Sydenham Hospital in Harlem. Eighteen months later she was named executive director of Martland Hospital in Newark, a 600-bed teaching hospital, the first African-American woman in the country to head a major teaching hospital.

From 1976 to 1980, Gaynor directed hospital and health services at Meharry Medical College in Nashville, and for four years after that she was director of a community mental health group in Philadelphia. She died of a brain hemorrhage in 1993 at the age of seventy-two.

WHO WAS THE FIRST WOMAN TO HEAD PLANNED PARENTHOOD?

Faye Wattleton was the first woman and the first African-American to become president of the Planned Parenthood Federation of America, the largest family planning organization in the country. Wattleton was born in 1943 in St. Louis and graduated from Ohio State University Nursing School when she was twenty-one, the first in her family to earn a college degree. She went on to earn a master's from New York's Columbia University in maternal and infant health care.

Affected by her experience with a young woman who died after an illegal abortion and by her work with teenage mothers and neglected children, Wattleton became a volunteer with Planned Parenthood in Dayton, Ohio, where she worked as a public health nurse. She eventually became executive director of that agency and in 1978 was named president of the Planned Parenthood Federation of America. The youngest person to hold that position, she work diligently and effectively for the reproductive rights of women until her resignation in 1992. In October 1993, Wattleton was inducted into the National Women's Hall of Fame.

WHO WAS THE COUNTRY'S FIRST AFRICAN-AMERICAN WOMAN NEUROSURGEON?

Alexa Canady was born in 1950 in Lansing, Michigan, where her father was a dentist. She earned her medical degree from the University of Michigan College of Medicine in 1975 with a specialty in pediatric neurosurgery.

From 1976 to 1981 Canady served a residency in neurosurgery at the University of Minnesota. She then held a fellowship in pediatric neurosurgery at Children's Hospital in Philadelphia and taught at the University of Pennsylvania's medical school. In 1983 she took a position as a pediatric neurosurgeon at Children's Hospital of Michigan in Detroit, and became a clinical instructor of neurosurgery at Wayne State University, also in Detroit.

WHO WAS THE FIRST NEUROSURGEON TO SUCCESSFULLY SEPARATE SIAMESE TWINS JOINED AT THE HEAD?

Appointed director of pediatric neurosurgery at Johns Hopkins University Hospital in Baltimore in 1984, when he was only thirty-three years old, Dr. Benjamin S. Carson became the youngest person in the country to hold that position. He soon made medical history.

In 1985 Carson performed a medical procedure known as a hemispherectomy, removing half the brain of a four-year-old girl who was suffering 150 seizures a day. The other half of her brain took over all functions, and the girl went on to grow and develop normally. Carson made news again in 1987 when he led the medical team that for the first time in history successfully separated Siamese twins joined at the head.

Dr. Carson had to overcome almost overwhelming obstacles to reach his prestigious position. When he was eight years old, living in a poor Detroit neighborhood, his father abandoned the family and his mother took domestic jobs to support her two sons. To instill in them the importance of education, she made the boys read at least two books a week and write her a report of each. Although he was a poor student in elementary school, Carson graduated third in his high school class and won a scholarship to Yale University. After graduating he entered the University of Michigan School of Medicine.

Carson's autobiography, Gifted Hands, chronicles his road from poverty and a broken home to his distinguished position in the field of medicine. His motivational book, Think Big, outlines his philosophy for a successful life.

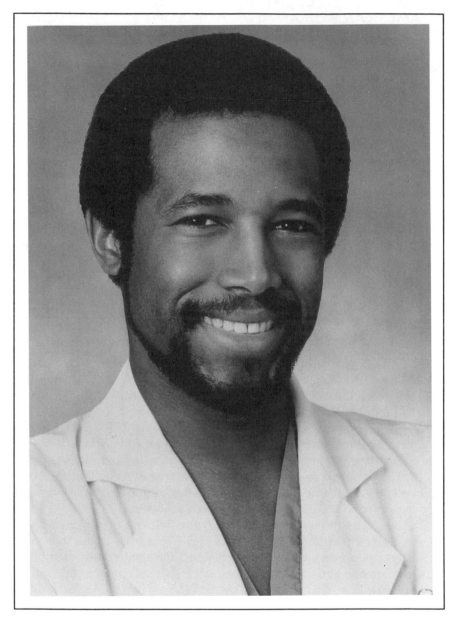

Dr. Benjamin S. Carson

WHO WAS THE FIRST AFRICAN-AMERICAN TO BE ELECTED PRESIDENT OF THE AMERICAN METEOROLOGICAL SOCIETY?

An internationally recognized expert on atmospheric science and climate research, Dr. Warren M. Washington added another title to his list of prestigious positions in 1993 when he was elected the first African-American president of the 11,000-member American Meteorological Society. Crediting his Portland, Oregon, high school teacher with exciting his interest in science and research, Washington earned degrees in physics and meteorology at Oregon State University and a doctorate in meteorology at Pennsylvania State University.

As a scientist and researcher at the National Center for Atmospheric Research (NCAR) in Boulder, Colorado, which he joined in 1963, Washington was given the responsibility of overseeing programs to study changes in global climate and developing computer models to monitor and analyze these changes. Scientists at NCAR have created climate models that include features like radiation, clouds, thunderstorms, oceans, and sea ice, and continue to develop models to help understand such phenomena as the greenhouse effect, the ozone hole, and deforestation.

In 1989 Washington founded the Black Environmental Science Trust to focus attention on the special environmental problems experienced by minority communities, such as exposure to lead, exhaust fumes, and contaminated drinking water, and to increase the number of African-American scientists in environmental fields. "There is a history of environmental problems being dumped on the poor and disadvantaged people, not only in this country but worldwide," Washington said in a 1993 newspaper interview.

An advisor to several presidential administrations, Washington is co-author of a book considered to be the standard reference on climate modeling, *An Introduction to Three-Dimensional Climate Modeling*.

WHO WAS THE FIRST AFRICAN-AMERICAN SURGEON GENERAL?

Dr. Joycelyn Elders spent her childhood in the tiny rural town of Schaal, Arkansas, where a visit to a doctor was a rare occurrence. But Elders grew up to be a pediatrician, the director of the Arkansas Health Department, and, in 1993 at the age of fifty-nine, the first African-American Surgeon General of the United States.

The eldest of eight children whose parents were sharecroppers, Elders graduated from college at the age of eighteen and joined the U.S. Army, where she was trained as a physical therapist. She attended the University of Arkansas Medical School on the G.I. Bill, and after graduating in 1960

Warren M. Washington

worked as an intern at the University of Minnesota Hospital and as a pediatrician at the University of Arkansas Medical Center in Little Rock. She went on to earn a master's degree in biochemistry, became a pediatrics professor at the University of Arkansas Medical Center, and in 1978 was certified as a pediatric endocrinologist. She published more than 150 articles based on her studies of growth in children and the treatment of hormone-related illnesses.

In 1987, Bill Clinton, then the governor of Arkansas, appointed Elders as the first woman and the first African-American to head the Arkansas Health Department. And in December 1992, President Bill Clinton nominated Elders to be the United States Surgeon General. But because of some who opposed her progressive and outspoken views on family planning, sex education, and abortion rights, the Senate did not confirm Elders as Surgeon General until September, 1993. Among Elders's goals at the time of her appointment were the establishment of school-based medical clinics and the introduction of comprehensive health education in the schools.

SPORTS

WHO WAS THE FIRST AFRICAN-AMERICAN PLAYER IN ORGANIZED BASEBALL?

John W. "Bud" Fowler, a native of Cooperstown, New York, joined a white team in New Castle, Pennsylvania, in 1872. Fowler could play any position in baseball, but was especially talented as a second baseman. For twenty-five years he played throughout the country, mainly for white teams. When he couldn't find a job he organized an African-American team called the All-American Black Tourists, who played in top hat and tails.

WHO RODE THE WINNING HORSE IN THE FIRST KENTUCKY DERBY?

From the early days of horse-racing until about 1900, most of the handlers, trainers, grooms, and jockeys were African-Americans. In the first Kentucky Derby, run in 1875, fourteen of the fifteen jockeys were black. In that race, an African-American jockey, Oliver Lewis, rode the winning horse, Aristides.

WHO WAS THE FIRST JOCKEY TO WIN THE KENTUCKY DERBY THREE TIMES?

Considered by some to be the greatest jockey of the nineteenth century, Isaac "Ike" Murphy was born near Lexington, Kentucky, in 1861. His mother did laundry for a racing stable, and when Murphy was young he exercised horses for stables in the area. He ran his first professional race at the age of fourteen; since most jockeys of the time were African-American, it wasn't difficult for Murphy to enter the profession.

During his twenty-year career Murphy raced 1,412 times and won 628 victories. In Saratoga, New York, in 1882, he won forty-nine of his fifty-one races. He won his first Kentucky Derby in 1884 and won it again in 1890 and 1891. Five years later, at the age of thirty-five, Murphy died of pneumonia. He was entered in the Halls of Fame of two racetracks—Pimlico, Maryland, and Saratoga.

WHO WAS THE FIRST AFRICAN-AMERICAN TO PLAY MAJOR LEAGUE BASEBALL?

Moses Fleetwood Walker was born in 1857 in Mt. Pleasant, Ohio, one of the stops for runaway slaves along the Underground Railroad. His family moved to nearby Steubenville, where his father, one of the first African-American doctors in the state, opened a practice. Fleetwood and his

Isaac "Ike" Murphy

younger brother Welday both entered Oberlin College, and in 1881 they were the only African-Americans on the school's baseball team.

In 1882 Walker enrolled in the University of Michigan Law School, where he played ball for two seasons before leaving to enter professional baseball as a catcher for the Toledo Mud Hens. When Toledo entered the

Moses Fleetwood Walker with the Toledo Mud Hens

American Association, a major league, in 1884, Walker became the first African-American ballplayer in the majors. During his season with Toledo he often had to contend with racial insults, especially when traveling in the South. After Toledo let him go he played for nine more years in the minor leagues.

When he was thirty-three Walker left baseball and worked as a mail clerk for a time in Syracuse, New York, before returning to Steubenville, where he and his brother Welday managed an opera house and started a newspaper. In 1908 he published a book entitled *Our Home Colony: A Treatise on the Past, Present and Future of the Negro Race in America.* After Walker died in 1924, Oberlin alumni put a headstone on his grave that read "First Black Major League Baseball Player in U.S.A."

WHAT WAS THE FIRST SALARIED AFRICAN-AMERICAN BASEBALL TEAM?

During the summer of 1885, the headwaiter at the Argyle Hotel in Babylon, New York, whose name was Frank Thompson, formed a baseball team composed of his fellow African-American waiters. They called themselves the Athletics. When the hotel closed on October 1, the ballplayers hit the road as a professional team.

Impressed by their talents, a wealthy man from New Jersey bought the team, hired an African-American manager, and renamed them the Cuban Giants. So they wouldn't be discriminated against as black Americans, the players spoke a kind of doubletalk on the field that they hoped would sound like Spanish.

The first team known to receive weekly paychecks, the Cuban Giants played semipro teams, college teams, and minor league clubs, and almost always won.

WHO WAS THE FIRST AFRICAN-AMERICAN JOCKEY TO WIN INTERNATIONAL FAME?

William Simms, known as Willie, was born in Georgia in 1870. In 1893 Simms won five races at Sheepshead Bay in New York and repeated the feat a year later at New York's Jerome Park. A hero of the racetrack, he won the Kentucky Derby twice, in 1896 and 1898.

Hired to ride in England, Simms became the first American jockey to win on an English racetrack with an American horse. He stayed in England for a lengthy period, becoming known throughout the world.

WHO WAS THE FIRST AFRICAN-AMERICAN TO WIN A NATIONAL SPORTS TITLE?

Marshall Taylor, nicknamed "Major," was a leading bicycle racer who became world-famous. Born in Indiana in 1878, Taylor entered the sport as a trick rider for a bicycle shop and a participant in local amateur races. He was a member of an African-American cycling group called the See-Saw Club, and in 1895 when he moved to Worcester, Massachusetts, he joined another black club. Often a victim of racist attacks, he defended himself by teaming up with two white cyclists.

In 1898, when he was twenty years old, Taylor became the cycling champion of America; he was the first African-American to capture a championship in any sport. During his twelve-year career he won more than one hundred races in the United States and abroad, and was given the title "The Fastest Bicycle Rider in the World."

WHEN WAS THE FIRST GOLF TEE CREATED?

In December 1899 Dr. George F. Grant, a graduate of Harvard University and a well-known dentist, patented the wooden golf tee. Before this invention, golfers had to balance their balls on mounds of dirt.

WHO WAS THE FIRST AFRICAN-AMERICAN BOXER TO WIN A WORLD TITLE?

Joe Gans, born Joseph Gaines in Baltimore, Maryland, in 1874, worked on the docks as an oyster shucker until he caught the attention of a local restaurant owner and boxing fan, who sponsored his professional debut. Gans became a pro fighter in 1901; a year later he won the lightweight title in a fight in Ontario, Canada, knocking out Frank Erne in the the first round.

Gans, who was called the "Old Master," won a savage fight in 1906 against a Danish boxer called Battling Nelson. Two years later they fought again. Gans, weakened by tuberculosis, lost by a knockout. He died two years later at the age of thirty-six.

WHO WAS THE FIRST AFRICAN-AMERICAN PROFESSIONAL FOOTBALL PLAYER?

When Charles Follis signed with the Shelby Blues in Shelby, Ohio, in September 1904, he became the first African-American professional football player. Born in Cloverdale, Virginia, in 1879, Follis moved with his family to Wooster, Ohio, when he was a youngster. At Wooster High School, Follis organized the first football team and was elected captain.

He continued to play football after entering the College of Wooster, first for a local amateur team and then for the Shelby Blues, with whom he signed a contract after he graduated in 1904. Follis was severely injured in a Thanksgiving Day game in 1906 and retired from football. He joined the Cuban Giants baseball team, playing with them until 1910, when he died of pneumonia at the age of thirty-one.

WHO WAS THE FIRST AFRICAN-AMERICAN ATHLETE TO WIN AN OLYMPIC MEDAL?

In the 1904 Olympics in St. Louis, Missouri, George Poage, a hurdler and quarter-miler, finished fourth in the 400-meter dash and third in the 400-meter hurdles, becoming the first African-American to win a medal in the Olympic Games. Poage, who represented the Milwaukee Athletic Club, had set a college record for the 440-yard dash and the low hurdles while a student at the University of Wisconsin.

WHAT RODEO STAR WAS THE FIRST TO PRACTICE BULLDOGGING?

Bill Pickett, a native Texan born in 1860, learned to ride horses and rope cattle while working as a ranch hand when he was a teenager. He eventually joined a Wild West show, soon becoming a star. One of the most popular rodeo performers of all time, Pickett gained fame for inventing the art of bulldogging, in which he rode after a steer, grabbed its horns, twisted its head back, sank his teeth into its upper lip, and wrestled it to the ground. The hair-raising feats of Pickett and his horse, Spradley, attracted crowds to rodeos throughout the country.

In 1932, while roping a bronco on his Oklahoma ranch, the seventy-two-year-old cowboy was kicked in the head, suffered a fractured skull, and died eleven days later. Pickett was inducted into the Cowboy Hall of Fame in 1971, the first African-American to receive this honor.

WHO WAS THE FIRST AFRICAN-AMERICAN WORLD HEAVYWEIGHT CHAMPION?

John Arthur Johnson was born in Galveston, Texas, in 1878 and was nicknamed Li'l Arthur as a boy. Leaving school after the fifth grade, he worked at different jobs until he was fifteen, when he was hired as a stevedore on the Galveston docks. A year later he went to Dallas, took boxing lessons, and by 1895, Jack, as he was now called, started fighting for a living. Eight years later he won the black heavyweight championship and by 1906 his record was ninety-seven victories, three defeats. During those years he fought only black boxers because whites refused to fight African-Americans.

Johnson kept trying to arrange a match with the Canadian boxer Tommy Burns, the white world heavyweight champion. Burns finally agreed and the fight took place in Sydney, Australia, the day after Christmas in 1908. Johnson defeated Burns in fourteen rounds to become the first African-American world heavyweight champion.

Bill Pickett on Spradley

The boxing establishment, upset with Johnson's win, began to search for a white boxer who could dethrone him. The promoters succeeded in getting former champion Jim Jeffries to agree to a match and billed him as the "Great White Hope." The fight took place in Reno, Nevada, on July 4, 1910. Called the "battle of the century," the brutal match ended in the fifteenth round and Johnson was declared winner by a knockout. Johnson successfully defended his crown until 1915 when, at age thirty-seven, he fought Jess Willard in Havana, Cuba, and was knocked out in the twenty-sixth round.

In 1922 Johnson served a one-year sentence at Leavenworth Federal Prison on an old charge having to do with transporting a white woman over a state line. Few people know that while he was doing his time, Johnson received patents for two inventions: an improved wrench (see patent drawings in Science & Medicine chapter) and a theft-prevention device for vehicles.

Johnson, who had held the heavyweight title longer than anyone up to that time, crashed into a light pole in his new Lincoln Zephyr car while traveling to New York and died in a North Carolina hospital on June 10, 1946. He was buried in Graceland Cemetery in Chicago.

WHO WAS THE FIRST AFRICAN-AMERICAN FOOTBALL PLAYER TO PLAY IN THE ROSE BOWL?

Although he wasn't very big—only five feet seven and 150 pounds—Frederick Douglas "Fritz" Pollard was chosen to play football for Brown University after he entered in 1914. He soon became known as the team's most elusive running back.

Pollard was born in a Chicago suburb where his father, a former championship boxer, ran a barber shop. His three older brothers were outstanding football players, and Pollard was chosen for the high school team after one of his brothers threatened to quit if he was rejected. Some members of the wealthy Rockefeller family saw Pollard play in a high school game in New York and took an interest in him. They paid his tuition at Brown University, where he was the first African-American student to live on campus. He opened a tailor shop, doing cleaning and pressing for fellow students, and became a campus favorite, which helped when he tried out for the football team.

On New Year's Day 1916, Pollard became the first African-American football player to play in a Rose Bowl game when Brown played Washington State. When some officals objected to his presence, his Brown University teammates refused to play if he was barred from the game. After graduating from Brown, Pollard attended the University of Pennsylvania dental school and coached at Lincoln University. In 1919 he signed up to play for the Akron Pros, becoming one of the first African-American players in professional football.

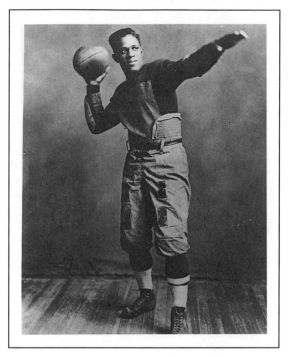

Frederick Douglas "Fritz" Pollard

WHO FOUNDED THE FIRST AFRICAN-AMERICAN PROFESSIONAL BASEBALL LEAGUE?

Andrew "Rube" Foster, born in Calvert, Texas, in 1879, organized his first baseball team in elementary school, and after finishing eighth grade he left to become a professional player. He joined a traveling Texas team called the Waco Yellow Jackets and went on to pitch for the Chicago Union Giants, the Cuban X Giants, and the Philadelphia Giants. Some considered the six-foot-four, 200-pound ballplayer one of the greatest pitchers of all time. In 1907 Foster joined the Leland Giants of Chicago, later becaming manager, and four years later became part-owner of a team called the American Giants.

In 1920 "the father of black baseball," as Foster has been called, formed the National Association of Professional Baseball Clubs, which became known as the Negro National League. His aim was to provide stability and financial equity for African-American ballplayers. With Foster as president, the league's first teams were the Kansas City Monarchs, the Indianapolis ABCs, the Chicago American Giants, the Detroit Stars, the St. Louis Stars, and a team of traveling Cubans, the Western Cuban All-Stars.

Andrew "Rube" Foster

Foster worked night and day running both the league and his own team. The strain took its toll; he suffered a breakdown in 1926 and was committed to a mental hospital. Never recovering completely, he died in 1930. Among the tributes at his funeral was a 200-pound baseball made of white chrysanthemums and roses sent by the directors of the Negro National League.

WHO WAS THE FIRST AFRICAN-AMERICAN ATHLETE TO WIN AN INDIVIDUAL EVENT AT THE OLYMPICS?

A native of Cincinnati, William DeHart Hubbard enrolled at the University of Michigan in 1921. While a student there, Hubbard won and set records in several track and field competitions. In 1924, at the Olympic Games in Paris, he became a gold medal winner with a long jump of twenty-four feet, five and one-eighth inches.

WHO WAS THE FIRST AFRICAN-AMERICAN BOXER TO WIN THE MIDDLEWEIGHT CROWN?

In February 1926, Theodore Flowers became the first African-American middleweight boxing champion when he won the title over Harry Krebs in New York City's Madison Square Garden. Flowers, who loved to read the Bible, was known as the "Georgia Deacon."

WHO WAS THE FIRST AFRICAN-AMERICAN GOLFER TO BELONG TO THE PGA?

Dewey Brown learned the game of golf as a caddy in New Jersey, and by the time he was sixteen he had begun his apprenticeship as a professional golfer. He was an assistant for a time to the veteran golfer Willie Norton, who hired him as a pro at the Buckwood Inn resort in Pennsylvania. Brown was known among visiting professionals and the resort's other guests as an excellent teacher and clubmaker—President Harding was one of his customers.

A Professional Golfers Association publication noted that Brown was the first African-American member of the PGA, but the date of his mem-

Dewey Brown

bership is unknown. Brown was a pioneer in a sport dominated by white men, and he was held in high esteem by all the big-name golf pros. In 1947 he moved to the tiny town of Indian Lake in New York's Adirondack Mountains, where he bought the Cedar River House, a resort hotel with its own nine-hole golf course. He owned and operated the resort for twenty-five years, leaving it to his son when he retired in 1972.

WHO WAS THE FIRST ATHLETE TO WIN FOUR GOLD MEDALS IN ONE OLYMPIC GAMES?

James Cleveland Owens was born in 1913 in a small Alabama town, the seventh child of poor cotton farmers. His family called him J.C., which his teachers and friends changed to Jesse. While he was still in elementary school, Jesse talked of someday attending college. To help him reach this goal, his parents moved to Cleveland, Ohio, in search of better employment.

In his school in Cleveland, young Jesse Owens was encouraged by the track coach to start training for the high school team. He became a record-breaking high school track star and went on to make history at Ohio State University when, at a Big Ten track and field meet in May 1935, in less than an hour he set a world record in the broad jump, tied his own world record in the 100-yard dash, and broke two more world records in the 200-yard dash and 220-yard low hurdles.

Owens will always be remembered for winning four gold medals at the 1936 Olympic Games in Berlin, where Hitler had hoped to prove that the Germans were the master race. Owens tied the world record in the 100-meter dash, set Olympic records in the broad jump and the 200-meter dash, and he and his team won gold medals in the 440-meter relay, setting a world record.

When Owens returned to the United States he was honored by a ticker tape parade in New York City and a reception at the Waldorf-Astoria hotel. He took a number of jobs in an effort to support his family, eventually working for the Illinois Athletic Commission. Owens died in March 1980 but his glorious victory in Germany will never be forgotten. At the opening ceremony of the 1984 Olympics in Los Angeles, his granddaughter, Gina Hemphill, carried the Olympic torch into the coliseum as a tribute to his memory.

WHO WAS THE FIRST BOXER TO HOLD THE HEAVYWEIGHT CHAMPIONSHIP FOR LONGER THAN A DECADE?

In what some consider the often corrupt and illicit world of boxing, Joe Louis was a shining star. Always honorable and dignified, he was idolized by African-Americans. He was born Joseph Louis Barrow in 1914 to a poor sharecropper family in Alabama. When his father died and his mother remarried, the family moved to Detroit, where Louis became enthralled by boxing. After winning a string of amateur bouts, he moved to Chicago and was taken on by a respected African-American businessman named John Roxborough.

By 1935 his reputation as a knockout fighter had earned him the nickname "Brown Bomber." That year Louis fought the ex-heavyweight champion Primo Carnera in New York's Madison Square Garden and another ex-champ, Max Baer, in Yankee Stadium. He knocked out both. But Louis didn't train hard enough for his next fight, with the German ex-champion Max Schmeling, and lost. His fans were distraught. Then, in 1937, Louis came back; he defeated James Braddock and was crowned heavyweight champion of the world.

In June 1938, with both black and white fans cheering for him, he faced Max Schmeling again. Two minutes and four seconds into the first round, Louis knocked out the German fighter. After going on to beat Billy Conn and Buddy Baer, he joined the army in January 1942 and played a major role in desegregating sports teams in army camps.

After a lengthy series of fights, Louis announced his retirement on March 1, 1949. He had been undefeated world champion for twelve years. But Louis was overwhelmed with financial problems and owed the government a million dollars in back taxes. He was forced to fight the younger boxers Ezzard Charles and Rocky Marciano, losing badly both times.

Louis wrestled professionally for a time, worked at public relations, and became a bouncer at a Las Vegas club. He suffered a massive heart attack in October 1977. Never fully recovering, he died on April 12, 1981.

WHO WAS THE FIRST AFRICAN-AMERICAN IN MAJOR LEAGUE BASEBALL IN MODERN TIMES?

On April 11, 1947, Jackie Robinson played his first game with the National League's Brooklyn Dodgers, becoming the first African-American ballplayer in the major leagues since the early days of baseball. (In 1884 Moses Fleetwood Walker was playing with the Toledo Mud Hens when the team joined the American Association, then a major baseball league.) Robinson was born in Georgia in 1919 and moved with his family to Pasadena, California. An outstanding athlete at the University of California at Los Angeles, he was forced to leave college in 1941 because he could no longer afford the expense. He played professional football before going into the Army to serve in World War II.

After his discharge Robinson signed with a Negro League baseball team, the Kansas City Monarchs. He was noticed by Branch Rickey, owner of the Brooklyn Dodgers, who signed him up in 1945. After a year with the

Dodgers farm team in Montreal, Robinson was brought up to the majors in 1947; that year he was named Rookie of the Year. He was chosen the National League's Most Valuable Player in 1949, and in 1962 was inducted into the Baseball Hall of Fame.

After his retirement in 1956, Robinson was active in business and social programs. He died in 1972 at the age of fifty-three.

WHO WAS THE FIRST AFRICAN-AMERICAN BASEBALL PLAYER IN THE AMERICAN LEAGUE?

In July 1947 Larry Doby signed a contract with the Cleveland Indians and became the first black baseball player in the American League. A World War II veteran and a former second baseman and infielder for the Newark Eagles, Doby became the first African-American to score a home run in the World Series in 1948 when he hit a 425-foot drive into right field in the third inning in Cleveland. Cleveland defeated the Boston Braves 4-2.

Doby played in the majors for thirteen years and was named to the American League All-Star team six times. In 1978 he was appointed manager of the Chicago White Sox, becoming the second African-American manager in baseball.

WHO WAS THE FIRST AFRICAN-AMERICAN PITCHER IN THE AMERICAN LEAGUE?

Dan Bankhead, who joined the Brooklyn Dodgers in 1947, was the first African-American pitcher in major league baseball, but his reputation could not match that of Leroy "Satchel" Paige. Not only was Paige the first African-American baseball player to pitch in the American League, he also was considered by many to be the greatest pitcher in the history of the sport. In the 1930s, while he was still playing for all-black baseball teams, white major leaguers like Dizzy Dean and Joe DiMaggio who faced Paige in exhibition games called him the best they had ever seen.

Paige was born in Mobile, Alabama. He said the year was 1906, but some have claimed it was earlier. In any case, when he was about seven years old he earned money carrying bags and satchels at the local railroad station. It is said that he dangled several satchels at a time from a long pole, causing the other kids to call him "satchel tree." Eventually shortened to "Satchel," the nickname stayed with him.

Paige also had a job cleaning up a local ball park, and it was there that he became interested in baseball. Not able to afford a ball, he practiced by pitching rocks. At age twelve he was caught stealing some cheap rings and was sent to a reform school, where the baseball coach helped him refine his pitching style and learn the game. In 1924 Paige signed on as a pitcher for the Mobile Tigers and two years later joined the Chattanooga Black

Leroy "Satchel" Paige

Lookouts. He continued to play for various teams in the Negro League, culminating in a nine-year stint with the Kansas City Monarchs, a team he led in a string of victories.

Finally, in 1948, a year after Jackie Robinson integrated major league baseball, Paige was signed by the Cleveland Indians. At age forty-two, the tall, lanky player, famous for his fast "bee" ball, became the first African-American to pitch in the American League. In 1952, while pitching for the St. Louis Browns, he was chosen for the American League All-Stars. His last job in baseball came in 1968, when he was hired as a coach by the Atlanta Braves. When Paige was elected to the Baseball Hall of Fame in 1971, his inclusion was based on his record in the Negro League. He died eleven years later, leaving a list of rules for a good life, including this one: "Don't look back. Something might be gaining on you."

WHEN DID THE FIRST AFRICAN-AMERICAN WOMAN WIN AN OLYMPIC GOLD MEDAL?

In 1948, at the Olympic Summer Games in London, Alice Coachman became the first African-American woman to win the gold, taking first place in the high jump. Her leap of five feet, six and one-quarter inches set a new Olympic record. This native of Albany, Georgia, attended Tuskegee Institute and earned a degree from Albany State College, where she won a dozen national high jump titles.

Coachman began entering track competitions when she was thirteen years old, winning a string of AAU championships. She began her track career as a sprinter, garnering titles in the 50-yard dash, 100-yard dash, and 440-yard relay. Some say that she chose the high jump competition for the 1948 Olympics because, at age twenty-two, she thought she was past her prime as a runner.

WHEN DID THE U.S. LAWN TENNIS ASSOCIATION ADMIT ITS FIRST AFRICAN-AMERICAN PLAYER?

Reginald Weir, an outstanding young tennis player, was captain of his team at City College of New York for three years in a row. Yet in 1929 Weir was barred from the National Junior Indoor Tennis Tournament of the U.S. Lawn Tennis Association, despite protests from the NAACP and the New York Tennis Association. It was 1948 before the Association allowed Weir to participate in a tournament.

WHO WAS THE FIRST AFRICAN-AMERICAN TENNIS PLAYER TO COMPETE AT WIMBLEDON?

Althea Gibson grew up in New York City where she played several sports, including paddle tennis. A local tennis coach noticed her talent, bought her a tennis racket, and introduced her to the game. Determined to be successful, she practiced whenever and wherever she could.

Gibson's persistence paid off. In 1950 at the age of twenty-three, she made it to Wimbledon, England, becoming the first African-American tennis player to compete in that prestigious tournament. Seven years later she returned to Wimbledon and won the women's singles, another first for an African-American athlete. When the triumphant champion returned to New York City, she was greeted with a ticker tape parade. Gibson went on to win many more competitions, becoming famous throughout the world.

WHO WERE THE FIRST AFRICAN-AMERICANS TO PLAY IN THE NATIONAL BASKETBALL ASSOCIATION?

Three African-American basketball players were signed by National Basketball Association teams for the 1950-51 season. They were Charles "Chuck" Cooper, who signed with the Boston Celtics; Earl Lloyd, who went with the Washington Capitols; and Nathaniel "Sweetwater" Clifton, who was signed by the New York Knickerbockers.

WHO WAS THE FIRST AFRICAN-AMERICAN TO WIN THE DECATHLON GOLD MEDAL IN THE OLYMPICS?

As a student in his Plainfield, New Jersey, high school, Milt Campbell was known as one of the finest athletes in the country, noted for his skill in track, swimming, wrestling, and football. Campbell's track and field talents were so outstanding that his coach decided to train him for the decathlon in the 1952 Olympics in Helsinki, Finland. The decathlon competition includes ten events: 100-meter dash, 400-meter dash, broad jump, shot put, high jump, 110-meter hurdles, discus throw, pole vault, javelin throw, and 1,500-meter run.

Campbell's home town residents raised $1,500 to send him to the West Coast for the Olympic tryouts. At the Games in Helsinki, the eighteen-year-old finished second in the decathlon competition. Four years later, while a student at Indiana University, he won a decathlon gold medal at the Olympics in Melbourne, Australia. After college, where he also played football, Campbell signed up with the Cleveland Browns, but he had a disappointing career in pro football and never became a star.

WHEN DID THE FIRST AFRICAN-AMERICAN TENNIS STAR WIN HIS FIRST NATIONAL TITLE?

Arthur Ashe began playing tennis as a ten-year-old in a segregated playground in his hometown of Richmond, Virginia. In 1960, at age seventeen, Ashe won his first United States Lawn Tennis Association national title, the Junior Indoors. A year later he became the first African-American member of the U.S. Junior Davis Cup Team.

Overcoming the experiences of his early years, when he was sometimes denied entry in tournaments because of his race, Ashe went on to achieve

Arthur Ashe

other firsts: he was the first African-American to be named to a United States Davis Cup team, in 1963; the first to win the U.S. Open, in 1968; the first to win men's singles at Wimbledon, in 1975, and, ten years later, the first African-American man inducted into the International Tennis Hall of

276

Fame. Not political at first, Ashe grew to be a quiet but firm fighter for civil rights, speaking out against injustice in the United States and apartheid in South Africa.

After piling up a multitude of victories and becoming tennis's first African-American millionaire, Ashe suffered a heart attack in 1979 and underwent quadruple bypass surgery. In April 1980 he announced his retirement from competitive tennis, and five months later he was named captain of the U.S. Davis Cup team, leading the United States to victory in 1981 and 1982. Ashe published a three-volume history of African-American athletes, *A Hard Road to Glory*, in 1988. Just four years later, in an emotional news conference, a gaunt, grim-faced Ashe announced that, apparently as a result of blood transfusions after a second open heart operation in 1983, he had contracted the virus that causes AIDS.

Ashe became a leading spokesperson in the fight to combat the disease, founding the Arthur Ashe Foundation for the Defeat of AIDS and speaking before the United Nations on World AIDS Day, December 1, 1992. On February 6, 1993, at the age of forty-nine, Ashe died of pneumonia, a complication of AIDS. In response to Ashe's death, New York City's mayor, David Dinkins, said, "words cannot suffice to capture a career as glorious, a life so fully lived, or a commitment to justice as firm and as fair as was his."

WHO WAS THE FIRST WOMAN RUNNER TO WIN THREE GOLD MEDALS IN ONE OLYMPIC GAME?

When Wilma Rudolph was a child, no one could have imagined that someday she would be a record-breaking athlete. Born in 1940 in Tennessee, one of nineteen children, she was a sickly child. She came down with scarlet fever and double pneumonia and, when she was four, she was left partially paralyzed by polio and forced to wear leg braces and special shoes. Her family learned to massage and exercise her legs, and by the time she was eight she could walk on her own.

In high school Rudolph was a star basketball player and top runner. She joined the track team at Tennessee State University, which she entered in 1958, and soon made history. At the 1960 Olympic Games in Rome, she became the first woman to win three gold medals in track, and the Associated Press named her Female Athlete of the Year.

WHO WAS THE FIRST HEAVYWEIGHT CHAMPION TO REGAIN THE TITLE?

Floyd Patterson, born in 1935 in Waco, North Carolina, caught the attention of boxing fans when he won a gold medal in the middleweight competition at the 1952 Summer Olympic Games in Helsinki, Finland. Patterson went on to become heavyweight champion, a title he held from 1956 to 1959, when he was knocked out by Ingemar Johansson. A year later, on June 20, 1960, Patterson KO'd Johansson and regained the title.

WHO WAS THE FIRST AFRICAN-AMERICAN GOLFER TO PLAY FULL-TIME WITH THE PGA TOUR?

In 1932, when he was ten years old, Charlie Sifford got a job as a caddy at the Carolina Country Club near his house in Charleston, North Carolina. It was then that he discovered the game of golf. When he was seventeen he dropped out of ninth grade and took a bus to Philadelphia, where he got a job as a shipping clerk. He began to play at a public golf course, the first integrated course he had ever seen.

In 1946 Sifford was hired as a private golf instructor by the popular singer Billy Eckstine. For ten years he toured with Eckstine in the winter and in the summer played with the U.S. Golf Association, which sponsored tours for African-American golfers. In April 1961 Sifford played in his first Professional Golfers Association (PGA) tournament in Greensboro, North Carolina.

Sifford played on the PGA circuit for fifteen years and became a regular player on the Senior PGA tour after it was instituted in 1980. In 1992 he published his autobiography, *Just Let Me Play.*

WHO WAS THE FIRST AFRICAN-AMERICAN FOOTBALL PLAYER TO WIN THE HEISMAN TROPHY?

Ernie Davis was an athlete with great potential. While still a high school student at Elmira Free Academy in upstate New York, he won eleven varsity letters. After he entered Syracuse University, his skills on the football field led some observers to call him the finest running back in the country. In 1961, his senior year, he became the first African-American to win the Heisman Memorial Trophy, which was awarded annually to the country's best college football player.

After college Davis was signed by the Cleveland Browns, and just before the 1962 season began he traveled to Chicago to play with a college all-star team against the Green Bay Packers. But a few days before the game, doctors sent him to the hospital for medical tests. He was diagnosed as having leukemia. Davis never got to play football with the Cleveland Browns; he died at the age of twenty-three.

WHO WAS THE FIRST BASKETBALL PLAYER TO SCORE 100 POINTS IN A SINGLE GAME?

Although he was physically huge—7'2" tall and 265 pounds—basketball star Wilt Chamberlain was admired for his speed, grace, and coordination.

Wilton "Wilt" Chamberlain

Chamberlain, born in Philadelphia in 1936, was an outstanding overall athlete in high school. He entered the University of Kansas but left in his third year to join the Harlem Globetrotters. In 1959 he signed with the Philadelphia Warriors, and in the 1961-62 season he became the first player to score 100 points in a single game as the Warriors beat the New York Knickerbockers 169-147.

Chamberlain, known as "Wilt the Stilt," was eventually traded to the Philadelphia 76ers, and got to play with his first NBA championship team in the 1966-67 season, leading the 76ers to victory over the Boston Celtics. He was traded to the Los Angeles Lakers in 1968, and in February 1972 became the first player in the NBA to score 30,000 points when he reached that total in a game with the Phoenix Suns. Two years later Chamberlain became a player-coach for the San Diego Conquistadors and in 1979 this legend of the courts was elected to the Basketball Hall of Fame.

WHO WAS THE FIRST AFRICAN-AMERICAN COACH OF A MAJOR LEAGUE BASEBALL TEAM?

John "Buck" O'Neil was a star hitter and a manager for the Kansas City Monarchs, a leading team in the early Negro League. O'Neil was named coach of the Chicago Cubs in 1962, becoming the first African-American coach in big league baseball.

O'Neil never lost his love for the game. In 1991, at the age of seventy-nine, he became chairman of the board of the Negro Leagues Baseball Museum in Kansas City, on a street near the spot where the Negro National League was started in 1920 by Andrew "Rube" Foster.

WHO WAS THE FIRST AFRICAN-AMERICAN TO BE SELECTED AS MVP OF THE AMERICAN LEAGUE?

After graduating from high school in St. Louis, Missouri, Elston Howard joined the Kansas City Monarchs, a Negro League team. In 1955 he became the first African-American member of the New York Yankees and in 1963 was named the American League's Most Valuable Player.

The catcher was honored with "Elston Howard Day" on August 29, 1964, at Yankee Stadium and was a Yankee coach until he died in 1980.

WHEN DID MAJOR LEAGUE BASEBALL APPOINT ITS FIRST AFRICAN-AMERICAN UMPIRE?

Emmett Ashford, who had spent fifteen years as an umpire for the minor leagues on the west coast, became the major leagues' first African-American umpire when he joined the American League in the spring of 1966, at the age of forty-eight. Before officiating at the opening game of the 1966 season, at which President Lyndon Johnson threw out the first ball, Ashford said, "I waited fifteen years for this, and now I'm finally here."

John "Buck" O'Neil

WHO WAS THE FIRST AFRICAN-AMERICAN TO COACH A MAJOR LEAGUE TEAM?

Even though Bill Russell was not an outstanding basketball player in his Oakland, California, high school, he was offered a basketball scholarship in 1952 by the University of San Francisco. There Russell improved greatly, becoming the team's captain in his junior and senior years and leading the players to two national championships.

In 1956 Russell was a member of a gold-medal-winning basketball team in the Olympic Games. He then signed with the Boston Celtics, leading them to eleven championships in thirteen years. In 1966 he was named coach of the Celtics, making him the first African-American head coach of a major league sports team.

WHO WAS MAJOR LEAGUE BASEBALL'S FIRST AFRICAN-AMERICAN MANAGER?

In October 1974 Frank Robinson was named manager of the Cleveland Indians, making him the first African-American manager in major league baseball history. Born in Texas in 1935, Robinson played baseball while growing up in Oakland, California, and in 1952 was signed by the Cincinnati Reds.

Robinson became the first major leaguer to be voted Most Valuable Player in both leagues—the National League in 1961 as a Cincinnati Red and the American League in 1966 as a Baltimore Oriole.

WHO WAS THE FIRST AFRICAN-AMERICAN GOLFER TO COMPETE IN THE MASTERS TOURNAMENT?

Like other African-American golfers, Lee Elder began playing golf while working as a caddy. Elder was born in Dallas, Texas, in 1935. After moving to Los Angeles with his family, he took lessons from the African-American golfer Ted Rhodes. Golf fans began to notice Elder in 1968 when he came in second to the famous golfer Jack Nicklaus at the American Golf Classic in Akron, Ohio.

In 1975 Elder became the first black golfer to play in the prestigious Masters Tournament, held yearly in Augusta, Georgia. Three years later he won the Westchester Classic, receiving $60,000 in prize money. He was the first African-American golfer to earn more than $100,000 in a season and the first to make the U.S. Ryder Cup team.

WHO WAS THE FIRST FIGHTER TO HOLD THE WORLD HEAVYWEIGHT TITLE THREE TIMES?

Muhammad Ali, born Cassius Clay, Jr., in 1942 in Louisville, Kentucky, became a professional fighter when he was eighteen years old. In 1964 he captured the professional heavyweight championship from Charles "Sonny" Liston, knocking him out in seven rounds. That same year, having earlier joined the Nation of Islam, he adopted his new name.

Refusing in 1967 to go into the Army because he was opposed to the Vietnam War on religious grounds, Ali was stripped of his title and barred from boxing for four years. In 1970 a court overturned his suspension from boxing and he began a comeback, reclaiming the championship four years later at the age of thirty-two by knocking out George Foreman in eight rounds.

Ali lost the title to Leon Spinks in 1978 but regained it before he retired in 1979. Thus, Ali was World Heavyweight Boxing Champion during 1964-67, 1974-78, and 1978-79. For most of his career he could, as he claimed, "float like a butterfly, sting like a bee." His autobiography, *The Greatest: My Own Story*, was published in 1975.

WHO WAS THE FIRST AFRICAN-AMERICAN TO WIN A PROFESSIONAL BOWLING TITLE?

In January 1987, George Branham of Arleta, California, then twenty-four years old, became the first African-American to win a Professional Bowlers Association event, the Brunswick Memorial World Open.

WHO WAS THE FIRST AFRICAN-AMERICAN ATHLETE TO WIN A MEDAL IN THE WINTER OLYMPICS?

A world-class figure skater and a winner of national and international titles, Debi Thomas became the first African-American to win a medal in the Winter Olympics when she was awarded a bronze medal in the 1988 games in Calgary, Canada. Born in 1967 in Poughkeepsie, New York, Thomas graduated from Stanford University in 1991 with a degree in engineering.

WHO WAS THE FIRST AFRICAN-AMERICAN MANAGER TO LEAD A BASEBALL TEAM TO A WORLD SERIES CHAMPIONSHIP?

In October 1992 the Toronto Blue Jays baseball team defeated the Atlanta Braves and became the first Canadian team to win a World Series. The victory marked another first for baseball: the Blue Jays' manager, Cito Gaston, was the first African-American manager to lead a team to a World Series championship. One year later, Gaston once again led his team to victory when Toronto triumphed over Philadelphia to win the 1993 World Series.

Born Clarence Edwin Gaston in 1944 in San Antonio, Texas, the victorious manager had been leading the Blue Jays since 1989, when he was promoted from batting coach. An All-Star outfielder who played for eleven seasons with Atlanta and San Diego, Gaston ended his playing career with the Pittsburgh Pirates in 1979.

He began his coaching career as a batting instructor with the Atlanta Braves and moved to the Toronto Blue Jays in 1982. He was the fourth African-American manager in major league history; the others were Frank Robinson, Larry Doby, and Maury Wills.

THEATER & DANCE

WHO WAS THE FIRST AFRICAN-AMERICAN ACTOR TO PERFORM BEFORE THE RULERS OF PRUSSIA, SWEDEN, AUSTRIA, AND RUSSIA?

Ira Aldridge was born in 1807 and attended the African Free School in New York City. He later joined a black theater troupe there, the African Company. When the troupe disbanded, Aldridge migrated to England, where he continued his career on the stage. In London, he appeared in the melodrama *The Revolt of Surinam, or A Slave's Revenge*, and in 1833 received wide acclaim for his performance in *Othello* at Covent Garden. Although known for his portrayal of Othello, he also gave memorable performances as Macbeth, Lear, Shylock, and Hamlet

For the rest of his life Aldridge toured England and the continent, performing Shakespearean roles before royalty and becoming one of the most celebrated actors of his day. Accounts of the time report that students in Moscow, thrilled by his performance there, unhitched the horses from his carriage and pulled him from the theater to his hotel. But Aldridge was never able to enact his most famous role, Othello, in his native land; he died in Poland in 1867 while making arrangements for a tour of the United States.

WHAT WAS THE FIRST NEW YORK CITY THEATER TO STAGE AFRICAN-AMERICAN PRODUCTIONS?

The African Grove, housed in a modest structure at the corner of Bleecker and Mercer Streets in lower Manhattan, presented all-black versions of Shakespearean plays and other dramas performed by a troupe of actors called the African Company. The famous tragedian, James Hewlett, who was the first black actor to play Othello, appeared at the African Grove in 1821. Ira Aldridge, another great African-American tragic actor, also starred in the company's productions.

The theater's actors were heckled by rowdy white customers and its productions were disparaged by a biased press. It finally was forced to close in 1823. Before disbanding, the African Company presented *The Drama of King Shotaway*, about the uprising of Carib Indians on St. Vincent's Island against the British navy. Some believe it was the first African-American drama to reach the stage.

WHO WAS THE FIRST ACTOR TO PLAY THE EMPEROR JONES?

Charles Gilpin was the first actor to play the lead in the Eugene O'Neill play, *The Emperor Jones*. Produced in 1920 at the Provincetown Playhouse in New York City, the play starred Gilpin in the role of Brutus Jones, a

Ira Aldridge as Othello, England, 1913

pullman porter who becomes the emperor of an island. The NAACP awarded Gilpin its Spingarn Medal for his achievement, the Drama League voted him one of the ten people who had done the most for the theater that season, and he was invited to appear at the White House.

Charles Gilpin in The Emperor Jones

Gilpin was born in Virginia in 1879. He performed in county fairs and minstrel shows trying to make a career in the theater. When he was in his twenties he helped organize an acting company in Chicago and in 1915 he played the lead in the first production of the Colored Dramatic Stock Company, *The Girl at the Fort*.

When Gilpin won the role of Brutus Jones, he was supporting himself as a printer and an elevator operator. *The Emperor Jones* gave him the opportunity to become the first African-American actor to win fame in a dramatic role, rather than as a singer or dancer.

WHAT WAS THE FIRST DRAMA BY AN AFRICAN-AMERICAN PLAYWRIGHT PRODUCED ON BROADWAY?

In 1923 the one-act play, *The Chip Woman's Fortune,* by Willis Richardson, was presented as part of a triple bill by the Ethiopian Art Players, a theater company from Chicago. Staged a week earlier at Harlem's Lafayette Theatre, *The Chip Woman's Fortune* appeared at the Frazee Theatre on Broadway on May 15, 1923.

Set in the home of a black family, the play focuses on the character of the "chip woman"—an old woman who wanders the streets collecting chips of wood and lumps of coal. As the first work by an African-American playwright to appear on Broadway, it was well received by critics.

WHO WROTE THE FIRST FULL-LENGTH PLAY BY AN AFRICAN-AMERICAN TO APPEAR ON BROADWAY?

Garland Anderson was working as a bellhop in a busy San Francisco hotel when he wrote his play *Appearances*. A self-educated man who read the Bible and studied psychology, Anderson had never taken a playwrighting lesson. Determined to have *Appearances* produced in New York City, Anderson traveled across the country by automobile. When he finally pulled up in front of New York's City Hall, his car was draped with a banner that read, "San Francisco to New York for New York production, 'Appearances' by Garland Anderson, The Black San Francisco Bellhop Playwright."

Once in the East, Anderson carried his play from producer to producer, invited New York's governor to attend a reading, and even went to Washington, D.C., in an attempt to get the support of President Coolidge. Anderson's efforts paid off at last; on October 13, 1925, *Appearances* opened at the Frolic Theatre on Broadway. The autobiographical story of a bellhop who believes he can accomplish anything if only he has faith, *Appearances* received little attention from critics. It lasted only twenty-three performances, but was revived in New York in 1929 and later was produced in London.

Having seen his dream come true, Anderson returned to the West Coast and in 1935 became a minister in the Seattle Center of Constructive Thinking.

Garland Anderson arriving in New York, 1925

WHO WAS THE FIRST AFRICAN-AMERICAN DANCER TO GAIN STARDOM?

When Bill "Bojangles" Robinson made his Broadway debut in *Blackbirds of 1928*, he was already fifty years old. As an orphaned youngster in Richmond, Virginia, Robinson had sold newspapers and shined shoes for pennies until he learned a few dance styles and began to earn money performing on street corners and in saloons. Around 1890 he joined a touring theater group and ended up in New York City, where critics praised his tap dancing skills in a string of Broadway shows. He was famous for his dance on a staircase and for the rhythmic, percussive sounds made by his wooden-soled shoes.

Although he was middle-aged when his career started to take off, Robinson remained in top physical condition. When he reached his sixtieth birthday he was starring in the show Hot Mikado. To celebrate, he danced sixty city blocks, from above Columbus Circle down Broadway to his theater.

It was in Hollywood that Robinson found his greatest fame. He is especially known for the four films he made with Shirley Temple, beginning with *The Little Colonel* in 1935. Although in his movie roles he was always a kindly, affable character, off-screen he was known for his hot temper. When he died in 1949, sixty thousand people filed past his coffin as it lay in state in a Harlem armory. After his funeral in the Abyssinian Baptist Church, thousands of people lined the streets as the procession wound down Broadway. It stopped on 47th Street while a band played "Give My Regards to Broadway."

WHO WAS THE FIRST AFRICAN-AMERICAN TO WIN A TONY AWARD?

Twenty-two years after she first appeared on the stage, singer Juanita Hall was honored with a Tony award for her performance as Bloody Mary in the 1949 Broadway production *South Pacific*. Her renditions of "Happy Talk" and "Bali H'ai" became hits throughout the country.

Hall, born in 1901, studied at the Juilliard School of Music and made her stage debut in 1928 in the chorus of *Show Boat*. For the next several years she was a soloist and an assistant director with the Hall Johnson Choir and in 1935 formed her own singing group, the Juanita Hall Choir. She gained increasing renown as a choral conductor, and at the 1939 World's Fair in New York City she led a church choir of 300 voices.

In the 1940s Hall played a number of musical and dramatic roles on stage, becoming a leading African-American star on Broadway. After her success in *South Pacific*, she appeared with Diahann Carroll in the 1954 production of *House of Flowers*, and later performed in nightclubs and concerts and on television. She died in 1968.

WHEN DID THE FIRST AFRICAN-AMERICAN DANCER PERFORM ON THE STAGE OF THE MET?

When Janet Collins danced in a 1951 performance of *Aida* at the Metropolitan Opera House in New York City, she became the first African-

Bill "Bojangles" Robinson

American artist to appear on that stage. Collins, born in 1923 and educated in Los Angeles, moved to New York City to pursue a career in dance. She studied and performed in California before making her New York City debut in 1949. A year later she appeared in the Cole Porter musical *Out of*

This World, dancing the role of "Night." After seeing her performance, one critic called Collins a "golden dancing girl."

The country's first African-American prima ballerina, Collins danced with the Metropolitan Opera Ballet for four years, appearing in *Carmen, La Gioconda*, and *Samson and Delilah*. During her career she taught at the School of American Ballet, performed in concerts, choreographed, and appeared on television.

WHO WAS THE FIRST AFRICAN-AMERICAN WOMAN PLAYWRIGHT TO WIN AN OBIE?

Alice Childress, born in 1920 in Charleston, South Carolina, came to live in New York City's Harlem when she was five years old. She attended city schools but had to drop out after her third year in high school when both her mother and her grandmother died.

Continuing her education by reading books from the public library, Childress worked at a number of jobs while establishing herself as an actress and writer. She made her acting debut in 1940 in the play *On Striver's Row*. In the early 1940s she helped found the American Negro Theater and participated in the organization as an actress and a director.

Two plays written by Childress, *Just a Little Simple*, 1950, and *Gold Through the Trees*, 1952, were the first by a black woman to be professionally produced on the American stage. A production of her play *Trouble in Mind* won Childress an Obie in 1955, making her the first African-American woman to receive this award for the best off-Broadway play. Throughout her career she wrote four novels and more than a dozen plays. Her novel about teenage drug addiction, *A Hero Ain't Nothin' but a Sandwich*, was made into a 1977 movie starring Cicely Tyson.

WHO WAS THE FIRST AFRICAN-AMERICAN TO BE A PRINCIPAL DANCER IN AN AMERICAN BALLET COMPANY?

When Arthur Mitchell graduated from the High School of Performing Arts in New York City in the early 1950s, he won a dance award and a scholarship to study at the School of American Ballet. In 1955 Mitchell made his debut with the New York City Ballet, performing in *Western Symphony*. Rising to the position of premier danseur with the company, he danced in all of the major ballets in its repertoire, including *Midsummer Night's Dream, The Nutcracker, Bugaku, Agon*, and *Arcade*, but he remained the only African-American dancer with the City Ballet until 1970.

The famous choreographer George Balanchine created the pas de deux from *Agon* especially for Mitchell and the white ballerina Diana Adams. Although Mitchell danced this role with white partners throughout the world, he could not perform it on commercial television in the United States before 1965 because Southern states refused to carry it.

Mitchell left the New York City Ballet in 1966 to appear in several Broadway shows and to direct a dance company. After the assassination of Dr. Martin Luther King, Jr., in 1968, Mitchell returned to Harlem determined to provide opportunities in dance for the children there. A year later he formed his own ballet school and company for African-American dancers, the Dance Theatre of Harlem.

WHAT WAS THE FIRST PLAY WRITTEN BY AN AFRICAN-AMERICAN WOMAN TO BE PRODUCED ON BROADWAY?

Lorraine Hansberry was born in Chicago in 1930, studied art and stage design at the University of Wisconsin, and moved to New York City in 1950. Having developed a love of the theater at school, she began writing plays, as well as poetry and short stories.

Hansberry's drama, *A Raisin in the Sun*, opened at New York's Ethel Barrymore Theater in March 1959, and starred Sidney Poitier, Ruby Dee, and Claudia McNeil. It was directed by Lloyd Richards, who later became dean of the Yale University School of Drama. The play, about a black family trying to solve its conflicts while seeking to leave a Chicago ghetto, had a highly successful run of nineteen months and was made into a movie.

This notable achievement was crowned with another when *A Raisin in the Sun* received the New York Drama Critics Circle Award as best play of the 1958-59 season, making Hansberry the first African-American woman playwright to receive this award. Soon she had another play, *The Sign in Sidney Brustein's Window*, on Broadway and was at work on her autobiography, *To Be Young, Gifted, and Black*. Sadly, Hansberry died of cancer in 1965 but her husband, Robert Nemiroff, completed and published her book.

WHO WAS THE FIRST AFRICAN-AMERICAN TO CHOREOGRAPH FOR THE MET?

Katherine Dunham, a choreographer and dancer whose company had performed throughout the world, was asked by the Metropolitan Opera to choreograph its new production of *Aida* for the 1963-64 season. It was the first time the Met had commissioned an African-American to choreograph dances for one of its operas.

Dunham's interest in dance began when she was a high school student in her hometown of Joliet, Illinois, where she was born in 1910. As an anthropology major at the University of Chicago, she won a scholarship that allowed her to study dance rituals, rhythms, and movements in

Martinique, Trinidad, Jamaica, and, particularly, in Haiti. Returning home with a collection of authentic West Indian dance forms, Dunham began performing and directing dance companies in Chicago and New York.

In the late 1940s she and her troupe of dancers performed in the all-black Broadway musical *Cabin in the Sky*, and she choreographed and appeared in several films. She opened the Dunham School of Dance in 1941, influencing future generations of dancers. Throughout her impressive career, Dunham received many awards and honors, and some of her works are still being performed today.

WHO WAS THE FIRST AFRICAN-AMERICAN PRESIDENT OF ACTORS' EQUITY?

Frederick Douglas O'Neal was born in 1905 in a small Mississippi town and named for the great nineteenth century statesman, Frederick Douglass. After his father, who was a teacher and a merchant, died in 1919, the O'Neal family moved to St. Louis, Missouri. It was there that the twenty-two-year-old aspiring actor made his professional stage debut. He and his friends organized an African-American theater group called the Aldridge Players, after the black Shakespearean actor, Ira Aldridge.

O'Neal went to New York City in 1936 to study acting. Four years later he helped found the American Negro Theater, an organization of African-American actors, playwrights, and producers, and starred in several of its productions. A tall, soft-spoken man, O'Neil made his Broadway debut in 1944 in *Anna Lucasta*; his striking performance earned him several awards. His other stage appearances included *House of Flowers* and *Lost in the Stars*, and he was featured in such films as *Pinky*, *No Way Out*, and *Something of Value*.

From 1964 to 1973, O'Neal was president of the Actors' Equity Association, an actor's union. A recipient of several honorary degrees and numerous awards, he died in 1992 at the age of eighty-six.

WHO WAS THE FIRST AFRICAN-AMERICAN ACTRESS TO PLAY MAJOR ROLES AT THE AMERICAN SHAKESPEARE FESTIVAL?

Ruby Dee, born Ruby Ann Wallace in 1923 in Cleveland, Ohio, graduated from New York City's Hunter College and studied acting at the American Negro Theater in Harlem. She began her stage career in the 1940s, and her first movie role was in the 1950 film, *The Jackie Robinson Story*, in which she played Robinson's wife. In 1959 she was acclaimed for her performance as Ruth in the Lorraine Hansberry play, *A Raisin in the Sun*, and later repeated the role in the movie version.

Ruby Dee

In 1965, at the American Shakespeare Festival in Stratford, Connecticut, Dee became the first African-American actress to play major classical roles, portraying Kate in *The Taming of the Shrew* and Cordelia in *King Lear*. She appeared in the stage and film versions of *Purlie Victorious*, written by her husband, Ossie Davis, and played Lena in the 1971 production of Athol Fugard's *Boesman and Lena*, winning an Obie award for her performance.

This talented actress has worked on many stage, film, and television projects with Ossie Davis, and has been a writer, poet, and civil rights activist. She appeared in the Spike Lee films *Do the Right Thing* and *Jungle Fever*, and in 1991 won an Emmy award for her role in *Decoration Day*, a Hallmark Hall of Fame television presentation.

WHAT WAS THE FIRST AFRICAN-AMERICAN BALLET COMPANY TO BE PERMANENTLY ESTABLISHED?

When Dr. Martin Luther King, Jr., was assassinated in 1968, Arthur Mitchell felt he had to do something positive in response. He made a decision to open a school in New York's Harlem where he could introduce young people to the beauty and discipline of dance. Thirteen years earlier, Mitchell had made his debut with the New York City Ballet; he was the first African-American principal dancer in a ballet company.

Mitchell's new organization, the Dance Theatre of Harlem, began as a small ballet school in the basement of a Harlem church and quickly grew to accommodate more than 400 students. The professional dance company made its debut in 1971 and continued to be enthusiastically received by audiences and critics alike. After its first major New York City season in 1974, the company danced all over the world, giving command performances for royalty and heads of state. It appeared at the White House and at the Kennedy Center for the Performing Arts in Washington, D.C.

In September 1992 the Dance Theatre of Harlem became the first multiracial performing arts group to visit South Africa. The dancers, including two who had emigrated from South Africa, appeared in a formerly whites-only theater in Johannesburg and performed and taught in neighboring black townships.

WHO WAS THE FIRST AFRICAN-AMERICAN PLAYWRIGHT TO WIN A PULITZER PRIZE FOR DRAMA?

An actor, director, and playwright, Charles Gordone was born in Cleveland in 1925 and educated in California. He then went to New York City, where he supported himself as a waiter in a Greenwich Village saloon and became involved in the theater community. His acting credits included roles in *Of Mice and Men*, for which he won a 1953 Obie award for Best Actor, and *The Blacks*. He directed about twenty-five plays, and taught at the New School for Social Research and in New Jersey prisons.

In 1970 Gordone was awarded the Pulitzer Prize for his play *No Place to be Somebody*. He was the first African-American playwright to win the

Pulitzer. His play, produced off-Broadway, was set in a bar much like the one in which he had worked, and dealt with the problems of a black bar owner and his customers.

WHO LED THE FIRST AMERICAN MODERN DANCE COMPANY TO PERFORM IN RUSSIA?

In 1970 the Alvin Ailey American Dance Theatre performed in Russia to enraptured audiences, receiving a twenty-three-minute ovation in Leningrad. This illustrious dance company had been formed twelve years earlier by dancer Alvin Ailey, who had always encouraged the work of African-American choreographers and composers, used the tunes and rhythms of spirituals and work songs, and provided a showcase for many talented black dancers. Under the auspices of the U.S. State Department, the company began its international travels in 1962 with a thirteen-week tour of Australia and the Far East, and toured widely in Europe, Africa, Asia, and the United States.

Alvin Ailey was born in the tiny farming town of Rogers, Texas, in 1931 and moved to Los Angeles while still in high school. There he saw a performance of the Katherine Dunham Company and was captivated. While a student at the University of California at Los Angeles, Ailey joined the Lester Horton Dance Theatre as a member of the stage crew. In 1953 he made his debut as a dancer and the following year he appeared in the movie *Carmen Jones* and on Broadway in *House of Flowers*.

Ailey moved to New York City to continue his dance training and performed in movies and on stage throughout the 1950s. He and his dance company won many honors, and in 1985 Ailey was named Distinguished Professor at City College of New York, the first choreographer to receive this honor. After Ailey's death from a rare blood disease in 1989, more than 4,000 devoted admirers attended his memorial service at the Cathedral of St. John the Divine.

VISUAL ARTS

WHO WAS THE FIRST KNOWN AFRICAN-AMERICAN PAINTER?

Although he was a slave, Scipio Moorhead, who was owned by the Reverend John Moorhead of Boston, was allowed the freedom to study painting. He is believed to be the first African-American in colonial America to receive formal training as an artist. Moorhead, who painted in the 1770s, was the object of a 1773 poem by the black poet Phillis Wheatley, "To S.M., a Young African Painter, on Seeing His Works."

There are no signed paintings by Moorhead in existence today, but he is known to have produced two works, *Aurora* and *Damon and Pythias*.

WHO WAS THE FIRST BLACK ARTIST KNOWN TO HAVE PAINTED A PORTRAIT OF ANOTHER AFRICAN-AMERICAN?

The Reverend G. W. Hobbs, a Methodist minister in Baltimore, was the official artist of the Methodist Episcopal Church in the late 18th century. His pastel portrait of Richard Allen, the co-founder and first bishop of the African Methodist Episcopal Church, was completed in 1785. It was the first known portrait of an African-American painted by a black artist.

WHO WAS THE FIRST AFRICAN-AMERICAN ARTIST TO BE RECOGNIZED AS A PORTRAIT PAINTER?

Although no one knows for sure if Joshua Johnston was a slave, it is certain that he was able to develop his artistic talent and pursue a career as a portrait painter. In 1798 he even advertised his services in a Baltimore newspaper. He claimed in his ad to be self-taught, but some art experts believe that Johnston studied with another portrait painter of the time, Charles Peale Polk, since their styles are similar.

Most of Johnston's subjects are white aristocrats, although one painting, *Portrait of a Cleric*, shows an African-American man. None of his paintings are signed, but all share certain characteristics: the faces are in three-quarter position with eyes looking forward and lips tightly compressed. He often seated his subjects on chairs studded with brass tacks, leading some to call him the "brass tack" artist. More than eighty works have been attributed to this early painter.

WHO WAS THE FIRST AFRICAN-AMERICAN PAINTER OF MURALS?

The first African-American artist to be recognized abroad, Robert Scott Duncanson was born in upstate New York in 1821 and sent to school in Canada. Duncanson moved with his mother to a town outside of Cincinnati, Ohio, in 1841 and a year later he exhibited his first paintings.

In 1848 Duncanson was hired by a wealthy Cincinnati political leader, Nicholas Longworth, to paint a series of murals for his new mansion. Completed over a two-year period, the murals consisted of eight poetic compositions in the tradition of French landscape painting. This accomplishment made Duncanson the first African-American muralist.

In 1853 the local Freedman's Aid Society sponsored Duncanson on a trip to Europe, enabling him to visit art museums in several countries. When he returned to Cincinnati he opened a photography studio but soon turned to painting full time. He became known as one of the country's leading landscape painters, and his fame spread beyond America. In the 1860s a London journal wrote that he was one of the best landscape painters in the world. But in 1872, at the top of his powers and fame, he experienced a mental breakdown and died in a Detroit insane asylum.

WHO WAS THE FIRST PROFESSIONAL AFRICAN-AMERICAN ARTIST IN CALIFORNIA?

Grafton Tyler Brown was born in Harrisburg, Pennsylvania, in 1841 and in the 1850s moved to San Francisco, where he lived in a boardinghouse called the What Cheer House and worked as a draftsman and a lithographer. In 1867 he founded his own business and became widely known for his lithographs of California towns and cities, which included a number of scenes of San Francisco. Brown is thought to have been the first African-American to work as a professional artist in California.

In 1882 Brown journeyed to Victoria, British Columbia, and joined a group that was conducting a geological survey of sections of Canada, later producing many detailed watercolors of places he had visited. He became a popular realistic painter in Victoria as well as in Portland, Oregon, producing works that evinced strong feelings for natural settings. His painting from the mid-80s, *Grand Canyon of the Yellowstone from Hayden Point*, may have been one of his last.

In the 1890s he traveled eastward, settling in St. Paul, Minnesota, and working for part of that time as a draftsman for the U.S. Army Engineers. His career as a painter apparently ended years earlier, since there is no evidence of his work in the 1900s. Brown died in a state hospital in St. Paul in 1918.

WHO WAS THE FIRST PROFESSIONAL
AFRICAN-AMERICAN SCULPTOR?

The daughter of a Chippewa Indian woman and an African-American man, Edmonia Lewis was born about 1843 near Albany, New York. Her parents died when she was young, and she went to live with her mother's sisters in Niagara Falls. The Chippewas named her Wildfire, and taught her to make baskets and embroidered moccasins.

Her brother, a California gold miner, arranged for her to enter Oberlin College in Ohio, where she stayed for two years. Moving to Boston, Lewis studied with a local sculptor and began selling her work. She opened her own studio, where she created a number of pieces, including a bust of Colonel Robert Gould Shaw, the commander of a black Civil War regiment from Massachusetts, and medallion portraits of the abolitionists John Brown and William Lloyd Garrison.

In 1865 Lewis sailed for Europe, settling in Rome to continue her studies. Influenced by the Greco-Roman sculpture she saw there, she began creating works in a neoclassical style. By the time she returned to the United States in 1874, her patrons included distinguished families in this country and abroad. She was given receptions in Philadelphia and Boston and was praised by prominent art critics. But her popularity dwindled and she eventually vanished from the art world. Lewis's surviving works include busts of Abraham Lincoln and the poet Henry Wadsworth Longfellow.

WHO WAS THE FIRST AFRICAN-AMERICAN
TO WIN A NATIONAL ART AWARD?

Edward Mitchell Bannister was born in 1828 in St. Andrews, a small seaport in New Brunswick, Canada, his mother's home. Bannister's father, who was from Barbados, died when the boy was two years old. His mother, who lived only twelve years longer, encouraged her son's interest in art. By the age of twenty, Bannister had settled in Boston, where he studied painting and supported himself as a photographer's assistant and as a barber.

In 1855 Bannister painted his first commissioned work, entitled *The Ship Outward Bound*, and his talents gained growing recognition in artistic circles. After the Civil War, Bannister and his wife, a successful hairdresser and wigmaker, moved to Providence, Rhode Island, where he achieved a wide reputation as a painter of pastoral landscapes. He became increasingly involved in the cultural life of the city and was one of the founders of the Providence Art Club, which evolved into the distinguished Rhode Island School of Design.

The high point of Bannister's career came in 1876 when his landscape, *Under the Oaks*, was awarded a medal at the Centennial Exhibition in Philadelphia, making him the first African-American to win a national art award. Upon learning the race of the artist, the judges attempted to revoke his prize, but the white competitors prevented them from doing it. After Bannister's death in 1901, the Providence Art Club honored him with a memorial exhibit of more than 100 of his paintings.

WHO WAS THE FIRST AFRICAN-AMERICAN ARTIST TO GAIN INTERNATIONAL FAME?

Henry Ossawa Tanner was born in Pittsburgh, Pennsylvania, in 1859, the son of a bishop of the African Methodist Episcopal Church. He started drawing when just a boy, and soon made up his mind to become an artist. He painted throughout his teens and at the age of twenty-one he enrolled in the Pennsylvania Academy of Fine Arts, where he was influenced by the famous artist, Thomas Eakins.

Tanner moved to Atlanta in 1888 and opened a small photo gallery, but closed it within a year and began teaching at Clark College. In 1891 he decided to travel abroad and sailed for Europe, settling in Paris, where he enrolled in a distinguished art school. Tanner's early paintings, *Banjo Lesson* and *The Thankful Poor*, portrayed African-American people in everyday life, but in the mid-1890s he began concentrating on religious themes. His first major religious painting was *Daniel in the Lion's Den* in 1895, followed by *The Resurrection of Lazarus* a year later.

Tanner received many honors, including membership in the National Academy of Design and the French Legion of Honor, and in 1900 he won a Medal of Honor at the Paris Exposition. He died at his home in Paris in 1937.

WHO WAS THE FIRST AFRICAN-AMERICAN MEMBER OF THE AMERICAN INSTITUTE OF ARCHITECTS?

A native of Los Angeles, Paul R. Williams was born in 1895 on downtown Olvera Street, where his parents owned a grocery store. At the age of twenty, Williams took a job with a prominent architect in nearby Pasadena and went on to study architecture at the University of Southern California, opening his own practice when he was twenty-three.

Known as the "architect to the stars," Williams designed hundreds of graceful, comfortable houses in such areas as Beverly Hills and Bel Air, including homes for entertainers like Cary Grant, Frank Sinatra, Lucille Ball, and Danny Thomas. He designed the Los Angeles County Courthouse, the Tudor mansion in Pasadena used in the "Batman" television series, and a number of landmark buildings in the African-American communities of Los Angeles, including the First African Methodist Episcopal Church, the Second Baptist Church, and the Golden State Mutual Life Building. Williams died in 1980 at the age of eighty-five.

WHO WAS THE FIRST AFRICAN-AMERICAN ARTIST TO HAVE A ONE-MAN SHOW AT THE MUSEUM OF MODERN ART?

Born around 1882 in Nashville, Tennessee, William Edmondson never received formal training as an artist. He worked at a number of menial jobs and for twenty-five years was an orderly at a Baptist hospital in Nashville. After his retirement, he lived alone, taking part-time work and selling his home-grown vegetables.

In 1934 Edmondson experienced a religious conversion and said that God had commanded him to find a mallet and chisel and create tombstones. Following his vision, he made his first works from pieces of limestone that had been dumped near his house. He began carving tombstones for members of Nashville's African-American community, and progressed to making rough limestone figures—birds, rabbits, squirrels, owls, preachers, angels, and brides.

His carvings were discovered by a magazine photographer who took pictures of Edmondson and his work and showed them to the director of the Museum of Modern Art in New York City. In 1937 Edmondson was given a solo exhibition, the first at that museum for an African-American artist. Edmondson was involved for a number of years with the Federal Artist's Project of the Works Progress Administration, a government program to support artists. Then, in 1947, he was stricken with cancer, and gradually grew too ill to work. He died in 1951 and was buried in an unmarked grave.

WHO WAS THE FIRST AFRICAN-AMERICAN WOMAN CARTOONIST TO CREATE NATIONALLY SYNDICATED COMIC STRIPS?

Inspired by her artist father, Jackie Ormes studied art as a teenager, and when she was about twenty years old joined the staff of the *Pittsburgh Courier*. She started as a feature writer but also contributed occasional drawings, eventually developing a comic strip called "Torchy Brown in Dixie to Harlem," which made its debut in the newspaper on May 1, 1937. The strip was about a young woman from the South who settles in New York City's Harlem intending to become an entertainer but ending up as a newspaper reporter.

In the early 1940s Ormes moved to Chicago, studying at the Art Institute and working for the Chicago Defender. She created another strip, "Patty Jo 'n' Ginger," and used her cartoons to address segregation and other forms of inequality. Her strips were syndicated to African-American newspapers around the country.

WHO WAS THE FIRST AFRICAN-AMERICAN ART HISTORIAN?

When James A. Porter's book, *Modern Negro Art*, appeared in 1943, it was the first comprehensive study of African-American art to be published. Porter, born in Baltimore in 1905, graduated from Howard University in 1927 and went to New York to study at Columbia University and the Art Students League. He was awarded a grant to travel to several countries, where he studied collections of African art and crafts, and he later earned a master's degree in art history from New York University.

Porter returned to Howard University as an art instructor and eventually was named chairman of the school's art department, a position he held until his death in 1971. During his tenure at Howard, Porter took several trips abroad to study art and to create his own paintings, including many that reflected his impressions of West Africa, Haiti, and Cuba. In 1966 Porter was honored by President Johnson as "one of America's most outstanding men of the arts."

WHO WAS THE FIRST AFRICAN-AMERICAN TO CREATE A BUST FOR THE HALL OF FAME?

In 1946, Richmond Barthé was commissioned to produce a bust of Booker T. Washington for the New York University Hall of Fame. This piece was only one example of a wide body of work by the sculptor, whose creations reflect both African-American and white themes. Barthé's sculptures range from a graceful African dancer and busts of the actors Paul Robeson and Sir Laurence Olivier to an American eagle that is displayed in front of the Social Security Building in Washington, D.C.

Born in 1901 in Bay St. Louis, Mississippi, Barthé studied at the Art Institute of Chicago, where he concentrated on painting until being persuaded by a teacher to try modeling in clay. He eventually chose to work in metal. He began showing his work in the 1930s in New York City, where he had exhibits at the Whitney Museum and the 1939 World's Fair. Throughout his long career, Barthé's work was popular with museums and private collectors. He died at his home in Pasadena, California, at the age of eighty-eight.

WHO WAS THE FIRST AFRICAN-AMERICAN PHOTOGRAPHER TO WIN A GUGGENHEIM?

Roy DeCarava, born in New York City in 1919, was awarded the prestigious Guggenheim Fellowship in 1952, the first African-American photographer to be so honored. DeCarava had started out pursuing a career as a painter, studying at Cooper Union and the Harlem Art Center. In the mid-1940s he began taking photographs to document his ideas for paintings, and in 1958 he gave up painting altogether and became a full-time photographer.

DeCarava's photographs have been featured in a number of publications and exhibited in many museums and galleries, including the Metropolitan Museum of Art, the Museum of Modern Art, and the Studio Museum of Harlem. *The Sweet Flypaper of Life*, a book combining DeCarava's black-and-white photographs of Harlem residents with a text by Langston Hughes, was first published in 1955 and has been reprinted twice. He worked as a photographer for *Sports Illustrated* magazine and taught at Hunter College.

WHO WAS THE FIRST FULL-TIME PHOTOGRAPHER OF AFRICAN-AMERICAN THEATER?

Bert Andrews, who was born in 1929 in Chicago and grew up in New York City's Harlem, started out as a songwriter, singer, and dancer. But his career path changed after he studied photography while in the Army in the early 1950s, and he later served as an apprentice to Chuck Stewart, a well-known photographer of jazz musicians. Andrews soon began chronicling African-American theater, photographing such productions as *A Soldier's Play*, *Ma Rainey's Black Bottom*, and *The Blood Knot*.

In 1985 Andrews saw thirty years of his work go up in smoke when a devastating fire struck his studio, destroying more than 40,000 prints and 100,000 negatives. With the help of the theater community, Andrews was able to reassemble much of his collection, and about 3,000 of his photographs were housed in Manhattan at the Schomburg Center for Research in Black Culture. Some of the work is reproduced in his book, *In the Shadow of the Great White Way*, which was published in 1989, four years before Andrews's death at the age of sixty-three.

WHO WAS THE FIRST AFRICAN-AMERICAN WOMAN TO BECOME A LICENSED ARCHITECT?

Norma Sklarek was born in Harlem and raised in the Crown Heights section of Brooklyn. Her parents encouraged their only child to enter a profession, and she decided to attend the School of Architecture at Colum-

Norma Sklarek and her U.S. Embassy building, Tokyo

bia University. She graduated in 1950, a time when few women were entering the field. She became a licensed architect in New York in 1954 and a year later was hired by Skidmore, Owings & Merrill, one of the largest architectural firms in the United States.

Relocating to Los Angeles, Sklarek was licensed in California in 1962. She worked for twenty years for another large firm, Gruen Associates, where she rose to the position of director of architecture and was involved in such projects as the U.S. Embassy in Tokyo and the Pacific Design Center in West Hollywood.

In 1980 Sklarek went to Welton Becket Associates, where she was the firm's first woman vice president and served as project director of Terminal One at Los Angeles International Airport. That same year she became the first African-American woman to be made a fellow of the American Institute of Architects.

WHO WAS THE FIRST AFRICAN-AMERICAN MAN TO WIN A PULITZER PRIZE?

Moneta Sleet, Jr., a staff photographer for *Ebony* magazine, was awarded a Pulitzer Prize in 1969 for his moving photograph of Coretta Scott King consoling her daughter at the funeral of Dr. Martin Luther King, Jr. Born in Kentucky in 1926, Sleet took his first pictures with a camera his parents gave him. He received a degree in business from Kentucky State University in 1947 and then took a six-month course in photography in New York City. After teaching photography at Maryland State College for a year he returned to New York to earn a master's in journalism from New York University.

Sleet reported on sports for a short time for the *Amsterdam News* and in 1950 began his career as a professional photographer for *Our World* magazine. Five years later he became staff photographer for the Johnson Publishing Company, publisher of *Ebony* and *Jet* magazines. He had many one-man shows in such venues as the City Art Museum of St. Louis and the New York Public Library, and participated in a number of group shows.

Sleet has photographed the most important events of African-American life, including the civil rights march from Selma to Montgomery, Alabama, and the 1963 March on Washington. He accompanied Dr. King when he went to Norway in 1964 to accept the Nobel peace prize, and he has traveled to Africa many times to photograph important leaders.

WHO WAS THE FIRST ARTIST TO WIN THE NAACP'S SPINGARN MEDAL?

Jacob Lawrence was honored as an artist, teacher, and humanitarian when the NAACP awarded him the Spingarn Medal in 1970 for his outstanding achievements. Throughout his lengthy artistic career, Lawrence concentrated on depicting the history and struggles of African-Americans.

Born in 1917 in Atlantic City, New Jersey, Lawrence moved to New York City's Harlem in 1930, eventually studying at the Harlem Art Workshops

Moneta Sleet, Jr.

of the Works Progress Administration. He was not quite twenty-one years old when his series of paintings of the Haitian general, Toussaint L'Ouver-ture, was shown in an exhibit of African-American artists at the Baltimore Museum of Art. This impressive work was followed by a series of portraits of Frederick Douglass and Harriet Tubman. Lawrence was only twenty-three when he completed the sixty-panel set of narrative paintings entitled *Migration of the Negro*. The series is a moving portrayal of the migration of hundreds of thousands of African-Americans from the rural South to the North after World War I.

In the 1940s Lawrence was given his first major solo exhibition at the Museum of Modern Art in New York City and became the most celebrated African-American painter in the country. In 1974 the Whitney Museum of American Art in New York held a major retrospective of his work and in 1983 he was elected to the American Academy of Arts and Letters. He taught at a number of schools and his works have been exhibited in some of the most distinguished galleries, museums, and universities in the country.

WHO WAS THE FIRST AFRICAN-AMERICAN ARTIST TO HAVE A SOLO EXHIBITION AT THE BOSTON MUSEUM OF FINE ARTS?

Known for her brilliant, decorative paintings of Haitian and African subjects, Lois Mailou Jones was a 1927 graduate of the Boston Museum School of Fine Arts, a prestigious art school in the city of her birth. At first she pursued a career as a textile designer, but soon turned to painting. She joined the art department of Palmer Memorial Institute in North Carolina, one of the country's first prep schools for African-American students, and two years later, in 1930, became a teacher of watercolor and design at Howard University. She was to remain a member of the Howard faculty for forty-seven years.

Jones's early work was influenced by African themes. After studies in France, she concentrated more on French landscapes, cityscapes, and figures. In 1953 Jones married a Haitian artist, and her travels in Haiti led to a gradual transformation of her paintings; she developed a bright, decorative, two-dimensional style. A visit in 1969 to eleven African countries made a further impression on her work, inspiring her to once again explore African motifs.

In 1973 the Boston Museum of Fine Arts mounted a solo exhibition of Jones's paintings. She was the first African-American artist to be so honored by the museum, a notable achievement for the time.

WHO WAS THE FIRST AFRICAN-AMERICAN WOMAN CARTOONIST SYNDICATED IN MAINSTREAM NEWSPAPERS?

Barbara Brandon, born in Brooklyn in 1958, was exposed to cartoon art early in her childhood; her father, Brumsic Brandon, Jr., was the creator of "Luther," a comic strip about an inner-city child that was syndicated na-

313

Lois Mailou Jones

tionally from 1968 to the mid-80s. As a youngster, Brandon assisted her father by filling in colors and drawing borders on his strips.

Brandon studied illustration at Syracuse University and then worked for the magazine, *Elàn*, for which she created her comic strip, "Where I'm Coming From." But the magazine folded before the strip appeared, and

Barbara Brandon

she went on to write for *Essence* magazine for five years. "Where I'm Coming From" was reborn in 1989 when it began appearing in the *Detroit Free Press*. Featuring the lives and thoughts of nine African-American women, the weekly strip was picked up by Universal Press Syndicate in 1990 and three years later it was appearing in nearly one hundred newspapers nationwide. A collection of the strips was published in 1993 in a book also titled *Where I'm Coming From*.

WHAT SCULPTOR CREATED THE FIRST MONUMENT COMMEMORATING THE BUFFALO SOLDIERS?

A monument in honor of the Buffalo Soldiers, the first African-American units commissioned in the regular army, was dedicated in July 1992 at Fort Leavenworth, Kansas. The monument was created by Eddie Dixon, an African-American sculptor from Lubbock, Texas. Dixon spent two and one-half years creating the monument, a twelve-foot bronze statue of a Buffalo Soldier reining in his horse.

Born in San Francisco in 1948, Dixon studied computer science, finance, medical statistics, and engineering, and held a variety of jobs. Wanting to learn more about African-American history, he began researching the sto-

Buffalo Soldier Monument, Fort Leavenworth, Kansas

ries of black cowboys in the Southwest. He decided to try to express this history in art, and started sculpting figures in wax using a stick and a butter knife. Encouraged by a Texas teacher named Verta Todd, who taught him discipline, he eventually sold his first piece, a statue of an Iberian warrior.

Reflecting on what would be the highest achievement for an artist, Dixon resolved to aim for the Smithsonian Institution. He reached his goal in the fall of 1992 when the Smithsonian's Air and Space Museum acquired his head of Eugene Jacques Bullard, the only African-American fighter pilot in World War I.

PICTURE CREDITS

Alphabetically, in the chapters in which they appear

BUSINESS

Delano, Lewis E., Courtesy Delano E. Lewis
Freeman, Capt. Louis L., Courtesy Capt. Louis L. Freeman
Norwood, Capt. William R., Courtesy Capt. William R. Norwood

EDUCATION

Berry, Mary Francis, Courtesy Mary Francis Berry
Green, Ernest G., Courtesy Ernest G. Green
Locke, Alain, State Historical Society of Wisconsin
Twilight, Alexander, Orleans County Historical Society, Inc., Orleans, Vt.

ENTERTAINMENT

Baker, Josephine, Wisconsin Center for Film and Theater Research
Carmen Jones, still from The Museum of Modern Art, Film Stills Archives
Cole, Nat King, Wisconsin Center for Film and Theater Research
Wade, Adam, by Emil Romano, CBS

FILM

Moten, Etta, Billy Rose Theater Collection, The New York Public Library
   for the Performing Arts, Astor, Lenox and Tilden Foundations
Perry, Lincoln Theodore (Stepin Fetchit), Wisconsin Center for Film and
   Theater Research
Stills from *Bright Road, Hallelujah!, Hearts in Dixie*, The Museum of Modern
   Art, Film Stills Archives

HISTORY

Allensworth, Col. Allen, California Afro-American Museum, Miriam Mat-
   thews Collection
Bluford, Guion S., Courtesy NASA
Coleman, Bessie, California Afro-American Museum, Miriam Matthews
   Collection
Jemison, Mae, Courtesy NASA
Thomas, Franklin A., Courtesy The Ford Foundation
Tubman, Harriet, Moorland-Spingarn Research Center, Howard University

JOURNALISM

Rowan, Carl, by Scott McLay
Stewart, Pearl, by Gordon Clark
Hunter-Gault, Charlayne, Courtesy The McNeil/Lehrer Newshour

LAW & GOVERNMENT

Barrett, Jacquelyn, Courtesy Jacquelyn Barrett
Blackwell, Unita, by Brian Lanker
Carter, Pamela, by Sid Rust
Dellums, Ronald V., Courtesy Ronald V. Dellums
Dinkins, David, by Joan Vitale Strong
Espy, Mike, Courtesy Mike Espy

319

Jones, Elaine R., by AsmanPhoto
Moseley-Braun, Carol, Courtesy Carol Moseley-Braun
Rush, Bobby L., Courtesy Bobby L. Rush
Sears-Collins, Leah, Courtesy Leah Sears-Collins
Ward, Benjamin, Courtesy Benjamin Ward
Wilder, L. Douglas, Courtesy L. Douglas Wilder
Williams, Willie L., Courtesy Willie L. Williams

LITERATURE

Dove, Rita, by Fred Viebahn
Lorde, Audre, by Dagmar Schullz
Wright, Richard, Courtesy Harper & Row

MILITARY

Brown, Wesley A., U.S. Naval Institute
Buffalo Soldier Monument: Jay Carey, photo; Eddie Dixon, sculptor; Buffalo Soldier Monument Committee
Davis, Brig. Gen. Benjamin O., Jr., Photographs and Prints Division, Schomburg Center for Research in Black Culture, The New York Public Library, Astor, Lenox and Tilden Foundations
Delaney, Martin, Moorland-Spingarn Research Center, Howard University
Gravely, Samuel L., Jr., U.S. Naval Institute
Harris, Brig. Gen. Marcelite, Courtesy Marcelite Harris
Smalls, Robert, State Historical Society of Wisconsin

MUSIC

Anderson, Marian, Moorland-Spingarn Research Center, Howard University
Cole, Robert, and J. Rosamond Johnson, The Billy Rose Collection, The New York Public Library for the Performing Arts, Astor, Lenox and Tilden Foundations
Europe, James Reese; Garner, Erroll; Gillespie, John Birks "Dizzy"; Hardin, Lil: Institute of Jazz Studies, Rutgers University
Jackson, Mahalia, Moorland-Spingarn Research Center, Howard University
Johnson, James P., Institute of Jazz Studies, Rutgers University
McFerrin, Robert, Sr., Metropolitan Opera Archives
Pratt, Awadagin, by Cynthia Johnson
Pride, Charley, Courtesy Charley Pride
Smith, Mamie, Wisconsin Center for Film and Theater Research
Still, William Grant, California Afro-American Museum, Miriam Matthews Collection

RELIGION

Allen, Richard, Moorland-Spingarn Research Center, Howard University
Harris, Bishop Barbara C., (c) Reginald Jackson
Streets, Rev. Frederick J., by Michael Marsland, Courtesy Yale University
Turner, Bishop Henry McNeal, Moorland-Spingarn Research Center, Howard University

SCIENCE & MEDICINE

Carson, Dr. Benjamin S., Courtesy Dr. Benjamin S. Carson
Ford, Dr. Justina, Black American West Museum, Paul W. Stewart Collection
Invention Drawings, U.S. Patent Office
Washington, Warren M., Courtesy NCAR

SPORTS

Ashe, Arthur, by Jeanne Moutoussamy Ashe
Brown, Dewey, Courtesy J. Peter Martin
Chamberlain, Wilton "Wilt", Courtesy Naismith Memorial, Basketball Hall of Fame
Foster, Andrew "Rube", Negro Leagues Baseball Museum
Murphy, Isaac "Ike", (c)1890 Churchill Downs, Inc./Kinetic Corp.
O'Neil, John "Buck", Negro Leagues Baseball Museum
Paige, Leroy "Satchel", Negro Leagues Baseball Museum
Pickett, Bill, Black American West Museum, Paul W. Stewart Collection
Pollard, Frederick Douglas "Fritz", Courtesy Brown University
Walker, Moses Fleetwood, Negro Leagues Baseball Museum

THEATER

Aldridge, Ira, Photographs and Prints Division, Schomburg Center for Research in Black Culture, The New York Public Library, Astor, Lenox and Tilden Foundations
Anderson, Garland, The Billy Rose Theater Collection, The New York Public Library for the Performing Arts, Astor, Lenox and Tilden Foundations
Dee, Ruby, Courtesy Dee & Davis
Gilpin, Charles, The Billy Rose Theater Collection, The New York Library for the Performing Arts, Astor, Lenox and Tilden Foundations
Robinson, Bill "Bojangles", The Billy Rose Theater Collection, The New York Public Library for the Performing Arts, Astor, Lenox and Tilden Foundations

VISUAL ARTS

Brandon, Barbara, Courtesy Barbara Brandon
Jones, Lois Mailou, by Scurlock Studio
Sleet, Moneta, by Vernon Smith
Sklarek, Norma, by Marc Schurer

SELECT BIBLIOGRAPHY

Abdul, Raoul. *Blacks in Classical Music.* New York: Dodd, Mead & Company, 1977.

Abramson, Doris E. *Negro Playwrights in the American Theatre 1925-1959.* New York: Columbia University Press, 1969.

Afro-American Artists. Edited by Theresa Dickson Cederhom. Boston Public Library, 1973.

Alexander, James I. *Blue Coats: Black Skin: The Black Experience in the New York City Police Department Since 1891.* Hicksville, New York: Exposition Press, 1978.

Alford, Sterling G. *Famous First Blacks.* New York: Vantage Press, 1974.

American Negro Short Stories. Edited by John Henrik Clarke. New York: Hill & Wang, 1966.

Asante, Molefi K., and Mark T. Mattson. *The Historical and Cultural Atlas of African Americans.* New York: MacMillan Publishing Company, 1991.

Ashe, Arthur. *A Hard Road to Glory, History of the African-American Athlete.* 3 vols. New York: Warner Books, 1988.

Balliett, Whitney. *American Musicians, 56 Portraits in Jazz.* New York and Oxford: Oxford University Press, 1986.

Benét's Reader's Encyclopedia. Third Edition. New York: Harper & Row, 1987.

Black Films & Film-Makers. Compiled by Lindsay Patterson. New York: Dodd, Mead & Company, 1975.

Black Leaders of the Nineteenth Century. Edited by Leon Litwack and August Meier. Urbana and Chicago: University of Illinois Press, 1988.

Black Leaders of the Twentieth Century. Edited by John Hope Franklin and August Meier. Urbana: University of Illinois Press, 1982.

Black Voices, Edited by Abraham Chapman. New York: New American Library, 1968.

Black Women in America, An Historical Encyclopedia. Edited by Darlene Clark Hine. Brooklyn, New York: Carlson Publishing Co., 1993.

Black Writers: A Selection of Sketches from Contemporary Authors. Detroit: Gale Research, Inc., 1989.

Blake & Martin. *Quiz Book on Black America.* Houghton Mifflin Company, 1976.

Bogle, Donald. *Blacks in American Films and Television.* New York: Garland Publishing, 1988.

Bogle, Donald. *Toms, Coons, Mulattoes, Mammies, and Bucks, An Interpretive History of Blacks in American Films.* New York: The Viking Press, 1973.

Book of Black Heroes, Great Women in the Struggle. Edited by Toyoma Igus. Orange, New Jersey: Just Us Books, Inc., 1991.

Branch, Taylor. *Parting the Waters, America in the King Years 1954-63.* New York: Simon & Schuster, 1988.

Brawley, Benjamin. *The Negro in Literature and Art*. New York: Duffield & Company, 1918.

Brown, Hallie Quinn. *Homespun Heroines and Other Women of Distinction*. New York: Oxford University Press, Shomburg Library of Nineteenth Century Black Women Writers, 1988.

Brown-Guillery, Elizabeth. *Their Place on the Stage: Black Women Playwrights* in America. New York: Greenwood Press, 1988.

Cantor, George. *Historic Black Landmarks, A Traveler's Guide*. Detroit: Visible Ink Press, a division of Gale Research, Inc., 1991.

Christopher, Maurine. *America's Black Congressmen*. New York: Thomas Y. Crowell Company, 1971.

Conyers, Charline Howard. *A Living Legend: The History of Cheyney University, 1837-1951*. Cheyney, Pennsylvania: Cheyney University Press, 1990.

Cooper, T.G., and Carole Singleton. *On Stage in America*. Bristol, Indiana: Wyndham Hall Press, 1987.

Cripps, Thomas. *Slow Fade to Black: The Negro in American Film, 1900-1942*. New York: Oxford University Press, 1977.

Dictionary of American Negro Biography, Edited by Rayford W. Logan and Michael R. Winston, New York: W.W. Norton and Company, 1982.

Drotning, Philip T. *Black Heroes in Our Nation's History*. New York: Cowles Book Company, Inc., 1969

Emory, Lynne Fauley. *Black Dance from 1619 to Today*. Princeton: Princeton Book Company, 1988.

Fletcher, Tom. *100 Years of the Negro in Show Business*. New York: Da Capo Press, 1984.

Franklin, John Hope. *An Illustrated Study of Black Americans*. New York: Time-Life Books, 1970.

Garr, Gillian G., *She's a Rebel: The History of Women in Rock & Roll*, Seattle: Seal Press, 1992.

Green, Mildred Denby. *Black Women Composers: A Genesis*. Boston: Twayne Publishers, 1983.

Greene, Robert Ewell. *Black Defenders of America, 1775-1973*. Chicago: Johnson Publishing Company, Inc., 1974.

Haber, Louis. *Black Pioneers of Science & Invention*. New York: Harcourt, Brace & World, 1970.

Handy, D. Antoinette. *Black Women in American Bands & Orchestras*. Metuchen, New Jersey: The Scarecrow Press,1981.

Harding, Vincent. *There Is A River*. New York: Harcourt Brace Jovanovich

Harrison, Daphne Duval. *Black Pearls: Blues Queens of the 1920's*. New Brunswick, New Jersey: Rutgers University Press, 1988.

Haskins, James. *Black Music in America*. New York: Harper Collins, 1987.

Haskins, James. *Outward Dreams, Black Inventors and Their Inventions*. New York: Walker Publishing Company, 1991.

Hedgepeth, Chester M. Jr. *Twentieth Century African-American Writers and Artists*. Chicago: American Library Association, 1991.

Henderson, Edwin B. *The Black Athlete: Emergence and Arrival.* New York: International Library of Negro Life and History, Publishers Company, Inc., 1968.

Hill, Dr. George H. *Ebony Images, Black Americans and Televison.* Carson, California: Daystar Publishing Company, 1986.

Hudson, Wade, and Valerie Wilson Wesley. *Book of Black Heroes From A to Z.* Orange, New Jersey: Just Us Books, 1988

Hughes, Langston, and Milton Meltzer. *Black Magic: A Pictorial History of the Negro in American Entertainment.* Englewood Cliffs, New Jersey: Prentice-Hall, Inc., 1967.

Hughes, Langston, Milton Meltzer and C. Eric Lincoln. *A Pictorial History of Black Americans.* New York: Crown Publishers, 1983.

Isaacs, Edith J.R. *The Negro in American Theatre.* New York: Theatre Arts, Inc., 1947.

Ives, Patricia Carter. *Creativity and Inventions, The Genius of Afro-Americans and Women in the United States and Their Patents.* Arlington, Virginia: Research Unlimited, 1987.

Jackson, Blyden. *The History of Afro-American Literature - Vol. 1.* Baton Rouge: Louisiana State University Press, 1989.

Jackson, Florence. *Blacks in America, 1954-1979.* New York: Franklin Watts, Inc., 1980.

Jones, LeRoi. *Blues People.* New York: William Morrow and Company, 1963.

Kane, Joseph Nathan. *Famous First Facts.* New York: The H.W. Wilson Co., 1981

Katz, Willliam Loren. *The Black West.* New York: Doubleday & Company, Inc., 1971.

Kelban, Stewart. *The Civil Rights Movement.* Minneapolis: Abdo and Daughters, 1990.

Kluger, Richard. *Simple Justice.* New York: Alfred A. Knopf, 1976.

Kranz, Rachel C. *The Biographical Dictionary of Black Americans.* New York: Facts on File, 1992.

Landay, Eileen. *Black Film Stars.* New York: Drake Publishers, Inc., 1973.

Lanker, Brian. *I Dream A World: Portraits of Black Women Who Changed America.* New York: Stewart, Tabori & Chang, 1989.

Larsen, Nella. *An Intimation of Things Distant, The Collected Fiction of Nella Larsen.* New York: Doubleday, 1992.

Leab, Daniel J. *From Sambo to Superspade, The Black Experience in Motion Pictures.* Boston: Houghton Mifflin Company, 1975.

Lee, George L. *Interesting People: Black American History Makers.* New York: Ballantine Books, 1989.

Lee, Irving H. *Negro Medal of Honor Men.* New York: Dodd, Mead & Company, 1967.

Lerner, Gerda. *The Majority Finds Its Past.* New York: Oxford University Press, 1979.

Lewis, Samella. *Art: African American.* Los Angeles: Hancraft Studios, 1990.

Lincoln, C. Eric. *The Negro Pilgrimage in America.* New York: Bantam Books, 1967.

Long, Richard A. *Black Americana.* Secaucus, New Jersey: Chartwell Books, Inc., 1985.

Low, W. Augustus, and Virgil A. Clift. *Encyclopedia of Black America.* New York: Da Capo Press, McGraw Hill, 1981.

MacDonald, J. Fred. *Blacks and White TV, Afro-Americans in Television Since 1948.* Chicago: Nelson-Hall Publishers, 1983.

Marsh, J.T.B. *The Story of the Jubilee Singers: With Their Songs.* Cambridge: Houghton Mifflin and Company, The Riverside Press, 1881.

Negro American Heritage. Edited by Arna Bontemps. San Francisco: Century Communications, Inc., 1965.

Notable Black American Women. Edited by Jessie Carney Smith, Detroit: Gale Research, Inc., 1992.

Patterson, Lindsay. *The Afro-American in Music and Art.* The Association for the Study of Afro-American Life and History, 1978.

Patterson, Lindsay. *The Negro in Music and Art.* New York: International Library of Negro Life and History, Publishers Company, Inc., 1967.

Perry, Reginia. *Free Within Ourselves.* Washington, D.C.: National Museum of American Art, Smithsonian Institution, 1992.

Peterson, Robert W. *Only the Ball Was White.* Englewood Cliffs, N.J.: Prentice-Hall, Inc., 1970.

Ploski, Harry A., and James Williams. *Reference Library of Black America.* Afro-American Press, 1990.

Powledge, Fred. *Free At Last?* Boston: Little, Brown & Company, 1991.

Profiles in Black. Edited by Doris Funnye Innis. New York: Core Publications, 1976.

Quarles, Benjamin. *The Negro in the Making of America.* New York: MacMillan Publishing Company, 1964.

Reynolds, Barbara. *And Still We Rise.* Arlington, Virginia: USA Today Books, 1988.

Robertson, Patricia. *The Guinness Book of Movie Facts & Feats.* New York: Abbeville Press.

Robinson, Wilhemena A. *Historical Negro Biographies.* New York: International Library of Negro Life and History, Publishers Company, Inc.,1969.

Rose, Thomas, and John Greenya. *Black Leaders: Then and Now.* Maryland: Garrett Park Press, 1984.

Rust, Edna and Art, Jr. *Art Rust's Illustrated History of the Black Athlete.* New York: Doubleday & Company, Inc., 1985.

Sammens, Vivian Ovelton. *Blacks in Science and Medicine.* New York: Hemisphere Publishing Corp., 1990.

Sampson, Henry T. *Blacks in Black and White.* Metuchen, New Jersey: The Scarecrow Press, 1977.

Schiffman, Jack. *Harlem Heyday.* Buffalo, New York: Prometheus Books, 1984.

Schuller, Gunther. *Early Jazz, Its Roots and Musical Development.* New York: Oxford University Press, 1968.

Shaw, Arnold. *Black Popular Music in America.* New York: Schirmer Books, 1986.

Southern, Eileen. *Biographical Dictionary of Afro-Americans and African Musicians.* Westport, Connecticut: Greenwood Press, 1982.

_____. *The Music of Black Americans, A History.* New York: W.W. Norton and Company, 1983

Story, Rosalyn M. *And So I Sing: African-American Divas of Opera & Concert.* New York: Warner Books

Sussman, Barry. *The Great Cover-Up: Nixon and the Scandal of Watergate.* New York: New American Library, 1974.

The Black American Reference Book. Edited by Mabel M. Smythe. Englewood Cliffs, New Jersey: Prentice-Hall, Inc., 1976.

The Negro Handbook. Chicago: Johnson Publishing Company, 1966.

The Reader's Catalog. Edited by Geoffrey O'Brien, New York: Jason Epstein, Publisher, 1989.

The Rolling Stone Album Guide, Edited by Anthony DeCurtis and James Henke with Holly George-Warren, New York: Random House, 1992.

The World Almanac and Book of Facts - 1991. New York: Pharos Books, 1990.

They Have Overcome. Warren Schloat Productions, Inc., Pleasantville, New York: A Prentice Hall Company, 1969.

Tirro, Frank. *Jazz: A History.* New York: W.W. Norton & Company, 1977.

Toppin, Edgar A. *A Biographical History of Blacks in America Since 1528.* New York, David McKay Company, Inc., 1971

Who's Who Among Black Americans, Fifth Edition (1988). Lake Forest, Illinois: Educational Communications, Inc.

Williams, Bert, photographs by. *In the Shadow of the Great White Way.* New York: Thunder's Mouth Press.1989.

Williams, Juan. *Eyes on the Prize, America's Civil Rights Years.* New York: Viking Penguin, Inc., 1987.

Woll, Allen. *Black Musical Theatre, from Coontown to Dreamgirls.* Baton Rouge and London: Louisiana State University Press, 1989.

Woods, Paula L. & Felix H. Liddell. *I, Too, Sing America.* New York: Workman Publishing, 1992.

Woodson, Carter G. *The History of the Negro Church.* Washington, D.C.: The Associated Publishers, 1921.

INDEX

328